WINNING WORLDWIDE

STRATEGIES FOR DOMINATING GLOBAL MARKETS

Other books published by Professor Lamont:

Managing Foreign Investments in Southern Italy
Foreign State Enterprises: A Threat to American Business
Forcing Our Hand: America's Trade Wars in the 1980s

WINNING WORLDWIDE

STRATEGIES FOR DOMINATING GLOBAL MARKETS

Douglas Lamont

BUSINESS ONE IRWIN
Homewood, Illinois 60430

Project editor: Karen Smith
Production manager: Bette K. Ittersagen
Compositor: Precision Typographers
Typeface: 11/13 Century Schoolbook
Printer: The Book Press, Inc.

Library of Congress Cataloging-in-Publication Data

Lamont, Douglas F.
   Winning worldwide : strategies for dominating global markets /
Douglas Lamont.
     p.   cm.
   Includes index.
   ISBN 1-55623-419-8
   1. International business enterprises—Case studies. 2. Success
in business—Case studies. I. Title.
HD2755.5.L35 1991
658.8'48—dc20   90–43329

Printed in the United States of America

1 2 3 4 5 6 7 8 9 0 BP 7 6 5 4 3 2 1 0

FOREWORD

As a researcher, writer, and teacher in the area of international business, Professor Lamont has well-established credentials in his field. In this, his latest work, he provides strategic approaches to global business and furnishes a background against which an international strategy may be developed and the success of operations may be gauged.

It is a work designed for those who are now players in the global marketplace and for those who wish to be. For both groups, Lamont offers a framework for developing an international business strategy and for evaluating the success of existing international ventures.

It is interesting to reflect on the critical fields of business where practice has run ahead of theory. In real estate and entrepreneurship, for example, we find case after case of winners and losers who operated in the absence of a reliable theory to guide them. In such areas, their only choice was to develop strategy along the way.

This condition applies also in international business, Lamont reminds us. He points out that while there has been much theory developed on certain aspects of the field such as finance and marketing, the overall study of international business still lacks a unifying theory. As he writes, with all the research on facets of the field, "no book melds these diverse intellectual ideas into a common train of thought of strategic thinking about international business."

The present work is grounded in practicality; it provides what Lamont calls his "10 international business strategies," offered in a readable format and supplemented by case studies. Nevertheless, I believe that it does represent the kind of research from which, in due course, a unifying theory can emerge.

While the book focuses on the three great centers of economic activity—Japan, the United States, and Europe—there is also an interesting emphasis on Canadian business and the importance of that nation as a market. Also, while the book provides models for business decisions in those developed markets, it may be useful for the future exploration of markets in regions that are currently suffering severe economic strains, like Central and South America.

It may also prove to be a useful guide to the evaluation of ventures in Eastern Europe, where the first step in developing new markets is helping potential business partners learn what a free market is.

It may be that business executives who fail to capture the spirit of global markets are consigning their firms to second-class status. It is evident that in the international arena there will be no room for the slow-footed. In *Winning Worldwide,* we are offered an approach for reviewing, evaluating, and succeeding in international markets.

> Donald P. Jacobs
> Dean, J. L. Kellogg Graduate School
>   of Management
> Northwestern University

FOREWORD

The 1990s marks the first truly global decade. Time and distance have shrunk rapidly with the advent of faster communication, transportation, and financial flows. Events in one part of the world—Eastern Europe, Middle East, Far East—profoundly effect the economies and politics in other regions of the world. Products developed in one country—Gucci purses, McDonald's hamburgers, Japanese sushi, Pierre Cardin suits, German BMW's—find enthusiastic acceptance in most other countries. A "global village" is emerging.

Although many companies have carried on international activities for decades—IBM, Nestlé, Shell, Bayer, Toshiba and many others—today's global companies are much more aggressive and expansive. Global competition has undergone a *quantum* intensification. Domestic companies that never thought about foreign competitors suddenly have found new competitors in their backyard. U.S. newspaper headlines daily scream about Japanese victories over U.S. producers in consumer electronics, motorcycles, and copying machines; the gains of Japanese, German, Swedish, and even Korean car imports in the U.S. market; the French firm Bic's successful attacks on Gillette; Nestlé's gains in the U.S. coffee and candy markets; and the loss of textile and shoe markets to Third World imports.

Every country urges its domestic firms to internationalize. Every country wants to export more and import less. Their companies will have to address some fundamental questions: What market position should our company establish in our country, on our continent, and globally? Which countries should we enter, how, when, where, and with what resources and partners? What are the major success factors?

Clearly many factors will affect a company's success in the global arena. Douglas Lamont has identified 10 such factors in the present book. He has tested the role of these factors through an in-depth study of a score of companies that operate in foreign markets. He presents a rich description of each company's objectives, strategy, and performance in its specific global adventures, drawing useful lessons for management. He is forging an "expert system" that can predict a company's performance as a function of its planned international strategy in a specific situation.

Professor Lamont's studies represent a new departure point for building better international business theory and practice. Managers can learn a great deal from his description and analysis of the global strategies used by Procter & Gamble, L'Oréal, Caterpillar, Komatsu, Kodak, Fuji, Unilever, Boeing, Airbus, Merck, Baxter, Beecham, Black & Decker, Quaker Oats, Electrolux, and several other companies. Lamont is to be commended not only for presenting a superb analysis of actual company strategies but for proposing a framework that synthesizes the principal international lessons learned from these company experiences.

Philip Kotler
S. C. Johnson & Son Distinguished Professor
   of International Marketing
J. L. Kellogg Graduate School of Management
Northwestern University

PREFACE

This book's aim is to advance knowledge about international business. The book identifies a group of strategies critical to international business and uses case studies to show how firms dominate global markets with the help of these international business strategies.

My intended audience is a mix of business professors, executives, and students who have an interest in how firms win worldwide. I believe that busy executives who read this book will be repaid for the time they spent by the increased success of their firms at home and overseas.

A strategic framework is needed because scholars have approached international business from their original academic disciplines—economics, finance, marketing, organizational behavior, and so on. Indeed, no book melds these diverse intellectual ideas into a common train of strategic thought about international business. Recent trends, however, are encouraging. Contributors such as Drucker, Ohmae, Porter, Dunning, and Rugman have made significant advances in developing descriptive approaches to international competition. However, this unfolding interdisciplinary revolution has yet to reach successfully into international firms and their global markets.

In attempting to provide such a framework, this book classifies strategies, tactics, and data in ways that not everyone will affirm. In some instances, I suggest solutions to controversial topics, such as the theory of contestable markets or the theory of internalization, before all scholars have been heard on these subjects. I do this because I have found these topics useful in explaining to students why firms succeed or fail in global markets.

Because this book contains a new approach to international business, I offer a few remarks by way of guidance. Each of the 10 international business strategies is presented individually in Chapters 1 thru 10. Although the case (or cases) in each chapter focus on the one international business strategy under discussion, other international business strategies are brought into the case discussion to give readers a complete picture of the firm.

All the cases have been examined quantitatively through an expert systems (or decision support) model that uses the chaos theory of mathematics, resampling statistics (the jackknife or bootstrap), and a Lotus 1-2-3® spreadsheet computer model as the means to examine the international business performance of firms. These details appeared in earlier drafts. Reviewers thought they were excessively technical and encouraged they be dropped from the text, and put in an appendix. I think this is good advice, and I encourage readers to review the appendix and supporting literature at their own convenience.

The book reflects contributions of numerous friends and colleagues. Among those who read parts of the manuscript are David Ricks, Phil Kotler, and William Ogram. The Kellogg Graduate School of Management of Northwestern University lent institutional support. Peter Lawyer and Robert Parsons, graduate research assistants, helped coordinate the case materials. Mark Knight wrote the macros for the first Lotus 1-2-3 spreadsheet model, and Robert Parsons wrote the macros for the the second Lotus 1-2-3 spreadsheet model, which is the one in current use. Robert Gayner, executive director of the Business Fund for Canadian Studies in the United States, gave timely financial support to the project.

ACKNOWLEDGMENTS

This book is dedicated to the management students of the Kellogg Graduate School of Management of Northwestern University, Evanston, Illinois; and of the Sasin Graduate Institute of Business Administration of Chulalongkorn University, Bangkok, Thailand.

The cases in Chapters 1 through 10 were developed from research these students carried out as part of their course requirements for the Masters of Management and Masters of Business Administration degrees. The students examined the international business performance of global firms by using the 10 international business decisions discussed in this book. When these decisions are grouped together as a set of independent variables, they help students make better decisions about whether or not these firms are better off and have created a competitive advantage.

As a part of their studies, these students used an application of Lotus 1-2-3 that was developed at the Kellogg School to study international business performance over time, across industries, and among diversified firms. This approach is referred to as an expert systems (or decision support) model of international business decision making. Without the active participation of Kellogg and Sasin students, it would not have been possible to move the frontiers of international business strategy forward toward model building, statistical analysis, and mathematical rigor.

Special thanks goes to the Business Fund for Canadian Studies in the United States for its support of a Kellogg study on the internationalization of Canadian-owned firms as they readied themselves for competition under the U.S.–Canada Free Trade Agreement. Three cases presented in this book—Molson, Labatt, and MacMillan Bloedel—were developed with support from the Business Fund. These cases were the first to be studied under the expert systems model of international business decision making discussed above, and they became the prototypes for the American, European, and Japanese cases also presented in the book.

Thanks also goes to the Kellogg faculty and administration, whose intellectual interest in the overlapping boundaries of strategy, marketing, organizational design, finance, economics, accounting, and international business nourished and sustained the development of the expert systems model on international business decision making over the last four years.

Douglas Lamont

CONTENTS

PART I
COUNTRIES AND INTERNATIONAL BUSINESS
How to Gain Competitive Advantage

PART II
MARKETING MANAGEMENT AND INTERNATIONAL BUSINESS
How to Maintain Competitive Advantage

PART III
ORGANIZATIONAL LEARNING AND INTERNATIONAL BUSINESS
How to Sustain Competitive Advantage

PART IV
GLOBALIZATION AND INTERNATIONAL BUSINESS
How to Gain, Maintain, and Sustain Competitive Advantage

LIST OF EXHIBITS

INTRODUCTION

HOW TO GAIN, MAINTAIN, AND SUSTAIN COMPETITIVE ADVANTAGE

To maintain a leadership position in any one developed country a business . . . increasingly has to attain and hold leadership positions in all developed countries world-wide. It has to be able to do research, to design, to develop, to engineer and to manufacture in any part of the developed world, and to export from any developed country to any other. It has to go transnational.[1]

Peter F. Drucker, *Clarke Professor of Social Sciences at the Claremont Graduate School.*

BOOM IN FOREIGN DIRECT INVESTMENTS

International business forces its attention on Canadians and Europeans because investments by American-owned firms overseas since the early 1950s amount to about $368 billion (in U.S. dollars). Our purchase of their factories and our control of their home markets cause them to fret about economic independence and national competitiveness Throughout the 1970s, their governments acted foolishly against these foreign direct investments by seeking to limit, restrict, or end American control over petroleum, minerals, steel, automobiles, telecommunications, and other national industries. These bans on foreign control did not work in Canada, Britain, France, nor elsewhere in the Western world.

OHMAE ON INTERNATIONAL BUSINESS

Global companies learn to withstand the disruptions created by government irrationality.[2]

Today, Americans also worry about foreign direct investments. During a much shorter period of time, essentially the 1980s, the Japanese became the second largest foreign investor in the United States after the British. All investments by foreign-owned firms, including the Canadians and Europeans, grew to about U.S. $390 billion. The speed at which foreigners gained parity with Americans causes the latter to fuss about foreign control over the U.S. economy, to ask whether foreign direct investments enhance or reduce America's ability to compete both at home and overseas, and to wonder what American executives must do to improve the international competitiveness of their firms. The tenor of these questions suggests that the United States is seeking to follow the habitual course of action of Canada and Europe, that is, swim against the transnational tide in foreign direct investments.

DRUCKER ON INTERNATIONAL BUSINESS

Going transnational may be the only rational strategy for any business aiming at a leadership position anywhere in the developed world, whether in a mass market (market segment) or in a market niche.[3]

Unfortunately for Canadians, Europeans, Americans, and now the Japanese, international business theory is without answers to these basic questions. Because it cannot distinguish between stocks and flows of capital, the theory says nothing about whether long-time investors (e.g. the British in the U.S.) are less threatening than new investors (the Japanese) or vice versa. Nor can the theory answer whether foreign direct investments help or hinder economic growth and the international competitiveness of national economies. The long-standing complaint of nationalists that foreign investors take out more in the form of profits than they ever invested in new capital has yet to be answered by international business theory. Finally, the theory fails to offer international executives a strategy for gaining, maintaining, and sustaining international competitiveness in the face of significant changes in how the world economy goes about increasing standards of living, improving the quality of life, and forging a managerial consensus about business success both at home and abroad.

These conflicts between practice and theory come from how international business first defined itself when it emerged as a separate field of study in the late 1960s. Two decades later, international business still draws on a wide variety of disciplines (e.g. economics, organizational behavior, production, marketing, finance, law, and cultural anthropology) to explain what happens when firms do business abroad.

DUNNING ON INTERNATIONAL BUSINESS

International business still has no way of identifying the strategically related characteristics of firms most likely to be associated with a robust international posture.[4]

However, there are plenty of surviving export and import "war stories" that antedate the coming of multinational firms but no comparable explanation about why, for some firms, exporting remains the strategy of choice for long periods of time and, for others, exporting is simply a prelude to foreign investment. Moreover, there are plenty of studies about exchange rates, market segments and niches, cultural biases, joint ventures, foreign direct investments, and a host of other problems but no single, useful framework to explain why international production occurs and what its impact upon global marketing is.

Today, international business executives (who are trying to find out which strategies work, and why and how they can be used) are still unable to develop a strategy to move from a business idea, to strong market share in a few countries, to competitiveness worldwide. These executives are impoverished because, according to Dunning, the hard work of defining

> the nature and scope of their core assets, their attitude to inovation and change ... the range and segment of critical markets served, their attitude to risk and uncertainty, their operational flexibility, their organizational and cultural ethos ... and their willingness and capacity to conclude cross-border alliances[5]

has not been done by professors and other researchers.

The aim of this book is to give international executives a clearer understanding of which strategies enhance international production and global marketing. With careful reading, executives can learn how to develop a consistent response to changes in overseas markets, examine strategic behavior in their firms on a systematic basis, understand interfirm interaction concerning the dynamics of international business, and expand their firm's worldwide assets for the purpose of maintaining sustainable competitive advantage both at home and abroad.[6]

If international executives want to strengthen the competitiveness of their firms, they must apply one or more of the 10 international business strategies discussed below. These strategies provide both a common, unifying framework for the field of international business and a way to distinguish between successful and unsuccessful international business performance.

INTERNATIONAL BUSINESS STRATEGIES: AN OUTLINE

The spectacular results of international business competitiveness are evident among firms from the United States, Europe, and Japan. These three groups moved quickly away from foreign trade activities to foreign direct investments and then to competitive links across all continents of the world. From their successful efforts in creating multinational firms comes the distillation of a set of international business strategies. The following is a brief sketch of the international business strategies discussed in detail in the 10 chapters in this book.

Countries and International Business

How do international firms gain competitive advantage? Discussions about international business start with raw materials, parts, goods, services, and people crossing national boundaries. The land within a national boundary forms a country with its own language, culture, history, economy, political system, flag, national anthem, and army different from those of its neighbors, friends, and allies. All of these make the United States different from Mexico, France different from Germany, Japan different from Korea. Therefore, the following are questions for executives: What do they find in each country? Can they use their core skills to export to or invest in each country? And, will they be able to overcome the entry barriers raised by local firms in their home markets? That risks are acceptable, skills are transferable, and barriers are surmountable means that international business does take place. More on these three strategies in the paragraphs below.

1. Success in Choosing Market Opportunities

Because international business crosses many national frontiers, executives must deal with political, currency, and cultural risks. Their task is to avoid high-risk countries, find high-growth market segments in low-risk countries, and capture significant market share in all mass consumer markets of the world. Given that Japanese executives prefer a longer time horizon for gaining market share and becoming profitable than do American executives, the former see less risk and more opportunities than do the latter.

2. Success in Fitting Core Skills

Not every product, manufacturing system, marketing strategy, or organizational technique crosses national boundaries with ease. Some countries show a great deal of similarity in their ability to absorb new technologies and in their willingness to copy consumer preferences established elsewhere in the world. Others do not. Given that customers worldwide prefer Japanese technology incorporated within an international (sometimes referred to as Western or American) life-style, executives across the globe must get new products out more quickly and commit themselves to foreign market development in all parts of the world.

3. Success in Overcoming Barriers

Incumbent firms use their home market advantages (such as scale economies, learning curves, links with distributors, etc.) to keep out foreign contestants. The latter must overcome these entry barriers through the use of new technologies, products, services, and markets. Through a combination of technological competition and home market protectionism, Japanese executives have emerged as active players in international business. This is a wholly new lens through which American and European business executives must learn to view international business.

Marketing Management and International Business

How do international firms maintain their competitive advantage? Discussions about international business continue with how executives manage product sourcing, customer selection, and the creation of value. Many manage entry into overseas markets with only a minimum of difficulty. They learn to deal with the reality of domestic firms that have fully depreciated plants, strong links with local wholesalers, and significant market share. Nevertheless, new foreign competitors do have several strikes against them: First, their sunk costs are not depreciated; second, their forward pricing strategies are racking up losses instead of profits; and third, their local competitors are doing everything legally possible to keep them from gaining significant market share. Therefore, foreign firms must find the least expensive offshore products, seek customers with the highest discretionary income, and create valuable new products and services. These three strategies are discussed in the next paragraphs.

4. Success in Sourcing

Executives look for raw materials, parts and components, and finished goods from low-cost areas of the world. They want products with high export sales potential and that meet the technological and life-style expectations of customers abroad. Their task is to adapt international products to national, regional, and local markets. In the past, American mass-market and European high-class products built strong market segments throughout the world. Today, products from Japan and other Asian countries are capturing market share with the expectation that Japanese executives have something to say about the long-term development of international business.

5. Success in Selecting Customers with High-Quality Demand

Executives seek to improve the quality of demand by going after customers with high incomes, refined tastes, and preferences for upscale goods. Executives seek out goods from countries whose reputation is good in the eyes of customers. This country-of-origin effect is one of several cues that convince customers of quality. Today, high-performance cars from Germany and low-, medium-, and high-priced cars from Japan have excellent ratings, whereas cars from the United States have fair or poor ratings. The key to long-term development of international business is to pitch products with the right price, quality, and service to the most appropriate customer, niche, and market segment irrespective of national boundaries or differences in language, culture, and history.

6. Success in Creating Value

Executives acquire brands, trademarks, and other intellectual property to create value for their firms. They measure the actual movement of the brand name products through the channel of distribution, and they develop promotional campaigns to pull products faster from manufacturer to customer. Today, valuable American and European brands are for sale to those who have the cash: the Japanese. The key to long-term development of international business is to create new brands, service marks, and other forms of intellectual property so that value is enhanced for customers everywhere in the world.

Organizational Learning and International Business

How do international firms sustain competitive advantage? Discussions about international business continue with an appreciation that organizational issues shape managerial effort and its response to the rapid rate of change in the world's markets. Information is the lubricant of organizations and helps executives decide which markets to enter, how many to enter, and at what pace to finance market expansion. To make an expansion strategy work requires capital, human resources, and other assets to be leveraged to their fullest, with an eye on the detail of national differences worldwide. More on these strategies in the following paragraphs.

7. Success in Using Information
Organizations use production, marketing, and financial information to determine how management should go about its job in international business. Sometimes information is kept internally within the multinational firm, whereas at other times information is used as the carrot to induce other firms to join in licensing deals and joint venture partnerships. Also, information is used to scan many markets and then to decide which of these are similar enough so that the cost of additional market penetration is not prohibitive. Moreover, information is used to help executives decide on a market expansion strategy, for example, concentration on a few markets versus diversification into many markets.

8. Success in Positioning Assets
After decisions are made concerning concentration versus diversification, executives then position capital, human resources, and other assets based on the firm's pro forma sales statements. All expansion strategies require executives to make a host of predictions about the chances for success, involving, for example: sales response functions, industry growth rates, competitive lead times, spillover effects, costs of product and promotional adaptation, distribution expenses, costs of managerial control, and the loss of revenue due to external constraints. The task of executives

is to leverage their assets to outperform their sales quotas so that the whole company grows internationally.

9. Success in Understanding National Differences

Information and assets are no good without executives who have a feel for the real local, regional, and national differences among countries. Some of these are specific to one language or one cultural group (e.g. the respect for the king and royal family among Thais). Others transcend cultural groups and bind peoples into nations (e.g. the Maple Leaf of Canada, or the Stars and Stripes of the United States). Still others cut across nations and bind market segments worldwide (e.g, the Union Jack of Great Britain as a symbol of quality on Reebok running shoes). These competitive connections among countries turn pro forma sales statements into international marketing plans that are integrated into a worldwide corporate strategy for enhancing the firm's international business. Knowledge of the detail of national differences is the all-important information that executives must know and utilize.

Global Business Network

To gain, maintain, and sustain competitive advantage, three crucial puzzle pieces must be put in place first. These are how countries, management, and organizational issues affect international business. If all are put in place successfully, then executives can go about the business of creating a global business network for their firms.

10. Success in Globalizing the Firm, Its Products and Markets

Finally, successful international business executives employ both global and local marketing strategies to increase competitive connections among countries. They also foster organizational learning about international business among all of their subsidiaries, affiliates, branches, and other affiliate firms. Moreover, these executives turn some subsidiaries into sole-source firms, others into export platforms, and still others into great international firms in their own right. The task of international executives is to "think global, yet act local." That is the genius of international business.

INTERNATIONAL BUSINESS PERFORMANCE: FOUR TESTS

By using the 10 business strategies just outlined, international executives gain a set of "behavioral-related variables [that can influence] the extent and pattern of international production,"[7] according to John Dunning, and they learn new ways to improve the performance of their international firms. After several years of study, the following conclusion was drawn: The set of 10 international business strategies correlates well with several measures of international business performance.[8] The following are the four tests of performance that were applied to each of the firms discussed as cases throughout this book:

Better-Off Test

Is the firm better off exporting (or investing) overseas in terms of increases in market share and higher returns on sales? Two examples follow.

Molson Breweries of Canada is better off because exports increased its market share of the imported beer market in the United States and because its higher returns on sales in the U.S. were invested in its brewing and other businesses in Canada. John Labatt Ltd. of Canada is better off because its exports and foreign investments increased its market share of both the imported and domestic beer markets in the U.S., and because its higher returns on sales (and investments) were invested in its brewing and other businesses in both Canada and the United States.

Cost-of-Entry Test

Is the firm paying back its cost of entry by increasing its returns from equity, assets, or investments?

Molson easily passed the cost-of-entry test. As an exporter to the United States, it simply had to cover its costs of distribution, advertising, and point-of-purchase selling. Because Labatt chose to acquire regional breweries in the U.S. as well as to export to the American market, it had higher entry costs, which take much longer to pay back. More on these two examples in Chapter 1.

Attractiveness Test

Is the firm making itself so attractive that it is restructuring the industry and becoming its dominant firm? One example follows.

Unilever made itself more attractive in the U.S. personal care products market by acquiring Chesebrough-Ponds and its famous brand names, such as Pond's face cream and Vaseline hand cream. From its position as an also-ran in the U.S., Unilever propelled itself into competing successfully with the giants of American brand management, Procter & Gamble, Colgate, and others. By restructuring American industry, Unilever was able to transfer its successful brands and product strategies back to Europe, where it is the dominant firm in personal care products, detergents, fats and oils, and other industries. See Chapter 6 for further details.

Sustainable Competitiveness Test

Is the firm ousting local firms from national markets, setting worldwide standards, and gaining long-term dominance in the United States, Japan, and Europe so that its sustainable competitive advantage is unassailable both at home and abroad? One example follows.

Electrolux used its long-term northern European dominance in three product lines (hot—stoves; cold—refrigerators, and freezers; and wet—washing machines) to oust Italian and Spanish firms from their home markets, to set product standards for hot and wet products in all major world markets, and to sustain its competitive advantage worldwide. Both U.S. and Japanese firms are having difficulty mounting an effective competitive challenge to such an entrenched multinational firm as Electrolux. See Chapter 10 for how Electrolux built up its competitiveness in Europe, the U.S., and Japan.

More on these relationships later. Just note one basic point right now: The successful outcome of one or more of the performance tests is dependent on the set of international business strategies used by the international executives to gain, maintain, and sustain the international competitiveness of their firms.

FOREIGN TRADE, DIRECT INVESTMENT, AND COMPETITIVENESS

Coming from studies of foreign trade and direct investment to those of international business firms that compete in all parts of the world today is like stepping out of darkness into a blaze of brilliant light. Exporters and importers are still around as middlemen and agents; their ways of measuring the risk of nonpayment by foreigners, cobbling a deal together through countertrade or for cash, shipping the merchandise across the oceans, and using letters of credit to collect funds owed have been incorporated into the contractual arrangements used by international firms. However, now more than one third of foreign trade is done internally within international business firms. Even the most sophisticated trading houses—those in Japan and Korea—look to international production and global marketing as the way out of their life cycle problem of decline and loss of market share. It challenges their imagination to create again the international firm, this time built on a set of mutually supported international business strategies. Their success depends on whether management sees the future and exercises leadership to make the future happen today.

WHY THIS BOOK ON INTERNATIONAL MARKETING COMPETITIVENESS

Executives need a framework within which to test their assumptions, plan their initiatives, and roll out strategies to capture increasing market share abroad. From research done at the Kellogg Graduate School of Management at Northwestern University (and financed in part by the Business Fund for Canadian Studies in the United States), international business relationships have been put into the strategic analysis of countries, industries, and firms.

Because the field of international business covers so many disciplines, this book focuses on international production and global marketing, and only the international marketing tactics for rolling out each of the strategies are discussed in detail. These sensible limits permit international executives to dwell on expanding their product markets, which is the fundamental strategic issue facing them as they compete for market share at home and abroad.

The 10 international business decisions and their accompanying international marketing tactics are simply the foundation on which executives may build their own more detailed, technical analysis of product markets, market segments, and market share. Their intuition about which decisions and tactics fit or do not fit is what counts. The 10 decisions are suggestive of the broad field called international business and the strategic problem facing international executives.

WHAT THE FUTURE HOLDS FOR
INTERNATIONAL BUSINESS FIRMS

The following are some of the futures that have already happened in the continuing battle for international competitiveness. A global international management consciousness exists among rival firms irrespective of their country of origin. This spills over into standardized product design concepts that are erasing local and regional identities as consumer preferences converge worldwide.[9] However, varieties in national and corporate culture require firms to exhibit flexibility in pursuing customers while pushing for global integration. The dynamics force firms away from both the commodity nexus of export-import trade and the power nexus of direct investment and ownership by multinationals and force them toward partnerships, joint ventures, research and marketing consortia, and so on.[10] This radical restructuring is required of firms that wish to sustain their international competitiveness in the face of changes in the political economy of the world.

With this brief introduction to international strategies, performance, and competitiveness, the first task is to apply these concepts to a famous export "war story": the invasion of the U.S. beer market by Molson Breweries of Canada. But we must be careful because there are other plots that lead to some new insights about risks and opportunities, core skills, and entry barriers.

PART I

COUNTRIES AND INTERNATIONAL BUSINESS

How to Gain Competitive Advantage

Risks
Skills
Barriers

CHAPTER 1

RISKS WORTH TAKING

Molson had to become something other than a Canadian brewing company.[1]

Norman Seagram, *executive vice president of Molson Cos., and former chairman of Molson Breweries of Canada.*

We have to consider North America as our marketplace.[2]

Peter N. T. Widdrington, *chairman and CEO of John Labatt Ltd.*

COMPETITIVENESS: THE IMPORTANCE OF A GOOD HUNCH

During the last two decades, first Molson and much later Labatt exploited the upscale U.S. market for imported beer. Norman Seagram of Molson and Peter N. T. Widdrington of Labatt learned the beer business in Canada, a highly protected home market where too many small-scale breweries sold high-priced beer to 25 million Canadians. Nothing in the business experience of these two executives suggests they could make the transition to an open market where fewer large-scale breweries sold low-priced beer to 250 million Americans, and where for two decades of all the industry's growth was in the imported market segment of European, Canadian, Mexican, and Australian beers. However, both Seagram and Widdrington viewed the move from Canada to the United States as a risk worth taking because it increased sales and improved overall business performance. These two cases offer good examples of how international business firms manage country risk, encourage trade reciprocity between countries, and identify market opportunities abroad.

Sometimes, naysayers refuse to believe even successful international executives. For example, in early 1989, Molson said it would export 40 million cases of beer to the United States during the next two years. But Martin Romm, a managing director and a beer industry analyst with First Boston Corp., turned opportunity into risk by concluding that Molson's forecast appeared to be optimistic because growth of the imported beer market in the U.S. had slowed to 2 percent in 1988 from 6 percent in 1987.[3] However, here is the answer to the naysayers: All international market opportunities have risks associated with them. Successful executives (such as Seagram and Widdrington) were able to use a good hunch to transform political, economic, and cultural risks into long-term sustainable international competitiveness.

In summary, three industrial markets captivate most international executives: the United States, Japan, and Europe. They are low-risk, high-growth, mass consumer markets with populations of 250 million, 120 million, and 350 million, respectively. Market size—together with high levels of disposable income among young urban professionals (or "yuppies"), cultural similarities between beer drinkers in Canada and the U.S., and long-term North American economic integration—caused Molson, Labatt, and others to compete for market share in the United States. Their continuing battle for international growth is carried out under the authority of the two-year-old U.S.–Canada Free Trade Agreement that discontinues tariffs and other barriers to trade and investment between the two countries.

Whatever the risks of freer U.S.–Canada–Mexico trade; whatever the opportunities in the European Economic Community (EEC) with changes in 1992 and new developments in central Europe; and whatever the problems caused by Japan's cultural, technological, and governmental barriers, marketing executives worldwide believe they must be in these three markets. Failure in one or more of these markets means losing skirmishes for increases in market share and returns on sales; battles for increases in returns on equity, assets, and investments;

and wars for dominance and long-term, sustainable competitive advantage.

STRATEGY INSIGHT

International competitiveness comes from marketing success in Europe, the United States, and Japan.

Read on, and you can be the judge as to whether or not Molson can make money in the United States during the 1990s as it has done every year since 1971, and whether or not Molson, Labatt, and others can market their American success stories in Europe and Japan.

MOLSON EXPORTS TO THE UNITED STATES[4]

For many decades, Molson Breweries was perennially number two, after John Labatt, in the Canadian beer market.[5] No combination of product market strategies within Canada alone could make Molson number one, that is, the dominant firm, the industry leader in Canada. Therefore, in 1971 Molson decided to export its beer to the United States, Canada's nearest neighbor and most important trading partner. This end-run strategy resulted in higher sales, increased market share, and greater profits for the firm. Most important, through its strong position in the U.S. market, Molson was able to challenge its chief rival back home by going into an equity joint venture with the Carling O'Keefe subsidiary of Elders IXL, an Australian firm. Molson's access to the U.S. market proved to be a valuable asset for Elders.

STRATEGY INSIGHT

Success in exporting leads not only to new competitive strength abroad but also to stronger market position at home.

Molson is better off because it increased its market share and return on sales both in Canada and the United States. Yet Labatt came back in the mid-1980s with a different strategy, namely, direct investment in the U.S. for the purpose of turning itself into a more competitive international brewery than Molson. Today, Labatt is also better off because of its greater attention to learning how to position assets in the United States.

MOLSON'S EIGHT INTERNATIONAL MARKETING TACTICS

- Exports to American market using nearest neighbor approach
- Tailors strategy to fastest growing product market segment
- Targets beer to specific market niche (yuppies)
- Gains scale economies or lower average costs of brewing
- Gains scope economies through product line extensions
- Overcomes entry barriers with investment in distributor
- Uses country of origin as cue for advertising
- Maintains first-mover advantage over Canadian competitor

A GREAT HUNCH ABOUT THE MARKET FOR IMPORTED BEER

The Molson "war story" is about chance, hunches, intuition, good guesses, and a little bit of forecasting. In the 1970s, Molson executives came across the fact that the imported beer market was the fastest growing segment of the U.S. beer market, whereas domestic beer sales were not growing at all.

Because Canada is known among U.S. beer drinkers as a country with excellent beer, Molson executives used this information (or cue) to promote its beer within the United States. They targeted their beer to "yuppies"—Americans who were between 18 and 34 years old, sports fans, and who could be reached through nationwide spot radio advertising. They also converted their brown beer bottles (the type preferred in Canada) to green (the type preferred in the United States), lowered the alcohol content of their beer to make it more suitable to American tastes, and produced a light beer specifically for the U.S. market.

Moreover, Molson executives brewed the following beers in Canada for both the Canadian and U.S. markets: Molson Gold, Molson Light, Canadian Export Ale, Brador Malt Liquor, Kirin (of Japan), and Steinlager (of New Zealand). These product line extensions gave Molson two important competitive advantages: (1) greater scale economies (or lower average costs of production) in its competition with other Canadian breweries and (2) increased scope economies (wide product breadth and depth) in its competition with other Canadian and foreign-owned breweries in the United States.

Finally, Molson established Martlet Importing Company, a U.S. subsidiary, to import Molson beer into the United States. This tactic of direct exporting helped Molson overcome American entry barriers, such as the 350 independent beer wholesalers that control access to the U.S. retail market.

In summary, Molson was the first Canadian brewer to see the export opportunity of the U.S. market. This good intuitive decision gave it place and position in the United States. Another very small Canadian brewer, Moosehead, followed Molson into the American market; Moosehead took fifth place and a 5 percent share of the imported beer market, ahead of both Labatt and Carling O'Keefe. Nevertheless, Molson remains the leading Canadian exporter of beer to the United States.

MARKET SHARE ANALYSIS

For 15 years, until 1986, Molson was number two (after Heineken of the Netherlands) in the imported beer market. Then Molson dropped to number three (after Heineken and Corona), and three years later, in 1989, Molson fell to fourth place after Heineken, Corona, and Beck's a fast-rising German import.[6] Although Molson did very well against its Canadian and most of its European competitors in the U.S. imported beer market, it failed to note the ground swell of interest in beer from America's other nearest neighbor and third largest trading partner, Mexico.

And what of Labatt? After many years of being one of the other 280 brands of imported beer in the U.S., Labatt finally showed up as number six in the imported beer market. In 1987, Labatt had a 4 percent market share compared to Molson's 11 percent share of the U.S. imported beer market. In 1989, Labatt moved to fifth place with a 5.7 percent share of this market segment.[7]

DECISIONS ABOUT EXPORTING AND INVESTMENTS AFFECT COMPETITIVENESS[8]

Molson executives needed to do more than make good guesses as they reviewed their opportunities under the 1989 U.S.–Canada Free Trade Agreement. Why? Because in the mid-1980s, Labatt's executives were seeking to overcome Molson's first-mover advantage by acquiring several regional breweries in the United States, including Latrobe Brewing Co., "maker of trendy Rolling Rock beer."[9] Jacques H. Kavafian, an analyst with McLeod Young Weir Ltd. in Montreal, said it this way: "If [Labatt] wanted to survive in beer, they had to go into the U.S."[10]

The results of these decisions are as follows: Molson is now competing only in the imported beer market segment. Because beer is currently excluded from the U.S.–Canada Free Trade Agreement, Molson's products could face higher U.S. tariffs, nontariff barriers, or other trade restrictions unless Canada puts beer under the agreement by 1994. U.S. breweries are unwilling to accept this single exception to free trade indefinitely. Labatt, on the other hand, is competing in both the imported *and* domestic beer segments of the U.S. market. The beer it brews in the U.S., which over time will become a large portion of its total brewing capacity, faces no such potential trade restrictions or other elements of country risk. Therefore, Labatt is much further along in becoming a North American-based brewery ready to face strong competition from U.S.-owned and Japanese-owned international breweries.

STRATEGY ANALYSIS OF MOLSON'S INTERNATIONAL BUSINESS PERFORMANCE

The Molson case helps explain the following crucial points for international marketing executives: First, overseas expansion through exporting is a viable strategy for small, medium, and large companies when market-defying trade barriers are not imposed by importing countries. These export sales make firms better off. Second, Molson's export expansion strategy included segment and niche analyses, preferences about country of origin, product line extensions, wholesale and retail distribution, market share analysis, and first-mover advantage. With effective marketing management, exporters can pay off their costs of entry and costs of ongoing business in import markets.

STRATEGY INSIGHT

Success in international business comes from the right combination of exports and investments to take advantage of overseas market opportunities.

Third, Molson's competitive advantage in the U.S. is now threatened because its chief Canadian competitor, Labatt, has chosen to expand overseas through foreign direct investments. With competent organizational learning, exporters become foreign investors. Eventually, they turn themselves into competitive international firms that can restructure their industries, set worldwide standards, and dominate local and foreign firms.

Therefore, Molson must revise current export expansion strategies and craft new international strategies to meet the challenges offered by domestic and foreign competitors, to reduce its exposure to country risk, and to become a North American-based international brewery. Because Labatt is combining exports to and production in the U.S. to gain competitive advantage within North America, it is only a matter of time before Labatt makes an outright challenge to Molson's dominant Canadian place within the U.S. beer market.

INTERNATIONAL MARKETING RESEARCH

Molson's initial study of the U.S. market was long on executive intuition and short on marketing research. This was not a crucial problem between 1971 and 1986. With additional research, Molson might have anticipated the changes in the U.S. beer market that were captured by Corona or Labatt's investment strategy for overcoming potential trade restrictions in the future. The task of Molson executives now is to deal with these important competitive developments on a more systematic basis. Exhibit 1–A shows the first international business decision, which Molson carried out quite successfully when it originally entered the U.S. market. Exhibit 1–B shows the marketing tactics for rolling out Decision 1; some of these need to be addressed by Molson executives before Molson loses more market share to Corona and Labatt. Exhibit 1–C shows the data elements for assessing country risk.

INTERNATIONAL MARKETING TACTICS AND DATA ELEMENTS FOR ASSESSING COUNTRY RISK

The following section provides an explanation of how Molson used the four tactics listed in Exhibit 1–B for rolling out Decision 1. It also includes an explanation of most of the data elements listed in Exhibit 1–C that were useful to Molson in assessing country risk.

Tactic: Choose Product Market Segments

Molson found sales opportunities in a nearby foreign market because its executives saw a gap in the imported beer market segment of the United States. Their corporate culture was to seek out low-cost, low-risk opportunities through geographic diversification (in Canada and then in the United States) so that the firm could escape the competitive restrictions imposed on it by its main home market competitor. Molson overcame Labatt by exporting to the U.S., building up a U.S.-based distribution system, and gaining the number two position in the imported beer market segment. Finally, Molson's internal management capability led it to stress product line extensions, niches, country of origin cues, and other core export marketing skills rather than alternative foreign direct investment strategies.

EXHIBIT 1–A
International Business Decision 1: Success in Choosing Market
Opportunities

Export
Foreign direct investment
Equity or contractual joint venture
Licensing or franchising

Note: Executives must specify decisions to fit the international business problems of the
firm. Is it an exporting problem? Is it a foreign direct investment problem? Is it a joint
venture problem? Is it a licensing problem? Or is it a combination of these problems?

EXHIBIT 1–B
International Marketing Tactics for Rolling Out Decision 1

Choose product market segments
Determine the level of country risk
Indentify sales opportunities
Master changes in terms of trade

EXHIBIT 1–C
Data Elements for Assessing Country Risk

Market-defying trade practices
Market-conforming trade practices
Firms as national champions
Reciprocity and free trade agreements
Cultural changes
Economic changes
Political changes
Foreign exchange rate forecasting (Forex)

MARKETING INTELLIGENCE

International competitiveness comes from success in segmenting
markets.

Initially, Molson faced little country risk in expanding to the United States. This is normal not only for Canadian firms but also for companies from Europe, Japan, and elsewhere in the world. Why? Among Canadian, U.S., European, and Japanese executives there exists a shared consciousness about the value of exporting and its rewards in terms of returns on sales from selling the same or similar products throughout the world.

Tactic: Determine Level of Country Risk

Molson, Moosehead, and Labatt chose to expand into a low-risk country, the United States. The country is politically stable. Moreover, its domestic economy is healthy so that profits earned there can be transferred back to Canada without cumbersome foreign exchange controls. Finally, Americans speak English, the language of most Canadians, and both peoples share the same cultural habits of drinking beer as they watch sporting events and enjoy themselves after work or on the weekends.

In fact, low country risk exists in the world's three most important industrial regions (North America, Japan, and Europe) as well as in several peripheral manufacturing regions (such as Australia and New Zealand). Sometimes foreign firms may have problems with regional preferences within the United States; the more intractable labor problems in Canada and Australia; the language and cultural differences among the European nations; and the unique language, cultural, and government intervention practices in Japan. However, none of these differences in customs, habits, and norms for living the good life is a reason to label these nations high-risk countries.

Data Element: Market-Defying Trade Practices[11]
Although all of the industrial countries are members of the multilateral General Agreement on Tariffs and Trade (GATT), virtually all of them have some market-defying restrictions on trade among themselves and between themselves and the less-developed countries. These bilateral restrictions are in the form of higher tariffs, nontariff barriers, and industrial policies. However, these restrictions are often waived when reciprocity, in

terms of access to each other's markets, is forged between culturally distinct nations.

For example, 12 European nations are members of the EEC which grants reciprocity among its members but which has a common external tariff against nonmember countries from North America and Asia. Moreover, under the U.S.–Canada Free Trade Agreement, the two countries encourage the free flow of goods (except beer) and services north and south rather than across the North Atlantic and Pacific oceans. Other free trade agreements exist; for example, there are agreements between Australia and New Zealand, and among six European countries that are not members of the EEC. The intention is to make country risk negligible while fostering greater international economic integration.

Data Element: Market-Conforming Trade Practices[12]

On the other hand, Japan's industrial policy of market-conforming government intervention through its Ministry of International Trade and Industry (MITI) slows the entry of foreign goods while Japanese manufacturers get ready for new competition and Japanese distributors find a place for these new foreign goods in their complicated wholesale-retail distribution system. The emphasis is on pushing new technology into Japanese firms to stave off foreign domination rather than on increasing demand among Japanese consumers. This form of government intervention (which came early in the product life cycle of data processing, computer software, and biotechnology and late in the life cycle of iron and steel, paper and pulp, and textiles) is generally considered adversarial by and unacceptable to Americans who believe in an autonomous, rational market economy.

Data Element: Reciprocity and Free Trade Agreements

The problem of government intervention is compounded by the following data: Imports as a proportion of Japan's gross national product were equivalent to 10 percent in 1970, 12 percent in 1980, and 13 percent in 1989 (versus 4.1 percent, 9.1 percent, and 18.1 percent, respectively, for the United States).[13] Therefore, the United States is demanding more reciprocity from Japan, whereas Japan is pushing for an East Asian trading bloc similar to those already in place in North America and Europe.

MARKETING INTELLIGENCE

International competitiveness comes from being realistic about reciprocity, free trade, and government intervention.

Thus, Japanese executives may find the U.S. a slightly more risky place to do business, whereas Canadian and Mexican executives are given treatment as if they were U.S. executives. That is what is meant by reciprocity. Nevertheless, the Japanese use a longer time horizon than their counterparts in North America and Europe, which encourages Japanese executives to see greater market opportunities where others might detect increased risk. Finally, Japanese executives will continue to build market share in North America through exports and direct investments while their government and MITI build a consensus for negotiating a reciprocity arrangement with the United States.

Tactic: Identify Sales Opportunities

Molson executives made excellent decisions concerning the sales opportunities awaiting them and in overcoming the entry barriers in the U.S. market. Initially, they also made several good marketing management decisions: products were sourced, customers were selected, and value was created for U.S. consumers.

MARKETING INTELLIGENCE

International competitiveness comes from making good, intuitive decisions.

Over time, their decisions were second best because Molson as an international firm was unwilling to learn from the accumulating sales and marketing information about the United States. Molson has not been able to use its North American base to build a global export sales network. Molson faces becoming an also-ran among Canadian, U.S., and Japanese breweries.

Tactic: Master Changes in Terms of Trade

In the Molson case, Heineken always ranked number one in the U.S. imported beer market, and for 15 years Molson ranked number two. Then in 1986 Molson was pushed to third place behind Corona, an imported beer from Mexico. Consumer preferences, the cultural terms of trade, and niche marketing all began to turn against Molson.

Data Element: Cultural Changes

Corona was first noticed by Californians vacationing in Mexico.[14] They liked its taste. When they returned home, its clear glass bottle reminded them of their unspoiled vacations on the beaches of Acapulco. Many cultural trends in the United States start in southern California and, through television, sweep eastward across the country. Corona became the imported beer of choice for Americans (especially yuppies) who wanted California good times, pleasant Mexican memories, and an escape from the harsh Canadian winter storms. Now, Corona, which used to be a working man's beer in Mexico, is also fashionable there among the market segment that copies upscale living tastes from California. Because of these two strong market developments, Cerveceria Modelo, the Mexican parent of Corona, built a new brewery on the Mexican side of the U.S. border to serve both North American markets and to take advantage of the one-way free trade in beer from Mexico to the United States.

CORONA'S FOUR INTERNATIONAL MARKETING TACTICS

- Exports to American market to earn foreign exchange
- Targets beer to specific market niche (yuppies)
- Uses country of origin as cue for advertising
- Gains scale economies in building brewery for two markets

Molson fought back with Molson Light and other product-line extensions. However, Molson was unable to come up with a clever advertising line such as that of Moosehead beer—"The Moose is loose!"—when its country of origin cue, Canada and cold weather, became less acceptable to Americans than Mexico and warm weather. Also, Molson's tie-in with sports through spot radio advertising was challenged by Labatt's use of its own television sports channel to promote National Hockey League teams such as the Nordiques, the Canadiens, the Maple Leafs, the Flames, and the Oilers.

With the expansion of Corona in the United States, both Molson and Labatt were faced with a declining market share for Canadian beer in the imported beer market of the United States. With this information, Labatt decided to shift its expansion strategy from exports to foreign direct investments. Labatt has also decided to downplay country of origin as an important theme in its advertising strategy.

Today, U.S. beer drinkers do not recognize Labatt as a Canadian beer, whereas they do think of both Molson and Moosehead as imported Canadian beers and of Corona as an imported Mexican beer. As regional identities lose their power to impede the convergence of consumer preferences in North America, Labatt's strategic decisions about managing cultural and corporate change made Labatt more likely to become a truly competitive international firm. This is the power of organizational learning within international business.

Data Element: Economic Changes

International executives also must manage economic changes in regional, national, and world economies. From the mid-1970s to the mid-1980s, Canadian-owned firms had to deal with a falling Canadian dollar vis-à-vis the U.S. dollar. Their profits in Canadian dollars were less valuable than their profits in U.S. dollars. Much of the sinking foreign exchange value of the Canadian dollar can be explained by the restrictive foreign investment policies of the Canadian government,[15] and some of it can be described by the lack of competitiveness of Canadian manufacturing exports in world markets.

Therefore, Molson's exports to the U.S. were a tonic for Canada and an example for other Canadian-owned businesses. Over the 10-year period, its earnings in U.S. dollars became even more valuable when repatriated in terms of Canadian dollars. Because Labatt did not have as strong a position in the U.S., it did not earn this same foreign exchange premium, and so it did less well across North America than Molson did before the former began earning U.S. dollars from its direct investments in the United States.

Poor Corona. Its home currency is the Mexican peso. During the early 1980s, Mexico suffered from hyperinflation, that is, changes in prices of over 100 percent or more annually. The peso went through multiple and substantial devaluations throughout most of the 1980s. As a consequence, the Mexican government did not have the foreign exchange to sell to those Mexican businesses that needed to pay for foreign imports. For Corona to pay for its imported raw materials, such as hops, it had to find a way to earn foreign exchange by exporting its beer to the United States. The rest of the story is California dreaming—or serendipity, chance, fortune, and good luck.

Finally, both Canadian and Mexican firms must deal with the integrative pull of the U.S. economy. For example, within one year after the beginning of the U.S.–Canada Free Trade Agreement, three regional economies have already begun to emerge within North America: (1) Quebec, New England, and New York; (2) Ontario and the Midwest; and (3) British Columbia, the Pacific Northwest, and northern California. Moreover, southern California, the Southwest, Texas, and northern Mexico have become a regional economy under special rules for trade and investment agreed to by both countries. Mexico has its border industry program for foreign direct investments, which permits Japanese, U.S., Canadian, and European firms to take advantage of low labor costs and proximity to the U.S. market. The U.S. agrees to charge very low or no tariffs for goods exported from these Mexican border plants to the United States.

These two new trade pacts among the three North American countries are designed to ensure reciprocity between the countries involved and to replace market-defying rules on trade and investment with those that are market-conforming. Irrespective of nationalistic pressures on the three governments, these new trading rules will bring the three national economies closer together, force national firms to do business throughout North America, and give North American executives a leg up in the competition with Europeans and Japanese.

Data Element: Political Changes
The U.S.–Canada Free Trade Agreement seeks to provide business executives on both sides of the border with full reciprocity and a set of market-conforming trade and investment rules. Because each country is the other's best trading partner, any agreement that ends tariffs on goods and reduces national restrictions on services and foreign investments will enhance the chances for success of business firms irrespective of their country of origin.

However, problems of organizational learning exist for both U.S. and Canadian firms. In the United States, government is viewed as an adversary or an impediment to business success. Canadian executives find that learning to manage the U.S. government relationship is one of the most difficult things about investing in the United States.[16] In Canada, government is a friend, a partner, and an agent for economic change. U.S. executives have trouble coming to grips with such cooperative governments whether they are Canadian, Japanese, or Mexican.

For example, since the late 1870s, the Canadian government has sought to create an east-west economy behind a high tariff wall that would have government support and depend on industry based primarily in Ontario. This industrial policy forced U.S. investors to set up branch plants across the border instead of simply exporting directly to Canada. After more than 100 years, this market-defying industrial policy has given way to north-south free trade with the United States. This new industrial policy is being greeted with enthusiasm by both U.S. and Canadian business executives.

Of course, the Japanese took another tack, one that suited their culture and societal traditions. Through consensus building among MITI, business, labor, and consumers, the Japanese government created export industries based on multinational firms that span the globe. After 40 years, this market-conforming industrial policy has taken the world by storm, with attempts to introduce it in other Asian countries such as South Korea and Thailand. Yet U.S. executives complain bitterly about it, and they charge that Japan is violating some higher economic ideal—an autonomous, value-free market economy that neither Canadians, Europeans, nor the Japanese find as acceptable to their national interests as do Americans.

For most of Mexico's 180 years of independence, Mexicans have been putting the government in the driver's seat of the economy, thereby limiting the freedom of executives to make independent judgments about investments, markets, and products. Mexicans took their cue from Spain, which imposed the state over the market throughout Latin America during 300 years of colonialism. Only once, at the turn of the century, did Mexicans permit foreigners to invest with reckless abandonment in mining, oil, and other crucial sectors of their national economy. This hiatus in state capitalism was cut short by the 1910 Mexican revolution and the new governing party's attempt for the next 70 years to reduce the impact of the U.S. economy on Mexico.

However, when Mexico's national economy collapsed in the 1980s over a failed oil policy, Mexican money and talent fled to the United States because few executives had faith in the economic development policies of the Mexican government. Although the Mexican government today is in retreat from active state ownership of crucial sectors of the economy, its market-defying industrial policy remains a club used by nationalists to keep out or restrict U.S. investment and hence limit economic integration within North America. If and when both the U.S. and Mexico enter into an expanded trade and investment pact, U.S. executives will have to spend more time learning how to deal with a government whose industrial policy is in transition from autarky and state capitalism to a more open market economy. Most U.S. executives, unless they are old Mexican hands, reject such macroeconomic information about a country because it does not fit within their understanding of the right and proper role of government in a market economy.

MARKETING INTELLIGENCE

International competitiveness comes from converting cultural, economic, and political risks into market opportunities.

These biases about the proper roles of government and business in the economy drive U.S. executives to see country risk where others find sales opportunities. If Molson and Corona (through their exports) and Labatt (through its direct investments) can overcome their biases about what the right and proper role for government in the economy is, then U.S. firms can do the same outside the United States. This type of learning about countries, societies, and traditions is the beginning of wisdom in international business.

STRATEGY ANALYSIS OF INTERNATIONAL MARKETING RESEARCH

One future has already happened in international business: Country risk among the industrial countries, and between them and the less-developed countries, is manageable through effective marketing management and a great deal of organizational learning by international executives. Trade and investment will expand among countries that agree to reciprocal market-conforming rules as long as international executives change their time horizons to suit the cultural, economic, and political conditions imbedded within each country's society. In this way, international firms gain competitive advantage.

CONCLUSIONS FROM THE CASES

Have Molson, Labatt and Corona created sustainable competitive advantage? What lessons were learned about international business decisions and international marketing tactics? How can international executives implement these lessons within their own business firms?

These questions can be answered by examining whether or not the three firms passed one or more of the four tests of international business performance. Between 1971 and 1986, Molson was definitely better off by exporting to the United States. Molson was successful in choosing export opportunities in a low-risk, high-growth, mass consumer market. The firm outperformed Labatt, its chief competitive rival. Then Labatt fought back with exports *and* acquisitions, and Corona entered the import market with a beer that matched the life-style preferences of Americans during the mid-1980s. No longer is it clear that Molson is better off.

Now, both Corona and Labatt are better off. However, it is not clear whether or not either of them can pay off cost of entry into the U.S. market. Corona has borrowed funds to build a new brewery on the Mexican side of the border, and Labatt has had to do the same to acquire regional U.S. breweries. Of course, Molson, with its smaller investment in distribution and advertising, paid off its cost of entry many years ago.

Nevertheless, Molson's low-risk, low-return strategy will not help it restructure the North American beer industry and become one of the dominant breweries on both sides of the border. Labatt's medium-risk, high-return strategy has the promise of doing what Molson cannot do. But that is so far in the future that new elements of country risk might overturn even the best-laid plans of international executives.

EXECUTIVE SUMMARY

Although several success stories are presented in this chapter about choosing export opportunities in the U.S., international executives should not be overconfident about the power of marketing research. They should not forget to give equal weight to consumer preferences, product quality, distribution practices, and other sociocultural aspects of marketing. International marketing executives go into exporting and foreign direct investments at their own peril when they fail to take into consideration the role of government and its impact on country risk.

CHAPTER 2

CORE SKILLS
WORTH MASTERING

The fact that L'Oréal was founded by a chemist is a key point. This is what differentiates us from most people in the cosmetics business. While other companies tended to cultivate the idea of selling hope in a jar, we on the contrary made a very basic choice that success for us would be our ability to innovate technically.[1]

Lindsay Owen-Jones, *president directeur general (or CEO) of L'Oréal.*

COMPETITIVENESS: THE IMPORTANCE OF AN INTERNATIONAL MANAGEMENT CULTURE

"No one thinks of me as a Brit, but as a familiar face in the company who happens to have a slightly strange sounding name. I am a classic product of a company which has only one nationality—not French, but L'Oréalienne,"[2] has said Lindsay Owen-Jones, president directeur general of L'Oréal, a French hair care and cosmetics firm. Mastery for L'Oréal, Procter & Gamble (P&G), and other international firms comes from their ability "to produce local products adapted to local markets, but reap world economies of scale in research and development, raw-materials sourcing, and production balancing."[3] Successful international executives, such as Lindsay Owen-Jones or Edwin L. Artzt (of P&G), create a community of interest within their firms and among suppliers, distributors, and customers centered on export sales, overseas markets, and international management strategy.

The spectacular success of these firms is bringing about the integration of the global goods markets, the manufacturing economy, and the service sectors (e.g. finance, accounting, distribution, and advertising). "The result is a relentless global competition on price and quality, a steady, even startling, worldwide increase in manufacturing productivity, ... solid increase in world output," and higher standards of living.[4] No markets are safe as international firms restructure their businesses to avoid humiliation at the hands of their competitors and as executives accept the vision, objectives, and performance criteria set by the global international management culture.

Moreover, successful international business executives direct the pace of industrial innovation, the diffusion of new technology, and the convergence of consumer preferences worldwide. On the other hand, unsuccessful executives stumble along without the right combination of core technical and marketing skills to create an international management culture within the firm.

STRATEGY INSIGHT

International competitiveness comes from marketing new, technically sophisticated products in Europe, the United States, Japan, and the rest of the world.

The L'Oréal and P&G cases offer good examples of how French and American executives diffuse new technology, reap scale economies, integrate global markets, and succeed (or fail) in performing at the high level expected of them by the international business community. Both L'Oréal and P&G determined the extent to which similar market segments existed between their home and host country markets. This is a must today as customer preferences for hair care products and disposable diapers become more alike all over the world. In terms of segmenting markets, these two firms competed as ardent members of the international business community.

Then P&G reverted to its U.S. origins. Its executives thought that what worked in the United States had to work in Japan. They imposed American pricing, advertising, and distribution practices on an Asian society. By doing so, these executives thrust a high level of unnecessary cultural risk on Pampers that led to a decade of lost sales opportunities in Japan.

L'Oréal introduced its products in the United States by following U.S. marketing practices in pricing, advertising, and distribution; these functional activities tend to be more culturally bound than other aspects of business. The firm also used cross-functional management teams to position new products more quickly throughout market segments identified as target customers by the firm's marketing research department.

Initially, L'Oréal had great success with its innovative product, a styling mousse for hair, called Free Hold. In 1984, when few competitors could manufacture mousse, Free Hold held a 45 percent unit share. Unfortunately, each year thereafter the product's unit share dropped until, in 1989, it was a low 0.5 percent, far below the 2.5 percent unit share needed to be a player in the hair care market.[5] L'Oréal was unable to leverage Free Hold's initial success into long-term dominance of the low-price end of the market. Instead, it took its cash and plowed it back into Studio Line, a more expensive product, which kept L'Oréal as a player in the U.S. market for hair care products.

Owen-Jones has summed up L'Oréal's results in the U.S. as follows: The cosmetics business "is a much longer term business than it seems. It takes between 20 and 30 years to build up a cosmetics name and you can destroy it in a much shorter period."[6] All international firms must make a long-term commitment to market development in Europe, the U.S., Japan, and the rest of the world.

L'ORÉAL SUCCESSFULLY EXPORTS TO THE UNITED STATES [7]

L'Oréal markets its products in more than 100 countries, with 43 percent of its worldwide sales in France, 23 percent in the United States, and 34 percent in the rest of the world. Its executives combine long years of product research and sales efforts to build and sustain competitive advantage. Theirs is a team effort whose goal is to create new products that can be sold in similar international market segments irrespective of nationality, cultural traditions, and country risk.

STRATEGY INSIGHT

Success in exporting depends on a long-term team effort in research, manufacturing, marketing, and management.

According to Owen-Jones, L'Oréal "has always adopted an almost Japanese policy to employment. Nearly all senior positions are filled by people promoted from within and nearly all of us started our careers in our twenties. [Such management continuity has long been regarded by L'Oréal as] one of the absolute key elements of success in the cosmetics business."[8] The firm's ability to master the core skills necessary for overseas market development and its willingness to take risks throughout the world are the hallmarks of L'Oréal's international business success.

L'ORÉAL'S SEVEN INTERNATIONAL MARKETING TACTICS

- Carries out behavioral research to determine latent demand
- Uses similar market segment approach in exporting to the United States
- Gains scale economies through product innovation
- Gains scope economies through mass merchandising
- Overcomes entry barriers with investment in distributor
- Uses elegant-sounding name as cue for advertising
- Emphasizes management continuity in overseas markets

INTUITION ABOUT LATENT DEMAND AMONG WOMEN CUSTOMERS

During a five-year period in the late 1970s and early 1980s, L'Oréal sought to fill a latent demand for a new product among women customers. Before they tried the product they did not know they wanted it, yet after they used it they realized they must make it a permanent part of their life-style. This new product from L'Oréal kept hair in place without the stiffness of traditional hairspray. From the merger of two formerly incompatible molecules into a foam substance, L'Oréal's research laboratories gave the world a new hair care product, mousse.

For two more years, L'Oréal tested mousse under the Valance brand name in the beauty salons of France and Great Britain. The product was a huge success. Then the firm packaged the new hair care product in aerosol cans and gave it the brand name Free Hold Styling Mousse. At the same time, L'Oréal bought Cosmair Inc., a U.S. distributor, for the purpose of immediately gaining access to established retailers of hair care products such as salons, better pharmacies, and upscale department stores. As competitors rushed to catch up, Free Hold became synonymous with mousse across the United States. By the mid-1980s, L'Oréal had captured over 40 percent of the U.S. market with its set of strategies in product research, distribution, pricing, brand management, and market segmentation.

Today, L'Oréal spends about 5 percent of its sales volume on research.[9] This is twice that of Revlon and three times that of Avon. L'Oréal has over 1,000 people employed on its research staff, whereas both Revlon and Estée Lauder rely on both in-house and contracted research. The exclusive use of in-house research gives L'Oréal a competitive edge in proprietary knowledge, product development, and innovation. From this system of research and development has come Preference, a hair color product that was under study for eight years in L'Oréal's laboratories, and of course Free Hold.

MARKET SHARE ANALYSIS

L'Oréal chose two European and American target markets in which to sell its hair care and cosmetics products. The first was the low- and middle-income, younger market, where women seek department store quality at low drug store prices. Although the name L'Oréal means nothing in the French language, among English-speaking people L'Oréal is an elegant, French-sounding name and thus the firm's products were accepted as the essence of quality even though its prices were lower than those of its competitors.

The second target group was the middle- and high-income market, where women seek quality, image, and occasional beauty tips from consultants in the department stores. L'Oréal's high-fashion brand, Lancome, possesses a 14 percent share of this market behind the segment leader, Estée Lauder, which controls a 37 percent share. In this second target market, L'Oréal positioned itself as the company with research-based products, controlled line offerings, heavy advertising support, and quality offerings at higher prices.

In the U.S., L'Oréal has had such high sales that it has become far more successful than both Coty and Max Factor. As early as 1984, L'Oréal unseated Revlon from second place in the U.S. cosmetics market. Part of this success was due to L'Oréal's concentration on the research and marketing of cosmetics, whereas Revlon decided to diversify its sales efforts into health care and pharmaceutical products.

Around the world today, L'Oréal's nail polish, lipstick, hair color, and styling mousse are global products. They are essentially the same in all 100 countries. L'Oréal does modify them ever so slightly in shade, fragrance, and taste to meet the special preferences of local national markets. Moreover, throughout Europe, North America, and Japan, L'Oréal has found from its marketing research that the traditional market for hair color is maturing. The average age has climbed to 35 when some customers accept gray hair as part of middle age and drop out of the market for hair coloring products. Therefore, L'Oréal is reconceptualizing these products and introducing them to younger people; for example, Zazu Colorburst and Colorwash lines of temporary hair coloring are to be introduced as fun products for those who want to change their hair color as often as they change their jewelry and clothes. Nevertheless, L'Oréal's overall corporate goal is to introduce new products that are not fads but that capture long-term changes in consumer preferences not only in Europe but also across the globe.

Throughout the world, L'Oréal ranks third, behind Avon and Shiseido, in the cosmetics business. L'Oréal is a collection of companies. Some of these it acquired, such as Helena Rubinstein. Others it has grown internally. Some 15 years ago, L'Oréal began investing in pharmaceutical research through its wholly owned subsidiary, Synthelabo. The latter now accounts for 15 percent of the group's annual sales. L'Oréal sees this as a long-term investment compared to the more short-term view taken by Revlon in its attempt at product diversification.

STRATEGY ANALYSIS OF L'ORÉAL'S INTERNATIONAL BUSINESS PERFORMANCE

The L'Oréal case reinforces some of the conclusions drawn from the Molson case. First, overseas expansion through exporting is a long-term, feasible strategy for companies that apply their core skills to opportunities in foreign markets. L'Oréal kept its costs of production competitive by not seeking market-defying subsidies from the French government to purchase raw materials, construct factories, or employ labor. Instead, L'Oréal used its increases in market share and higher returns on export sales to make itself better off in both the short and long run.

Second, L'Oréal's export expansion strategy built on in-house research, precise knowledge about customers, global products tailored to national preferences, acquisition of a local distributor, and product diversification. With effective production and marketing management, L'Oréal paid off its costs of entry and costs of ongoing business in both its home and import markets.

Third, L'Oréal's competitive advantage in Europe was strengthened by its strong market share in the United States. Even with competent organizational learning, exporters do *not* have to become foreign investors nor do they have to acquire local firms to sustain their competitive advantage over the long run. Through exports, L'Oréal has restructured its industry, set new standards for hair care preparations, and dominated U.S.-owned firms.

STRATEGY INSIGHT

Success in international business comes from the right combination of product market talents worthy of cultural, economic, political, and commercial risks inherent in host country markets.

Therefore, L'Oréal should continue to employ its export expansion strategy. The risks are negligible. On the other hand, the opportunities for increases in sales and cash flow are substantial as long as the firm's executives choose appropriate core research, production, and marketing skills for their international business. This is the correct international business strategy for L'Oréal in the United States and Europe.

PROCTER & GAMBLE UNSUCCESSFULLY SELLS PAMPERS IN JAPAN[10]

Through high-quality research and skillful brand management, Procter & Gamble (P&G) dominates the markets for detergents and personal care products in the United States. It is number one in the following product categories: detergent (Tide), deodorant (Secret), coffee (Folgers), cleanser (Comet), stomach remedy (Pepto-Bismol), toilet paper (Charmin), cough syrup (NyQuil), dishwasher soap (Cascade), peanut butter (Jif), shortening (Crisco), and fabric softener (Downy).[11] Colgate is a strong number two firm and Unilever is a weak number three firm. P&G knows what U.S. consumers want long before they realize something is missing from their life-style. P&G is a great success in the United States.

The firm also sells its goods in more than 140 countries, yet its chief rivals, Colgate and Unilever, are the dominant firms in most product market categories outside the United States. There they reap the benefits from scale economies and worldwide market integration while P&G remains humiliated as a weak third firm along with its Japanese rivals, Kao and UniCharm. P&G is not the same great success overseas.

All of these rival companies recognize the growing similarity (or convergence) of preferences among U.S., European, and Japanese consumers for soap, detergents, and personal care products. That is why Colgate went to Europe and Asia, Unilever to Japan and the U.S., and Kao to southeast Asia and the U.S. with exports and direct investments. Moreover, all of these firms were better than P&G at overseas market development because they used cross-functional teams between the parent firm and subsidiaries to implement the most effective set of international strategies and tactics possible. P&G chose to believe in the superiority of U.S. brand management, and from this managerial decision came P&G's initial success and prolonged failure in the sale of Pampers in Japan.

RESEARCH ON BRANDS FINDS SIMILAR MARKET SEGMENTS WORLDWIDE

In the 1960s, P&G introduced disposable diapers in the United States under the brand name Pampers. Within 10 years, P&G captured export markets in Canada and Europe. Then in 1978, P&G began exporting Pampers to Japan, where, because of first-mover advantage, it gained 90 percent of the market niche almost immediately.[12] Because its disposable diapers curtailed leaking and eliminated soaking, P&G was successful in taking market share away from Japanese manufacturers of cloth diapers and local providers of diaper services.

P&G had everything going for it. Within the parent firm in Cincinnati, Ohio, its aggressive brand managers sought to find out what consumers wanted before consumers even understood their latent preferences for new goods. These marketing executives believed in market share as the only sure way to keep P&G ahead of Colgate and Unilever in the U.S. market. After export successes in Canada, Great Britain, and Europe, P&G's brand managers believed their products could be sold anywhere because markets, tastes, and preferences were so similar that whatever was best for the U.S. was best for the world.

Moreover, P&G had everything going for it in Japan. Beginning as early as 1973, P&G went into a joint venture with the Nippon Sunhome Co. of Osaka. The latter's help was needed to set up the manufacture of soap and cleaning products and to gain entry into Japan's complex distribution system.

Because P&G already was exporting Pampers elsewhere in the world, its disposable diapers had the ring of an American success story for Japanese consumers. In 1978, prestige-conscious Japanese consumers were willing to pay a premium for products made in the United States. The Japanese began buying Pampers in very large quantities.

Within a year, P&G's success turned to failure. Japanese competitors came up with a better product, and Japanese customers began reacting negatively to P&G's advertising campaigns and distribution policies. However, P&G's management refused to adapt its U.S. strategies to the culture of Japanese business. The firm paid a heavy price with eight years in the wilderness before sales began to pick up once again in Japan for Pampers.

MANAGERIAL FAILURE IMPOSES HIGH LEVEL OF CULTURAL RISK

If P&G had not been so set in its ways, it would have noticed three significant cultural (or psychic) differences between Americans and the Japanese concerning diapers. First, the image cues P&G presented in its advertising were wrong for the Japanese culture. The firm sold Pampers with slice-of-life and testimonial advertising more suitable to the U.S. market.[13] The ads used a blonde, blue-eyed baby, who looked out of place among black-haired, dark-eyed Japanese. Moreover, the ads conveyed the idea that Japanese mothers need not bother changing their babies' diapers. This goes against an important social pattern in Japan—that is, Japanese mothers change their babies twice as often as do American mothers. Finally, the ads projected the image of the brand name rather than the corporate image. In Japan, the corporate image must be advertised to establish relationships with distributors and consumers. Therefore, these ads widened the cultural distance between Pampers and Japanese mothers rather than bringing them closer together.

Second, Pampers were too bulky for Japanese babies, and thus they tended to leak in Japan, which was not the case in the United States. Both UniCharm, which ultimately gained one half of the Japanese diaper market, and Kao, which gained 30 percent with its Merrys brand name, modified P&G's disposable diapers to suit the size and needs of Japanese babies.

Moreover, UniCharm introduced a "super-slurper" polymer product, which was invented in Japan, whereas P&G continued to make its disposable diapers with paper pulp. UniCharm's product soaked up wetness and held it in the form of a gel which kept babies drier longer.[14] Also, UniCharm shaped its disposable diapers in an hourglass form, added elastic legs to prevent leakage, and provided reusable adhesive closures for better fit.

Third, when things began to go wrong, P&G sought to keep market share by cutting its price and hence reducing margins to its distributors. In Japan, discounted goods do not generate enough profits for the vast number of retailers who have very limited shelf space and infrequent turnover. Once P&G introduced a price-cutting strategy, it devalued the Pampers brand name in the minds of Japanese consumers. There was no going back for P&G because Japan's Fair Trade Commission tightly restricts the number of free samples, gifts and discount coupons any firm can use to win back customers.

P&G'S INTERNATIONAL MARKETING TACTICS

Unsuccessful:
- Gains market share based upon similarity of preferences
- Uses advertising cues more appropriate to home market
- Fails to change product quality
- Chooses inappropriate distribution practices for host market

Successful:
- Improves product quality and introduces innovations
- Establishes teamwork with its local workers and technicians
- Chooses appropriate distribution practices for host market
- Uses advertising and promotional cues appropriate to host market
- Rebuilds market share by narrowing cultural differences

MANAGERIAL DEFTNESS LEARNED THE HARD WAY

By 1987, P&G was beginning to turn itself around in Japan. First, P&G introduced improved, compact, ultra-thin Ultra Pampers with a superabsorbent gel. The bulk of Ultra Pampers was one half that of Pampers so that Ultra Pampers could be stored more easily in Japanese homes where closet space is a great deal more limited than in the United States. This innovative technology has been introduced into Whisper (a sanitary towel) and Attend (a diaper for adults).

Second, P&G modernized and doubled the capacity of its plant in Akashi, Japan. The rank-and-file workers were given the responsibility for setting the criteria for quality control, and small teams of technicians were given the responsibility for reducing manufacturing time, cutting costs, raising productivity, and improving quality.

Third, P&G began visiting the vast number of small mom-and-pop stores, 7–11 convenience shops, and supermarkets to check shelf space and monitor the sales and turnover of Pampers. P&G has sought to make Japanese retailers and wholesalers members of the team so that more Pampers will be sold. P&G has formed a National Accounts Division to work with the top 10 chains and wholesalers in Japan.

Finally, P&G's ads now demonstrate a strong product in which a talking diaper shows viewers how to use it from beginning to end.[15] This ad is a hit because the Japanese prefer animation in their ads and because it has a closing with P&G's corporate signature. Also, P&G has formed a Pampers Club to build brand loyalty, and it gives proofs of purchase that can be redeemed for toys, children's books, and other premiums.

With all of these changes, P&G has regained a 30 percent market share in Japan. Yet P&G cannot regain its first-mover advantage nor recreate its long-term competitive advantage in the Japanese market. Overall, P&G's decision to take Pampers to Japan has made it a stronger firm worldwide because it has learned how to be competitive in one of the most difficult markets in the world.

STRATEGY ANALYSIS OF P&G'S INTERNATIONAL BUSINESS PERFORMANCE

The obvious conclusion is that P&G failed all four tests, but some things can be learned from its humiliation in Japan. Even though markets seem similar on the surface, cultural differences do wreak havoc on the firm's ability to implement preexisting manufacturing and marketing strategies. The tactics must change because perceptions differ about what is in good taste and whether product quality measures up to local standards. Only after being in Japan for a decade and losing $200 million (in U.S. dollars) did P&G learn these hard truths about international marketing competitiveness. The firm also stepped out of its American skin by making its Japanese staff a part of its worldwide team. Now P&G's Japanese employees have the important assignment of fitting the firm's core skills in research and brand management to market opportunities in Japan.

ARTZT ON P&G'S CHANCES FOR SUCCESS IN JAPAN[16]

We learned our lessons well and the hard way for 16 years in Japan.

The Japanese will be formidable competitors.

The Japanese have no inherent advantage in terms of cost or quality or attention to consumer needs.

In January 1990, Edwin L. Artzt was named CEO of P&G after a 37-year climb through the firm's marketing and management ranks. Like Owen-Jones, Artzt is the product of his firm's fondness for management continuity and its preference for almost lifetime employment for its senior executives. Whereas Owen-Jones is British and the CEO of a French firm, Artzt is American and the CEO of an American firm, as all his predecessors have been since the founding of P&G over a century ago. This management inbreeding led to the Pampers humiliation in Japan.

In 1981, Artzt took over responsibility for all of P&G's international business, including turning Japanese losses into profits. Thanks to his work, Ultra Pampers is the new market leader in Japan. When Artzt took over as CEO, P&G's international business had grown to 40 percent of its sales and 35 percent of its profits. The firm has first place abroad in the following product categories: diapers (Ultra Pampers) in France, toothpaste (Blend a med) in West Germany, and fabric softener (Lenor) in West Germany.[17] Artzt's assignment was to make the firm the market leader in each of P&G's 39 product categories in every national market throughout the world.

What does Artzt have to say about P&G's future in international business? "We need to develop the ability to deliver globally what we do well regionally. We have to adapt to overseas markets."[18] What does he think about himself as the CEO? "It is not enough that I [P&G] win; all others [Colgate, Unilever, Kao, and UniCharm] must lose ... Winning is the only result that matters."[19] This is how Artzt plans to develop an international management consciousness at Procter & Gamble.

INTERNATIONAL MARKETING TEAMWORK

Contrast L'Oréal with P&G. L'Oréal's initial studies of the British, European, and American markets were strong on executive intuition, product research, and brand management. The firm's marketing tactics were targeted to minimize the cultural risks faced by new products in all foreign markets. P&G surveys of the U.S. market were also strong on intuition, research, and marketing management. As long as foreign markets had few cultural differences with the United States, P&G could get away with using the same product anywhere in the world. In the case of Pampers in Japan, P&G's analysis should have included intuitive and research inputs from Japanese executives and employees. That is the essence of international marketing teamwork. The task of executives is to learn from successes and failures so that international business performance is enhanced throughout the world.

Exhibit 2–A shows the second international business decision. L'Oréal carried out this decision quite successfully when it entered the British, European, and U.S. markets; P&G did not do as well in Japan. Exhibit 2–B shows the marketing tactics for rolling out Decision 2; many of these had to be addressed by P&G before it could turn its Japanese business from losses to profits. Exhibit 2–C presents the data elements for assessing skills.

EXHIBIT 2–A
International Business Decision 2: Success in Fitting Core Skills

Research and development
Manufacturing
Brand management
Marketing
Organizational design
Financial services

Note: Executives must specify core skills to fit the international business problems of the firm. Is it a research and development problem? Is it a brand management problem? Is it a marketing problem? Is it an organizational problem? Or is it a combination of these problems?

EXHIBIT 2–B
International Marketing Tactics for Rolling Out Decision 2

Fit core skills
Use teamwork to postion products quickly
Determine similarity between home and host country markets
Stress commitment to overseas market development

EXHIBIT 2–C
Data Elements for Assessing Skills

Reduction in development time
Use of cross-functional teams
Availability of transferable knowledge
Research connections
Ability to discern cultural (legal) differences
Balancing business and government needs
Managing internationally
Integrating external markets (internalization)

INTERNATIONAL MARKETING TACTICS AND DATA ELEMENTS FOR ASSESSING SKILLS

The following section provides an explanation of how various firms have used the four tactics listed in Exhibit 2–B for rolling out Decision 2. It also provides examples for the data elements listed in Exhibit 2–C for assessing skills.

Tactic: Fit Core Skills

L'Oréal fit core research and development skills to market opportunities in Europe and the United States. Its administrative culture is to do in-house research for long periods of time and then to come up with products specially suited to meet the unmet demands of customers. However, new products do not go from test marketing to final production unless the sales force tells management that customers want these products. Free Hold, Preference, Zazu Colorburst, Colorwash, and Studio Line are examples of new products successfully launched on the advice of the sales force.

MARKETING INTELLIGENCE

International competitiveness comes from success in launching new products.

Moreover, L'Oréal's core product skills are easily transferable from France to England, to the United States, and now to Japan. Corporate management empowers local sales forces, wherever they may be, to decide the fate of new products developed in France.[20] After all, local sales personnel knew what their customers expected in terms of good taste, high quality, and effective service, and so they were able to convert short-term explosive demand for Free Hold into long-term steady demand for Studio Line. All of these efforts were in line with the CEO's dictum: Take as long as necessary to build up a brand name that conveys quality and luxury to customers. As a consequence, L'Oréal's executives are leaders in the development of an international management culture based on competitiveness in all markets of the world.

Tactic: Use Teamwork to Position Products Quickly

Speed and teamwork are the newest core skills found in the most profitable companies worldwide. Essentially, these firms start from scratch by wiping out approvals, setting up teams, worshiping the schedule, remembering to include distribution, and putting speed into the corporate culture.[21] What follows are comments about speed and teamwork from both sides of the Pacific Ocean.

Data Element: Reduction in Development Time

"We are doing everything possible to get development time down to under a year,"[22] says Hideaki Yasukawa, senior managing director of Seiko Epson in Japan. The firm puts more pressure on its engineers to do more group work with specialists in marketing, industrial design, and manufacturing all working together on project teams.[23] According to professor Hirotaka Takeuchi of Japan's Hitotsubashi University, Seiko Epson's "hand-picked, multi-disciplinary team works together from start to finish of the development process, has a high degree of autonomy and often includes representatives from key suppliers. The net result is a shorter development time."[24]

"Doing it fast forces you to do it right the first time,"[25] says John Young, the CEO of Hewlett-Packard (HP) in the United States. He ordered HP's break-even time—the interval between a new product conception and profitability, including covering all development costs—to be cut in half across the entire corporation.[26] Under Young's direction, HP's employees were forced to pull in the same direction; to decide how to implement new, Japanese-inspired management practices such as just-in-time inventory, quality circles, and worker incentives; and to develop HP's new DeskJet near-laser-quality printer within 22 months.[27] "My people like to win at business,"[28] says Young.

McKINSEY & CO. ON SPEED AND TEAMWORK[29]

High-tech products that come to market six months late but on budget will earn 33 percent less profit over five years. In contrast, coming out on time and 50 percent over budget cuts profits only 4 percent.

Data Element: Use of Cross-Functional Teams

Cross-functional teamwork in product design, new product development, and market introduction is crucial to positioning new products more quickly overseas. This team effort puts pressure on all employees to work together to roll out new products speedily without diminishing the flexibility of these goods to serve many worldwide markets. New design technologies such as computer-aided design manufacturing and a wide array of flexible components (e.g, semicustom microprocessors) are shrinking product life cycles and forcing the more rapid introduction of new products. Time and teamwork are the key variables.[30]

When speed and teamwork are applied to international marketing, the net result is shorter development time from product idea to market introduction in Japan, the U.S., and Europe. For example, during the 1980s, Japanese automobile manufacturers decided to release tentative (not final) design data to their tooling suppliers. Thus, the manufacturers reduced the average development cycle for cars from five years, which is the standard in Detroit, to three and a half years.

MARKETING INTELLIGENCE

International competitiveness comes from success in positioning products quickly in Japan, the United States, Europe, and the rest of the world.

Interestingly, Honda does not even have a formal marketing research department.[31] Instead, the analysis of future customer requirements is left to its technical research and development staff. Each year Honda's research staff receives 6 percent of the group's total sales. Research staff members have the dominant say over which research projects should proceed to development and then to commercial products. For example, in 1986, Honda introduced a new type of four-wheel drive in some of its cars; this had been the subject of research since 1978. Honda's teams number 30 persons—20 research and development people and 10 sales and marketing people. Even so, U.S. sales personnel are so close to customers that the parent firm empowers the U.S. sales force to say no when Honda Japan suggests models of motorcycles and cars unacceptable within North America.

Moreover, Xerox, a U.S.-owned international business firm, turned itself around by working closely with its suppliers to create a just-in-time inventory system.[32] It copied Epson and slashed the number of its suppliers. Then it involved them deeply in the design, development, and market introduction of its new products. Xerox also set up these groups as highly autonomous project teams with the objective of gaining tactical advantage over Canon.

Data Element: Availability of Transferable Knowledge

Epson, Honda, HP, and Xerox offer good examples of how knowledge (or organizational learning about new technologies, product design, and market innovation) crosses from Japan to the United States. Such effects of experience are the seeds from which an international management culture about speed and teamwork is emerging at L'Oréal, P&G, Epson, Honda, and HP.

Tactic: Determine Similarity between Home and Host Country Markets

Similarities in language, education, business practices, and culture (like those between the United States and Canada) encourage international executives to expect success in selling products overseas. These opportunities are seen as less risky than those in which significant cultural, economic, and political differences exist between countries (like those between the United States and Mexico or Japan). Therefore, overseas sales opportunities are rated in terms of how close they are to similar, perhaps less risky, opportunities at home. Those close by in terms of geographic proximity, cultural practices, and level of economic development are called nearest neighbor markets.

For example, Canadian products, such as Molson, Moosehead,

and Labatt beers, sell in the United States because the U.S. market is nearby in terms of physical location and the life-style of consumers. Canada's breweries are within 100 miles of the border. Convenience dictates shipping Canadian beer overnight by truck to New England, mid-Atlantic, and Midwestern states and within one week, via the interstate highway system, to the rest of the country. Because the two countries are each other's best foreign trade customer, customs procedures are routine, swift, and for the most part free of bureaucratic red tape.

Yet cultural differences do exist between the two countries. The Canadians lowered the alcohol content of their beer and changed the color of their beer bottle to match the preferences of Americans. Moreover, in Canada beer must be brewed in the province in which it is sold. Instead of exporting to Canada, U.S. breweries—such as Coors, Budweiser, and others—license Molson, Labatt, and Carling O'Keefe to brew U.S. beer in Canada.

Until 1994, beer is exempted from the U.S.–Canada Free Trade Agreement. Canada will continue to have a provincial beer industry, whereas the U.S. will have a national beer industry. Such psychic distance between two neighbors on how to organize the beer industry has several important implications for international marketing executives.

For example, the legal differences between Canada and the United States on federal, provincial, and state control impose additional costs on Canadian-owned breweries. They must brew beer in shorter production runs. Moreover, their incentive to introduce new products as quickly as their U.S. competitors is reduced when attention is given only to the Canadian market.

MARKETING INTELLIGENCE

International competitiveness comes from success in targeting the most appropriate home country products to host markets.

Nearest neighbor export markets are good sites in which to initiate overseas business because they are important places to get started and to learn about international business. However, they are not good sites over long periods of time. Because Canada has only 25 million people, it cannot provide U.S. manufacturers with the same potential for overseas sales growth as does Japan. Canadian executives must sell more goods and services to Europe, Asia, Latin America, and Africa before they can be considered successful international executives.

Tactic: Stress Commitment to Overseas Market Development[33]

As discussed in the cases presented in Chapters 1 and 2, both Molson and Labatt limit their overseas market development to their nearest neighbor, the United States. These two Canadian-owned firms lack the commitment to overseas market development and the breadth of international experience found in L'Oréal and P&G. For all firms, organizational learning is crucial to success in international business.

Executives must understand that the firm's size, proprietary technology, and unique new products offer substantial opportunities for creating competitive advantage overseas. They must have fire in their bellies about the desire for expansion, growth, and control of overseas markets. These executives must make sales overseas the most important business goal and have high expectations about the impact of international marketing on the firm's growth in revenues and cash flow.

MARKETING INTELLIGENCE

International competitiveness comes from winning at business all over the world.

Firms with high product visibility and well-known brand names have everything going for them. Their customers are potentially worldwide—in Europe, the United States, and Japan. Their international executives plan for the systematic exploration of overseas market opportunities and devote sufficient resources to international marketing activities, for example, gathering market information, assessing market potential, planning the marketing campaign, and financing the marketing effort. Favorable expectations lead management to commit additional resources to the marketing effort. Yet very few international firms have the long staying power of the Japanese, for whom increasing market share rather than short-term profits is the overarching goal in the United States, Europe, and elsewhere in the world.

STRATEGY ANALYSIS OF INTERNATIONAL MARKETING TEAMWORK

A second future has already happened in international business: Speed, teamwork, management continuity, and an international consciousness are now all part of the work of marketing executives. These are their crucial core skills. With them, international executives take advantage of marketing opportunities in similar and distant overseas markets, commit their firms to the emerging international management culture, and gain competitive advantage.

CONCLUSIONS FROM THE CASES

Clearly, L'Oréal created sustainable competitive advantage in hair care products in France, Western Europe, the United States, and elsewhere in the world. The lessons learned from this case are that research and marketing go together; they are twin members of the team. Research must lead to product innovation, whereas marketing must lead to product extensions in the right markets both at home and abroad. L'Oréal is better off today than it was before because of its export marketing success in the United States. It paid off its cost of entry and continues to make substantial returns on its investment, equity, and assets. However, L'Oréal did not make the U.S. markets in which it does business more structurally attractive to itself and did not force local firms into second, third, or fourth place.

P&G did not pass any of the four tests of international business performance. Although it had first-mover advantage with a new, innovative product in a distant, somewhat similar market, P&G failed to improve on its product's quality and found itself faced with strong local competitors. The competitors were so good that they humiliated P&G within the first year of the sale of disposable diapers in Japan. Today, the firm is only just coming back from a long period of shrunken sales, inadequate market share, and substantial losses in the Japanese market.

EXECUTIVE SUMMARY

Although both successes and failures are presented in this chapter about fitting core skills to overseas market opportunities, international executives must remember the essential theme of the discussion. Teamwork is crucial to getting new products out more quickly into similar and dissimilar markets. The sales force must be empowered to represent the firm's customers before production engineers and other technical personnel. The management of L'Oréal understands well the process of overseas market development. P&G's management had to learn a hard lesson before it came around to doing a better job at product innovation and quality, advertising, distribution, and pricing in Japan. All of these are important lessons for international marketing executives.

CHAPTER 3

ENTRY BARRIERS
WORTH OVERCOMING

The costs of our six-year plant modernization program to reduce production costs by one-fifth at our 32 factories don't 'bother us a bit, because we are absolutely convinced of the payoff in the long term. We have to play the long-term game because the competition is playing the long-term game."[1]

George A. Schaefer, *chairman and CEO of Caterpillar, Inc.*

COMPETITIVENESS: THE IMPORTANCE OF BEATING RIVALS

"Schaefer is probably the best manager the construction machinery industry has ever had,"[2] says John Stark, editor and publisher of *Off-Highway Ledger*, a trade newsletter. George A. Schaefer has been with Caterpillar (Cat) so long that he has his "coat of yellow paint," a phrase used at Cat to show corporate loyalty and continuity among senior management.[3] In this regard, Schaefer is no different from Widdrington of Labatt, Owen-Jones of L'Oréal, or Artzt of P&G. In another regard, Schaefer is very different. He has taken the offensive against his rivals to their home markets and has beat them there, in the United States, and elsewhere in the world.

Since 1985, when Schaefer was named CEO, he has stepped up the defense of Cat's leading world position against determined competitors, such as Japan's Komatsu.[4] Cat's global strategy is to force its Japanese competitors always to be playing catch-up ball. For example, the firm continues to invest in more efficient manufacturing systems, such as its 1990s project called Plant with a Future (PWAF). Its costs are 50 percent higher than original projections, which has reduced CAT's 1989 earnings. Moreover, Cat matches (or beats) its Japanese rivals in capital spending per employee, returns on equity, and cash flow from operations. Finally, Cat blocks the sales growth of its Japanese rivals in their home market to limit their increases in market share and cash flow.

Schaefer has also had the good sense not to let Cat's senior management become inbred with Americans. He brought in Cat's top manufacturing manager from Europe, a Frenchman named Pierre Guerindon, to run the firm's six-year PWAF modernization program. What Schaefer wanted was good advice and someone who would take charge of one of Cat's most ambitious investment projects. The following quote is a sample of what he got: "We are not going to compete with the Japanese by doing what they did five years ago. That's not enough,"[5] says Guerindon, now the group president in charge of PWAF.

Guerindon also told Schaefer to avoid the star wars trap of General Motors and stick with computerized machine tools, laser-read bar codes, and automated carrier systems. He advised Schaefer not to get caught with unproven paperless integration of everything from engineering to finance.[6] And Guerindon insisted that the entire layout of the plant be changed to reduce inventories, speed up assembly time, improve quality, and boost efficiency. Dan Coyle, the PWAF project manager at Cat's East Peoria, Illinois, transmission factory has said, "I'll tell you, the teamwork around here has been unbelievable."[7] Again, it is speed and teamwork that drives international competitiveness, even at Cat.

Schaefer's impact on his firm's chief rival, Komatsu, shows up in statements of how the latter deals with Cat. For example, in 1981, Ryoichi Kawai, then Komatsu's president and now chairman, said: "We eagerly want to catch up with Caterpillar by modelling ourselves on them."[8] Just four years later with Schaefer as CEO, Shoji Nogawa, the group president of Komatsu, was singing a different tune: "I'm not interested in being number one or number two. What is important is to have enough of a share so that we can exist and cooperate in this market."[9] By the time the decade was up in 1989, the new president of Komatsu, Tetsuya Katada, knew his firm had been beaten by Cat. The following are his excuses for losing to Cat: "We had a high export dependence of 60%. We were always at the mercy of exchange rates and we were at the centre of trade frictions."[10]

Komatsu was bloodied very badly by Caterpillar. Unlike Kao and UniCharm, which succeeded over P&G, Komatsu is unable (as the incumbent firm in Japan) to deny Cat market share, distribution channels, and selling space in Japan. Komatsu cannot raise entry barriers high enough to keep Cat (as the new contestant firm) out of Japan. The industry has a high degree of seller concentration with a few very large firms manufacturing the equipment. According to some economists, the Japanese construction and materials handling market is contestable.[11] Cat has put a practical twist on this new academic idea by using its worldwide dominance in technology, marketing, and service to reduce Komatsu's strength in Japan.[12]

STRATEGY INSIGHT

International competitiveness comes from using worldwide competitive advantage to take away profit sanctuaries of rivals in their home markets.

At no time, not even when the U.S. dollar's foreign exchange value was rising against the yen in the mid-1980s, did Cat think about exiting the Japanese market. Cat made its initial investments there as early as 1963 through a joint venture with Mitsubishi Heavy Industries and has kept putting capital in for three decades to deny Komatsu strength in its own home market. Over the years, Cat has become as much an incumbent in the Japanese market as is Komatsu. Even more important, Cat's sunk costs there (just like those of Komatsu) have become the variable costs of doing business in Japan.[13] Cat bet correctly that its future profitability (even discounted over time) would be greater than its ongoing expenses plus the costs of withdrawing completely from one of the three most important markets of the world.[14]

When P&G faced the choice of staying in or withdrawing from the disposable diapers in Japan, it stayed in even while its losses mounted to more than $200 million (in U.S. dollars) during the 10-year period it took to break even once again in Japan. Cat was never in such dire straits in Japan. Schaefer wisely recognized that the potential increases in market share and cash flow from its Japanese business and the technological and marketing spinoffs back in the United States and worldwide outweighed all potential difficulties and losses in Japan itself.

Global corporations such as P&G and Cat must stay in Japan and compete there indefinitely. In fact, they are foreclosed from exiting any major market in the world. Instead, these global firms must compete everywhere with technical innovations, modernization programs, marketing tactics, and global strategies crafted to be effective in individual national markets.

CATERPILLAR IN JAPAN[15]

Caterpillar designs and manufactures earthmoving, construction, and materials handling machinery at 30 plants worldwide. It contains between 35 and 50 percent of the construction equipment market in all countries except Japan.[16] More than one half of Cat's sales revenue comes from outside its home market.[17] Its worldwide rival, Japan's Komatsu, is the second largest producer of materials handling equipment, with a 60 percent Japanese market share, a 13 percent world market share, and a 10 percent U.S. market share.[18]

In 1963, by making what is now considered a farsighted strategic move, Cat entered into a joint venture with Mitsubishi Heavy Industries. Through this strategic alliance, Cat overcame the entry barriers imposed by its rivals in Japan (Ishikawajima-Harima, Hitachi, and Kubota) and took away the profit sanctuary of its chief rival, Komatsu.

DRUCKER ON STRATEGIC ALLIANCES[19]

1. The dynamics of the world economy are shifting to partnerships, joint ventures, research and marketing consortia, cross-licensing, and so on.
2. The major driving forces behind the trend toward alliances are technology and markets.
3. These joint ventures require extreme clarity in respect of objectives, strategies, policies, relationships, and people.
4. These alliances help international firms unbundle support services and put them in the hands of competent outside professionals.

Cat crafted the following deal with its Japanese partner. Cat transferred technology and after-sales support services to Japan. In return, Cat received local distribution outlets and long-term support in its negotiations for market-conforming rules on trade and investment with Japan's MITI. Cat's objective was to serve on one of MITI's joint government-industry boards so that the Japanese would recognize the joint venture as a domestic firm that happened to have one U.S. parent.

For almost 30 years, this partnership has worked quite well. First, it took place when the construction and materials handling industry in Japan needed restructuring; there were too many local firms with no one of them having the competitive strength of Cat, and so none of the incumbents could raise entry barriers high enough to keep out the dominant global firm and new contestant. Moreover, both Cat and its Japanese partner worked hard at integrating original equipment manufacturing (OEM) and after-sales services. Finally, both partners had a precise set of expectations about strategy, tactics, and results.

CATERPILLAR'S FIVE INTERNATIONAL MARKETING TACTICS

- Sets up equity joint venture
- Establishes strong nondominant market position

- Transfers technology and after-sales support services
- Negotiates sourcing and distribution alliances
- Builds consensus on market-conforming industrial policy

RIVALS FORCE EACH OTHER TO
MODERNIZE AND INVEST ABROAD

Cat's strategic alliance with Mitsubishi Heavy Industries forced Komatsu to beef up its investment at home and to seek opportunities overseas. Some economists report that such geographic diversification by rivals occurs in industries with high degrees of concentration, product differentiation, and research and development.[20] These scholars conclude that the results from cross-border investments among rivals are higher rates of technological innovation, changes in market share (usually a loss for dominant firms), and additional capital investment in most markets of the world.

When Cat went into Japan, the strongest incumbent was Komatsu, which was then a small firm with technologically inferior products. For 10 years, Cat had first-mover advantage over Komatsu in Japan. This did not last. All throughout these early years, MITI encouraged Komatsu to license newer, more up-to-date technology from other U.S. firms such as Cummins, International Harvester, and Bucyrus-Erie so that Komatsu could become a more competitive firm against Cat in Japan.

In the 1970s, Komatsu shed its partners, cut prices drastically, and ended Cat's first-mover advantage. Cat's share of the Japanese market, a modest 15 percent, was maintained by strengthening its dealer and service network, introducing higher quality products, and building up its joint venture with Mitsubishi.

Yet throughout the early 1980s, Cat's Japanese joint venture was limited to producing for the local market. It never had a world product mandate from its U.S. parent firm. Because of this, Cat's Japanese operations lacked both product breadth and economies of scale. Cat was in the throes of being overwhelmed by Komatsu's lower cost and price structure in Japan. Komatsu was able to undercut Cat by 40 percent in Japan, the United States, and the rest of the world. Then Schaefer came on the scene to end

Cat's Japanese agony with factory modernization, foreign investments, and debundling of support services.

MARKET SHARE ANALYSIS

But there is more to Cat's success than management skill. As early as 1987, Japanese demand for earthmoving, construction, and materials handling equipment began reaching all-time highs once again. The forecast was for demand to grow by 5 to 8 percent annually for the rest of the decade.[21] For American and European firms, this product category jumped to the top of the list of highest potential exports to Japan. Furthermore, through an in-depth analysis of market segments, Japanese demand was shown to be driven by the building boom in the Tokyo metropolitan region; the construction of a new airport for Tokyo; and an upgrading of industrial, housing, transportation, and service facilities throughout Japan. With demand high in Japan, Schaefer's risks turned into opportunities for protecting Cat's market share and limiting Komatsu's profits at home.

FOREIGN EXCHANGE ANALYSIS

When the U.S. dollar was high and the yen was cheap (from 1981 to 1986), Cat preferred to lose money rather than to give up market share. Finally, in the latter half of the 1980s, with the Japanese yen high and the U.S. dollar low, exports of Caterpillar parts, components, and equipment to Japan became cheaper and hence more competitive than products made by Komatsu. Schaefer's operations began to mint money, whereas Komatsu first sued for a truce and then accepted its fate as the number two firm, an also-ran, in the construction and materials handling industry.[22]

DECISIONS ABOUT STRATEGIC ALLIANCES AFFECT COMPETITIVENESS

With the coming of Schaefer as CEO, Cat made several tactical decisions to rebuild its core skills in Japan. First, it increased its investment in Japan by $105 million (in U.S. dollars).[23] Also, it emphasized the production of hydraulic excavators, which is the largest market segment in Japan, rather than a wide product line; products with a lower demand were imported from neighboring countries in Asia or, when the dollar was cheap in terms of the yen, from the United States. Moreover, Cat provided its dealer-distribution network with more financing and gave its local managers more control over pricing decisions.

Cat was not totally successful in beating back its chief rival. Cat still took 10 years to bring out a new product, whereas Komatsu cut new product development time in half. And Cat was slow in selling its older, out-of-date manufacturing plants, whereas Komatsu benefited from a modernization program that reduced the costs of production. This lasted until Schaefer introduced his PWAF program in the United States, Japan, Europe, and elsewhere in the world.

Schaefer also pursued his global strategy to expand all over the world. Today, Cat has wholly owned subsidiaries in Australia, Belgium, Brazil, Canada, France, Mexico, and Great Britian. It owns 80 percent of its Indonesian factory and 50 percent of its facilities in Japan and India. Cat also has production contracts with Eder of West Germany to make hydraulic excavators, Tanguay Industries of Quebec to make forest products equipment, and CMI of Oklahoma to make asphalt paving equipment. Such global sourcing reduces the cost of products to Cat's worldwide network.

Moreover, Cat licenses Daewoo, a Korean firm, to make lift trucks for sale in Korea, Japan, and the United States. Cat also licenses the People's Republic of China to make construction equipment for sale in China and other less-developed Asian countries. Both licensing arrangements enable Cat to let others produce its standard technology products at the lowest cost possible, whereas Cat in the U.S. can produce those products with the highest value-added possible for the most technologically sophisticated markets in the world. Such deals give Cat the ability to diversify its product line and match parts, components, and finished goods with the needs of local markets.

STRATEGY INSIGHT

Success in international business comes from the right combination of entry strategies for all national markets worldwide.

To tie all of its production sites together, Cat has 212 dealers, with more than one half of these outside the United States. These help it to integrate its 30 manufacturing centers worldwide and to shift manufacturing based on production costs, the foreign exchange value of local currencies, and the needs of each national market. Through its logistics program of "48 hours anywhere in the world or Cat pays,"[24] Cat is able to minimize downtime at construction sites and excessive freight charges for itself and its customers. Cat pays its dealers to maintain this stock of inventory even when rivals, such as Komatsu, threaten Cat's local market share.

All of this has come about because Schaefer is the CEO and architect of purpose for Caterpillar. Kawai, Nogawa, and Katada now say that Komatsu never stood a chance against Cat.

STRATEGY ANALYSIS OF CATERPILLAR'S INTERNATIONAL BUSINESS PERFORMANCE

The obvious conclusion is that Cat passed all four tests of international business performance, but some things can be learned from its success in Japan. Even though industries seem to be similar on the surface, the market power of incumbent firms forces foreign contestants to choose from among several alternatives for overcoming entry barriers. Molson and L'Oréal chose exporting, P&G decided to make a foreign direct investment, and Cat worked out a strategic alliance with a local firm. Also, the tactics must be different because of dissimilar underlying cost structures, technological capabilities, and managerial strengths. Only now that Cat has been in Japan for almost three decades is the wisdom of Cat's initial choice recognized; its local partner gave Cat access to

MITI in a way not open to other foreign firms with equally pressing needs to be seen as loyal players within the Japanese economy. Early on, Cat stepped out of its American skin by making its local partner, suppliers, and distributors members of the worldwide team. This is the international business strategy of Caterpillar.

INTERNATIONAL MARKETING MIX POLICY[25]

Caterpillar's success in becoming the dominant seller of earthmoving, construction, and materials handling equipment is due to the quality of its products, the appropriateness of its links with distributors, and the management of its worldwide support and service business. Moreover, Cat's success comes from how well it manages these three elements of its marketing mix (i.e., product, distribution, and service) in the face of its rival's demand for modernization and investment abroad. Finally, Cat's success is the result of management's willingness to unbundle transportation, distribution, and logistics activities and to let them be done through alliances with outside business firms.

In the mid-1970s, Komatsu, with the backing of MITI, began challenging Cat's first-mover advantage in Japan through cross-licensing deals and plant modernization programs. Once Komatsu was strong enough in its home market, it also began confronting Cat in the United States and the rest of the world through strategic alliances and foreign direct investments. Nevertheless, Komatsu never became the dominant firm in any place except Japan. Komatsu failed in two crucial things: distribution and service.

Exhibit 3–A shows the third international business decision. Cat carried out this decision successfully when it entered the Japanese market; Komatsu is now trying to do the same in the U.S. market. Exhibit 3–B shows the marketing tactics for rolling out Decision 3; some of these have to be addressed by Komatsu as it seeks to strengthen its business in the U.S. and Europe. Exhibit 3–C shows the data elements for assessing distribution barriers.

EXHIBIT 3–A
International Business Decision 3: Success in Overcoming Barriers in
Contestable Markets

Entry
Mobility
Exit

Note: Executives must specify decisions to fit the international business problems of the
firm. Is it a problem of getting into the market? Is it a problem of moving from one
segment to another in the same market? Is it a problem of leaving the market?

EXHIBIT 3–B
International Marketing Tactics for Rolling Out Decision 3

Overcome barriers in contestable markets
Prepare products for local market conditions
Select appropriate channels of distribution

EXHIBIT 3–C
Data Elements for Assessing Distribution Barriers

Long-term commitments from trading companies
Quality and service (after-market costs)
Equity and nonequity joint ventures
Indirect exporting
Direct exporting
Intrafirm exporting
Internalization of foreign trade

INTERNATIONAL MARKETING TACTICS AND DATA ELEMENTS FOR ASSESSING DISTRIBUTION

The following provides an explanation of how various firms have
used the three tactics listed in Exhibit 3–B for rolling out Decision 3. It also discusses most of the data elements listed in Exhibit
3–C for assessing distribution barriers.

Tactic: Overcome Barriers in Contestable Markets

A winning strategy for contesting foreign markets includes strong links with incumbent distributors (such as those described in Chapters 1 and 2 concerning Molson and Martlet, and L'Oréal and Cosmair) and with incumbent original equipment manufacturers (such as that between Caterpillar and Mitsubishi Heavy Industries). These marketing teams must prepare products to meet local market conditions, select the appropriate channel of distribution, and know when to go into joint ventures or make foreign direct investments. Sometimes these teams must include outside suppliers, distributors, and transportation firms because the international firm finds it more cost-effective to do these marketing activities externally through agents, middlemen, and freight forwarders. These strategic alliances stem from the desire of firms to unbundle or farm out work that is not part of the career ladder for senior management.

MARKETING INTELLIGENCE

International competitiveness comes from success in distribution, service, and support.

Data Element: Long-Term Commitments from Trading Companies

"The mechanics of Japanese distribution are something only the Japanese really understand,"[26] says Anthony Greener, the CEO of Dunhill Holdings, the British tobacco and fashion group. For most foreign firms, including such well-known American firms as P&G, Caterpillar, IBM, and McDonald's, the Japanese distribution system is a significant barrier. The following describes how Dunhill has overcome the high costs of getting its products introduced into Japan.

Dunhill sells its products in Japan through a subsidiary of C. Itoh, one of Japan's largest *sogo-shosha*, or trading companies. C.

Itoh is responsible for importing, breaking bulk, transporting, storing, and positioning Dunhill's high-status lighters, watches, shirts, and other fashion goods on retail shelves. Dunhill's marketing office in Japan takes care of local advertising, new business development, and liaisons with the head office in London.

Three things are necessary for success in Japan: (1) a physical presence in the country by the foreign firm, (2) the use of the right local distribution firm, and (3) an eye for detail and quality. According to Greener, "The Japanese have an extremely highly developed sense of quality, [not only for the product itself], but also about the quality of distribution, presentation, packaging and promotion."[27] Today, Dunhill is seen in Japan as a purveyor of high-quality British merchandise.

If Dunhill had left its Japanese operation in the hands of an occasional visit by its London-based export manager, it could not have been as successful as it is today in Japan. Dunhill made the correct strategic decision in selling its products directly to and integrating its export marketing organization with C. Itoh.

Tactic: Prepare Products for Local Market Conditions

Sales overseas require an attention to details, some of which are different from those in domestic sales. In Japan, P&G learned the hard way about consumer preferences for more form-fitting diapers that almost never leaked. Dunhill could not break into the retail market until it guaranteed its local distributor the quality that Japanese consumers preferred. Even Caterpillar had to concentrate its customer sales on hydraulic excavators rather than on other products in its product line.

No foreign contestant can modify product market arrangements in Japan unless a consensus has been reached between the industry and MITI. In the case of fast food firms such as McDonald's, Kentucky Fried Chicken, and Pizza Hut, U.S. firms go into strategic alliances with local partners, and the latter work with the Japanese business community to convince MITI that fast foods—such as hamburgers, french fries, fried chicken, and pizza—are socially desirable commercial products. Neither P&G nor Cat could overcome MITI's determined resistance to foreign control over local markets when strong Japanese rival firms existed to do the job just as well. So Cat unbundled half of its ownership and all responsibility for distribution and after-sales service to its local Japanese partner.

MARKETING INTELLIGENCE

International competitiveness comes from success in supplying national markets with socially desirable commercial products.

Data Element: Equity and Nonequity Joint Ventures

Cat moderated its global strategy in Japan. Instead of full ownership, it went into an equity joint venture. Moreover, instead of offering a complete product line, Cat limited the type of products it would sell to those recommended by its local partner and to those that fit into MITI's idea of what Cat's relationship to Komatsu should be in Japan. The benefit to Cat has been as follows: Cat has a strong position in the Japanese market from which it draws new technological strengths and through which it expands into other countries in Asia.

Tactic: Select Appropriate Channels of Distribution[28]

International marketing executives make several crucial decisions concerning overseas distribution: Should they use indirect or direct exporting? Who are the most appropriate export and import middlemen? When should these contractual arrangements be given up in favor of intrafirm transactions between the parent firm and its overseas subsidiaries? That is, when should international firms, such as Caterpillar, internalize or bring within the firm the entry barriers they face in overseas markets? And when should they unbundle them to take advantage of the professional competence of outsiders in transportation, distribution, logistics, freight movement, and service?

Data Element: Indirect Exporting

Penetrating foreign markets through indirect exporting means that the entry risk, the control over operations, and the quest for competitive advantage is in the hands of export and import middlemen, their local distributors, and domestic retailers.

For example, commission agents search for merchandise that can be sold by foreign firms. They are paid a commission on all goods that foreign companies buy from domestic manufacturers. Many commission agents also arrange purchases for foreign governments.

On the other hand, export management companies (EMCs) act as the export department for several manufacturers of noncompetitive products. EMCs usually do not take title to the goods; however, they do business in the name of the manufacturers. Larger EMCs may purchase the goods for resale (in this case, they do take title and act similar to a trading company, like the *sogoshosha* used by Dunhill); arrange for financing; and pay manufacturers immediately instead of upon collection from foreign customers. Very successful EMCs are able to gain complete control over the export sales of manufacturers; this power restricts the ability of manufacturers to shift from indirect exporting to direct exporting.

Finally, export remarketers purchase goods directly from manufacturers, then package and mark the products with their own labels. Remarketers sell goods under their own names. Manufacturers give up complete control over their products when they are sold to remarketers.

Smaller international firms tend to use these indirect sales and distribution methods because they do not have the organizational capacity to manage export marketing on their own. This lack of sufficient international marketing talent is a major entry barrier for smaller firms, and they overcome this barrier by selling their products worldwide through long-term contracts for indirect exporting with the types of middlemen listed above. When larger firms use indirect exporting, they are trying to rid themselves of goods that are being closed out, being taken out of the product line, or being dropped from manufacturing altogether. Their contracts are for one-time sales, and they do not presume any long-term relationship between large manufacturing firms and export middlemen.

Data Element: Direct Exporting

Manufacturers may decide to treat export sales no differently from domestic sales, or they may set up a separate internal export marketing department to take care of overseas transactions. When export sales become 5 percent or more of total sales (that is, when the firm's export intensity is 5 percent or greater), manufacturers usually shift to creating a separate export department. This is because the details of exporting—such as the preparation of customs documents and country of origin certificates, the selection of freight forwarders, the purchase of foreign exchange, and the adjudication of demurrage liability—require specialized skills unfamiliar to domestic businesspeople.

Sales representatives are agents who use the literature and samples of manufacturers to present the manufacturer's products to potential buyers. "Reps" work on commission, and their contracts with manufacturers define territories, terms of sales, methods of compensation, and other details.

Distributors are merchants who purchase goods at a discount from exporters and resell them at a profit. Moreover, distributors maintain an inventory of products and spare parts, and they service what they sell. Sometimes manufacturers establish their own captive distributors to service their products overseas. (See the examples of Molson and Martlet in Chapter 1, and L'Oréal and Cosmair in Chapter 2.)

Foreign retailers are merchants who buy consumer items from manufacturers or from sales representatives. As mentioned earlier, Dunhill uses C. Itoh, a Japanese trading company, to sell its products to Japanese retailers.

Direct sales to end users usually come about when foreign buyers are governments, hospitals, banks, and schools. Exporters (in this case, manufacturers) are responsible for shipping, payment collection, and product servicing. These costs must be built into the export price.

Large international firms that produce brand name consumer products (i.e. firms similar to P&G) use all types of sales and distribution methods, from deals with Japanese trading companies to direct sales with end users that are very large customers. These big firms want to push products through the channel of distribution with the intent of maintaining their control over retail shelf space, their sales strength among consumers, and their intimate knowledge of what product characteristics are being favorably received by customers. Through these efforts, large international firms overcome some of the entry barriers put in their way by incumbent rival firms in the contest for increased market share abroad.

Data Element: Intrafirm Exporting

Intrafirm exporting is in-house or captive trade. It is carried out within the international firm. For example, roughly 35 to 40 percent of U.S. imports and exports are between parent firms and their manufacturing subsidiaries.[29] These intrafirm transactions keep growing as more U.S. firms source components and finished products from their overseas subsidiaries.

Intrafirm exporting is not only an American phenomenon. Japanese manufacturers in Great Britain import over 84 percent of their components, parts, and finished goods from their parent firms in Japan.[30] This is also true for Japanese manufacturers in the United States. The most important reason for this is that many of these products are consumer durables that require after-sales support. Other reasons include changes in the value of foreign currencies, in labor usage and productivity rates, and in sources of technological innovation.

Data Element: Internalization of Foreign Trade[31]

Equity links with overseas subsidiaries (P&G) and joint venture partners (Caterpillar) increase the penetration of exports into foreign markets. Joint ventures are strategies for entering foreign markets without committing the substantial resources needed for building a new plant or acquiring an ongoing business. Some joint venture deals include the export of parts and semifinished goods, the licensing of technology, and the payment of fees for managerial and marketing expertise.

Cat uses its global network of wholly owned subsidiaries, joint venture partnerships, and contractual deals with licensees to service domestic and foreign markets. Cat's internal network protocols include delivery dates for parts, transfer prices for transactions, functional currencies for accounting consolidation, and repatriation of revenues between the parent firm and its wholly owned and majority-owned subsidiaries. Cat's external network protocols also include contractual agreements for the supply of components, the calculation of sales prices, and the payment of royalties between itself and licensees as well as charges for the use of warehouses, freight services, and distribution outlets.

Cat offers its global network proprietary knowledge about earthmoving and materials handling equipment, computerized manufacturing and logistics, and dealer and distribution contracts. In this way, Cat keeps control over its patents and other intellectual property. However, Cat is still able to broaden its product line and to diversify itself internationally. Cat's joint venture with Mitsubishi enabled Cat to create, expand, and maintain its competitive advantage in Japan.

Cat enforces quality control of its parts, components, and products among its subsidiaries, partners, offshore suppliers, distributors, and after-market service personnel to build confidence among its industrial buyers for its earthmoving and materials handling equipment. With assets at risk in many locations throughout the world, Cat must calculate the costs and benefits of internalizing exports and imports versus those of buying parts, components, and products from independent firms.

MARKETING INTELLIGENCE

International competitiveness comes from success in moving socially desirable products to national markets through the most cost-effective method of distribution.

Large international firms that manufacture expensive industrial goods prefer to carry out export-import transactions internally. These big firms want to push products through the channel of distribution with the intent of maintaining their control over wholesale inventories, their sales strength among customers, and their intimate knowledge of what product characteristics are being favorably received by end users. Through these efforts, large international firms overcome some of the entry barriers put in their way by incumbent rival firms in the contest for increased market share abroad.

STRATEGY ANALYSIS OF INTERNATIONAL MARKETING MIX POLICY

A third future has already happened in international business: Distribution, transportation, logistics, and other services are being unbundled from parent international firms as the latter farm out these marketing mix activities to those better able to do them on a more cost-effective basis. These firms hire outsiders (agents, middlemen, forwarders, and other logistics professionals) to handle the complexities of freight movements via oceangoing vessels and air freight. The movement of freight, its costs, insurance and packing, and the need to avoid expensive demurrage charges force manufacturers to integrate their international marketing organization into global freight, distribution, and logistics networks. Otherwise, these firms would face very high entry barriers and would be unable to sell their products in foreign markets. Unbundling of these support activities applies to small and large international firms as well as to consumer and industrial firms. Unbundling calls for international marketing executives to rethink completely their international marketing mix policies so that they can gain competitive advantage.

CONCLUSIONS FROM THE CASES

For three decades, beginning in the 1960s, Caterpillar has had sustainable competitive advantage in earthmoving and materials handling equipment in the United States, Japan, Europe, and elsewhere in the world. It has accomplished this through research and development, foreign direct investments with or without local partners, product sourcing and licensing contracts, and careful manufacturing and logistics management. Only once has the Japanese government raised a serious entry barrier, with its support of Komatsu as its national champion. Although in the 1980s Komatsu became an arch rival of Cat, Cat stopped Komatsu in its tracks through time and teamwork, plant modernization, investments and alliances, and astute marketing mix policies.

Cat was better off once Japan was no longer Komatsu's profit sanctuary. Cat invested more money in its U.S. factories, its Japanese joint ventures, and the rest of its worldwide manufacturing and product sourcing network. The results are impressive: a $10,000 increase in sales per employee, and a 5 percent increase in its return on assets.

The increase in the return on assets reflects Cat's investments away from the high labor cost areas of the United States, Europe, and Japan, and into the newly industrialized countries of Asia. Some of the increase in revenues and profits from its Japanese joint venture reflects the high value of the yen rather than real changes in the performance of its business in Japan.

Cat has not gained dominance in Japan. However, its accomplishments there fit neatly into its global strategy. In the U.S., Europe, and the rest of the world, Cat has been a great success in dominating Komatsu and imposing its standards upon the construction and materials handling industry.

EXECUTIVE SUMMARY

Like most U.S. and European firms, Cat needs Japanese partners, suppliers, distributors, wholesalers, and retailers to get its products through the long channels of distribution common in Japan. Most foreign firms find these distribution channels to be high entry barriers and, like Dunhill, never think of going it alone in Japan. Large-scale industrial companies whose products are for specialized markets must weigh the gains from internalizing the export-import business versus the costs of unbundling international marketing services. The choice is not always so clear-cut; nor is the choice made today the one most appropriate for tomorrow. Drucker sees the future as one of farming out or unbundling services best performed by outside professionals.[32]

STRATEGY ANALYSIS OF COUNTRIES AND INTERNATIONAL BUSINESS: THE COUNTRY RISK FORECAST

The focus of Part I has been on countries and their impact on three decisions faced by international firms: What are the risks worth taking? What are the core skills worth mastering? And what are the entry barriers worth overcoming? The answers to these questions yield a great deal of information necessary to the success of firms in foreign markets. Concerns about politics, economics, culture, import trade restrictions, investment potentials, technological and managerial skills, and distribution barriers are the substance of the country risk forecast.

Country risk is manageable through reciprocal market-conforming rules on trade and investments among countries and between countries and international firms. Country risk is made even more manageable with the development of an international management consciousness and the availability of supporting trading and distribution services for markets that are especially difficult to penetrate. Clearly, three things help firms gain competitive advantage: (1) a good hunch, (2) an international management culture, and (3) beating rival companies.

Success in international business is guaranteed by segmenting markets, being realistic about government intervention, making good intuitive decisions, converting risks into opportunities, launching and positioning new products, targeting new markets, farming out support services, and winning at business all over the world. These and other pieces of marketing intelligence provide international executives with a treasure trove of new ideas about improving international marketing competitiveness.

PART II

MARKETING MANAGEMENT AND INTERNATIONAL BUSINESS

How to Maintain Competitive Advantage

Product Sourcing
Customer Selection
Value Creation

CHAPTER 4

MANAGING PRODUCT SOURCING UNDER THE U.S.–CANADA FREE TRADE AGREEMENT

[International] risks are increased by currency variations and unfamiliarity with the foreign environment,[1]

Peter F. Drucker, *Clarke Professor of Social Sciences at the Claremont Graduate School.*

The dollar's [steep decline in 1986 and 1987] has been an extremely significant factor in the rise of paper exports.[2]

Norma Pace, *a senior economist at the American Paper Institute.*

In late 1987 and 1988, Canadian stocks like MacMillan, which are cheaper on a price-earnings basis than U.S. counterparts, may be the best plays [particularly] if prospects for freer U.S.–Canadian trade pan out.[3]

A brokerage executive who follows the paper industry.

The move toward a regional headquarters in North America (to take advantage of the U.S.–Canada Free Trade Agreement) is fast becoming an essential part of almost every successful company's transition to global competitor status.[4]

Kenichi Ohmae, *head of McKinsey & Company's office in Tokyo.*

COMPETITIVENESS: THE IMPORTANCE OF BEING AN INSIDER

Since January 1989, free trade has been a fact between the United States and Canada. Canadian-owned companies such as

Labatt, MacMillan Bloedel, and Northern Telecom are able "to hedge exposure to currency fluctuations through sound operating decisions and not simply through shrewd use of financial instruments."[5] Their investments in the U.S. and the location of their North American regional headquarters in Atlanta, Chicago, Dallas, and New York make them privileged insiders, empowered to do business anywhere in the 50 states and Puerto Rico as well as in the 10 Canadian provinces, the Yukon, and the Northwest Territories. Under the rules of the U.S.–Canada Free Trade Agreement, Canadian firms are given national treatment in the U.S.— that is, they cannot be discriminated against because they are foreign firms with headquarters in Toronto, Montreal, or Vancouver.

Moreover, "by becoming, in effect, an insider in key markets, a global corporation can make its costs independent of home country currency—that is, at a par with those of domestic competitors in each of its markets."[6] During the heyday of Canada's "no truck or trade with the Yanks" policies (i.e. when the Foreign Investment Review Agency, the National Energy Programme, etc. were at their fullest strength), the Canadian dollar fell in terms of the U.S. dollar. Canadian companies were earning their profits in these low Canadian dollars, thereby increasing the costs of foreign investments, particularly in the U.S., from which came crucial cash flow to offset everything going haywire in Canada. All that could be tangled, made amiss, done completely wrong, or put out of order in terms of market-restricting rules on trade and investment was implemented by the Canadian federal government between the mid-1970s and early 1980s.[7] Because of these mistaken government policies MacMillan Bloedel Ltd. became an insider within the paper products market of the United States.

The following explains how the firm did it.

> To maintain both short-term earnings and long-term investments in the future, multinationals out-source parts, components and products. Thus they are able to cut costs fast and sharply, when they need to, by shifting the burden of short-term currency and cost fluctuations to outside, off-shore suppliers.[8]

> Cost-cutting measures that forest products companies [such as MacMillan Bloedel Ltd. of Canada] implemented to survive the

tough times mean that they are raking in profits now [in 1987] that times are better.[9]

MacMillan Bloedel's labor costs, which were rising by about 10 percent annually in the early 1980s, increased by only 1 percent annually in the mid-1980s, and its energy costs were significantly lower as well.[10] Even as Canada once again opened itself up for increased U.S. investment and as the political groundwork was being laid for free trade, Canadian companies were looking for cheaper sources of supply in the United States.

The global corporation "can also pull the trick of using cheaper sources of inputs from elsewhere in the world, something local players cannot easily duplicate."[11] MacMillan Bloedel went into the American South to acquire forests with quicker growing trees (seven years in the South versus three decades in British Columbia). "The strength of a global corporation derives, in no small measure, from its ability as a full-fledged insider to understand local customers' needs."[12] MacMillan Bloedel found it could make more money in the U.S. by running the sales and marketing end of its containerboard, corrugated, and box businesses from Atlanta rather than Vancouver.

STRATEGY INSIGHT

International competitiveness comes from staying in international markets when the going gets tough and investing in processes, products, services, markets, and people to maintain the firm's wealth-producing capacity in the future.

"Global companies that are in markets for the long haul have to prepare to absorb these fluctuations [in currencies, market-restricting policies, costs, and customers' needs] themselves."[13] Or, these companies have to internalize fluctuations through equity links between parent firms and subsidiaries, and contractual links with suppliers, distributors, and other affiliates. MacMillan Bloedel did not cut and run from Canada when things got tough, nor did it stick completely to Canada when global opportunity beckoned in the United States. Rather, it integrated production and marketing among all of its business entities in both countries. For MacMillan, being a global player means viewing the whole of North America as its home market.

MacMILLAN BLOEDEL IN THE UNITED STATES[14]

MacMillan Bloedel is one of North America's largest forest products companies, with integrated operations in Canada and the United States, major investments in Europe, and distribution in Japan and worldwide. Because the largest share of its sales revenues comes from commodity products such as pulp and paper, its profitability is sensitive to the ups and downs of the business cycle. After the 1982 recession and its accompanying losses, MacMillan Bloedel decided to concentrate more on producing higher value-added products such as building materials, containerboard, and packaging materials. It also reorganized itself into five profit centers, closed unprofitable operations, reduced corporate overhead, and went into profitable overseas joint ventures. The result: Today, the firm makes good money from its worldwide operations.

COUNTRIES DEMAND NATIONAL FLEXIBILITY FROM INTERNATIONAL FIRMS

The boom in international business (with more than $600 billion in U.S. dollars in direct investments worldwide) records the success of international corporate capitalism. However, governments consider successful international firms controversial, and MacMillan Bloedel is no exception. Its home country, Canada, wants the firm to be loyal to the trade and investment policies of the federal government. But that is not to be.

Data Element: Market-Defying Government Practices
When Ottawa pursued market-defying trade and investment policies, MacMillan Bloedel made a good international business de-

cision and escaped to the United States. Nationalists condemn flight capital, for they want locally owned firms to follow the flag, something that MacMillan Bloedel has not done. Government bureaucrats want foreign investors to obey the local flag, an obedience not given easily by U.S. investors in Canada. Even though both sets of firms have global functions, local politicians want domestic firms to be national champions and to make productive investments, create high-paying jobs, pay additional taxes, and export more high-value products. These same officials expect foreign investors to be good citizens, too.[15] Nevertheless, both sets of international firms work very hard to slip the leash of nationalists and gain additional independence within the international economy. In 1984, Canadian market-restricting policies were rejected by the voters and a new government came to power in Ottawa.

Although this new group of politicians began pursuing market-conforming policies (including the 1989 Free Trade Agreement with the United States) in favor with Canada's international executives, it was too late to reverse the removal of MacMillan Bloedel, Seagrams, Labatt, and others to the United States. Throughout the 1980s, MacMillan Bloedel's U.S. assets rose from 34 percent to 41 percent of its total assets, with the remainder in Canada's forests, saw mills, and containerboard factories. By the end of the decade, 11 percent of MacMillan Bloedel's forest lands were in the southeastern United States. In addition, Alabama (not Ontario) got the go-ahead to manufacture the firm's new, unique, reconstituted lumber product, called Parallam (or parallel strand lumber), for the North American market.

On the positive side, the new government's schemes did reopen the Canadian market to substantial new U.S. investment, such as Stone Container's acquisition of Consolidated-Bathurst, another Canadian newsprint and pulp maker. These government programs permitted American firms such as GE to designate their Canadian subsidiaries as sole-source suppliers of products (e.g., lights for automobiles) to the firm's global business network. Moreover, these pro-free-trade policies permitted McDonald's Canada to take the lead in building up the fast food business in the Soviet Union.

Unfortunately, the government's policies could not reduce the higher level of labor strife in Canada versus the United States. MacMillan Bloedel has 15,300 employees, who are represented by the following unions: International Woodworkers of America (Canada) with 4,700 employees; the Canadian Paperworkers Union and the Pulp, Paper, and Woodworkers of Canada with all 4,000 hourly employees at the pulp and paper mills in British Columbia; and the United Paperworkers International Union with 800 employees in Alabama.

MacMillan Bloedel has rarely experienced labor harmony; its six-month strike in July 1986 was one of the longest and most bitter in the history of the province. The International Woodworkers of America (Canada) lowered MacMillan Bloedel's operating earnings by an estimated $88 million. For the five years ending December 31, 1987, about 6.8 percent of the company's total available hours for operations was lost due to labor disputes. American unions are generally less hostile to the company than their Canadian counterparts. After almost two decades of trying, MacMillan Bloedel has begun to feel more like an insider in the United States, not unlike Quaker Oats, which started out as a Canadian firm more than 75 years ago.

Data Element: Firms as National Champions

Canada as the host country wants foreign firms to make investments locally that challenge domestic rivals, strengthen market competition, and increase Canadian exports. However, Canada does not want U.S. and other foreign firms to oust domestic incumbents from their domination of local Canadian markets. This is what caused the explosion of market-defying laws in the 1970s. The fine line between private investment and national control is especially hard to draw for Canada because its primary supplier of investment capital is the United States, and 80 percent of its foreign trade (even before the U.S.–Canada Free Trade Agreement) is with the United States.

Therefore, Canada directed MacMillan Bloedel to be its national champion in the international economy. The national government applauded MacMillan Bloedel's decision to beat its U.S. competitors to the punch by offering a 5 percent rebate for full contract performance by newsprint customers in the western

United States. This is the firm's largest newsprint market, and to lose it would mean a decline in exports from British Columbia.

Moreover, the government praised MacMillan Bloedel's willingness to tailor its products to the Japanese market. For example, its Alberni Pacific Division in British Columbia manufactures an entire line of finished products designed specifically for the Japanese housing market. In addition, MacMillan Bloedel finds specific woods, such as coastal cyprus and yellow cedar, that are of the same genus as Japan's most prized scarce wood, hinoki. The company markets this hinoki substitute for premium prices in Japan. Also, the firm markets hemlock, Douglas fir, western red cedar, and Sitka spruce in Japan for use in a variety of products from shoji screens to traditional wood-frame housing systems. These sales mean jobs for Canadians, exports for Canada, and tangible benefits from freer trade for the government.

Data Element: Balancing Government and Business Needs

For MacMillan Bloedel and other international firms not to run aground once again against the siren call of Canadian nationalists, their executives must show more national flexibility toward local employment and exports while pursuing more integration with the United States.[16] Success at combining political and business imperatives is the essence of becoming a market insider.

MacMILLAN BLOEDEL'S EIGHT INTERNATIONAL MARKETING TACTICS

- Overcomes foreign exchange risk
- Gains cheaper source of inputs
- Introduces cost-cutting measures
- Internalizes external market fluctuations
- Combines national flexibility and global integration
- Transforms upstream scale economies into downstream scope economies
- Improves raw materials and finished products
- Turns North America into export platform

RIVALS FORCE INTERNATIONAL INTEGRATION

Although a global forest products industry exists, market opportunities are regional and depend on the resources available nearby, for example, the newsprint market of the western United States and the forests in British Columbia. Some regions, such as Europe, have more demand for than supply of high-quality fiber resources, and they are big importers of pulp from Canada. Within North America, the business is heavily dependent on the business cycle to determine whether over- or undercapacity exists in the industry.

On the other hand, product prices are determined in global rather than in domestic markets. Unfortunately, MacMillan Bloedel does not participate in any one regional market in such a major way as to unilaterally determine prices. Because the firm tends to be a price taker rather than a price giver, it is trying to introduce special wood and paper products that give added value to its customers.

Through foreign investments (especially in the United States), equity joint ventures in Europe and Japan, and significant and ongoing investments in technology development, MacMillan is beginning the investment integration of Europe with North America while servicing Japan and the "southern" countries through exports from North America. MacMillan Bloedel is turning North America into an export platform that services Europe, Japan, and the less-developed countries of the world.

Technically, MacMillan Bloedel is using three market integration tactics to lower its costs of production and broaden its product line: (1) internalization, (2) intrafirm (and intranetwork) foreign trade, and (3) the transformation of upstream scale economies into downstream scope economies.

Data Element: Integrating External Markets (or Internalization)

According to some economists, internalization (i.e., bringing external markets into the firm) refers to the equity ties that bind a parent firm and its subsidiaries together across national frontiers.[17] These academics say that when external markets charge excessive transaction costs the result is internalization. In terms of MacMillan Bloedel, the market-defying Canadian laws on trade and investment and the resulting low value of the Canadian dollar caused the firm to move assets to, set up a subsidiary in, and do export business from the United States.

Moreover, until the U.S.–Canada Free Trade Agreement went into effect in 1989, MacMillan Bloedel and other Canadian forest products firms were subject to U.S. complaints that the Canadian government was giving unfair subsidies (or stumpage fees) to its lumber mills forcing the latter to impose a 15 percent tax on softwood lumber shipped to the United States.[18] A major reason for the U.S. grievance is that Canadian firms boosted their share of the U.S. lumber market from about 25 percent to 33⅓ percent when the Canadian dollar was weak and when these companies were making productivity gains through technological improvements and labor-saving practices. American competitors demanded and got the U.S. International Trade Commission to impose countervail duties equal to the federal and provincial stumpage fees. The unilateral imposition of higher tariffs by the U.S. ended with the initiation of the U.S.–Canada Free Trade Agreement.

Academics say that when external markets are regulated by tariffs, nontariff barriers, regulations on subsidies and dumping, and other anachronisms of an era when currencies fluctuated regularly and unpredictably, the result is internalization. Because the theory leads to the practice of marking prices up or down every time currencies rise or fall, prices of imported parts, components, and finished goods have a lot more to do with government shortsightedness than with the real needs of customers, hence the need to internalize these fluctuations within the firm (or to unbundle them within the firm's global network of subsidiaries and affiliates, suppliers and distributors, and customers).

Finally, economists suggest that if external markets are missing altogether from the international economy the result is internalization. When MacMillan Bloedel financed its own research and development and created Parallam, the hinoki substitute, the resulting sales within North America and to Europe and

Japan were to market segments that did not exist before the product was created.[19] For marketing executives, internalization means discovering latent demand and then tailoring new products to unmet customer needs.

Data Element: Integrating Intrafirm Foreign Trade (or Internalization)

Throughout the 1980s, MacMillan Bloedel achieved high levels of international integration through intrafirm (or intranetwork) exporting and importing. The firm set up strategic alliances among its Canadian parent, U.S. subsidiary, Dutch joint venture partner, Japanese marketing partner, and worldwide suppliers and distributors. MacMillan Bloedel's administrative protocols included delivery dates, transfer (or sales) prices, functional currencies, charges for warehousing and freight, licensing fees, and royalty payments. Through these equity, contractual, and cooperative exchanges, MacMillan Bloedel internalized foreign trade within its global business network. In short, MacMillan Bloedel made a success of its integration strategy by retaining sufficient national flexibility to please both its home government and its host government.

Data Element: Integrating Upstream Scale Economies and Downstream Scope Economies

Upstream (or backward) integration is from forests, lumber mills, and pulp and paper mills to corrugated or containerboard manufacturing operations. This type of integration produces economies of scale or lower costs of production.

Downstream (or forward) integration is from manufacturing operations to processors of newsprint, building and packaging materials, and fine paper to partners, distributors, and sales offices worldwide. This type of integration produces economies of scope and widens the product line.

When upstream scale economies are transformed into downstream scope economies, international integration helps the firm match appropriate products to appropriate markets worldwide. The following explains how MacMillan Bloedel is carrying out international integration in the face of competition from rival Canadian and U.S. firms.

Five Operating Units. Three manufacturing units are in British Columbia: the Nanaimo Region, the Alberni Region, and the Powell River Region. These units specialize in different forest products. The other two units are the containerboard group and the marketing group both of which are in Canada *and* the United States.

Mill Specialization. Within Canada, the firm's lumber mills specialize in supplying raw materials or semiprocessed products to paper and containerboard operations in the United States and Europe. Often, the finished products are returned to Canada.

An example of mill specialization is the Harmac Mill in the Nanaimo Region. The Harmac mill produces fully bleached northern softwood pulp, a great deal of which is manufactured and blended to meet the specific requirements of its customers, who produce a wide variety of grade paper products. Approximately 61 percent of Harmac's pulp is sold in Europe, 22 percent in the Pacific Rim, and 17 percent in North America.

MacMillan Bloedel is modernizing its old sawmills or replacing them with smaller, more efficient mills that specialize in particular grades and species of logs. Each mill matches its unique mix of logs to those end uses that best fit the value to be realized from the company's timber resources.

Harmac's largest customer is Koninklijke Nederlandse Papierfabrieken N.V. (KNP), a Dutch affiliate in which MacMillan Bloedel owns a 28.5 percent interest. KNP is one of Europe's largest producers of coated and uncoated printing papers, and an important pulp customer for MacMillan Bloedel. Fine paper produced by KNP is marketed in the United States through the U.S. subsidiaries of MacMillan.

MacMillan Bloedel concentrates its standard newsprint operations in the western U.S. (where prices are lower than in the east due to a difference in the supply and demand),[20] Canada, the Pacific Rim countries, and Latin America.

Containerboard Group. MacMillan Bloedel has a corrugating medium mill in Sturgeon Falls, Ontario. The firm also has a fully integrated containerboard complex in Pine Hill, Alabama. This plant is located in one of the finest and most market-accessible fiber markets in the world, and it is one of the lowest cost container board operations in North America. The Alabama plant supplies linerboard and corrugating medium to the British joint venture, MacMillan Smurfit SCA Limited (U.K. Corrugated), which is the second largest producer of corrugated containers in England.

MacMillan Bloedel merged its packaging operations in Great Britain and Canada with those of other industry leaders. This increased the firm's market share for containerboard. Through this effort at rationalizing combined packaging operations, the company earns a greater return on its 50 percent share of the merged operations than it used to obtain from the 100 percent share of its previous holdings.

However, the majority of MacMillan Bloedel's containerboard-producing assets remains in the United States because 79 percent of the company's sales in 1987 were in the United States, the key market for containerboard in the world.

MacMillan Bloedel Containers is based in Atlanta, Georgia, and operates 11 corrugated container plants in the American Midwest, South, and East. These plants produce a wide range of corrugated containers from huge, bulk-bin industrial containers to small, custom-designed, and printed display packaging for lamp wrappers. MacMillan Bloedel Containers sells its fruit and produce containers internationally in South America and Africa.

Moreover, the firm has benefited from the decision of Japanese and European companies to reduce their efforts in packaging paper. Since both the Scandinavians and the Japanese do not have the access to the cheap fiber that is available to American and Canadian companies, the former are concentrating their efforts on higher-end specialty papers where the profit margins are higher.[21]

Marketing Group. MacMillan Bloedel has 38 building materials distribution centers throughout the world. Their task is to help MacMillan Bloedel become more competitive overseas through improved customer service. Moreover, the company has sales offices in Tokyo, Hong Kong, Kuala Lumpur, and Sydney to market pulp and newsprint into the low-risk, high-growth, mass consumer markets of the Pacific Rim. The western U.S. is serviced from four offices along the Pacific coast. The Canadian market is serviced from Vancouver; European customers from London and Brussels; and British customers from Twickenham, England.

Twenty percent of MacMillan Bloedel's lumber production is now shipped to Japan. Through its building materials distribution center, MacMillan Bloedel is able to service Japan's large demand for high value-added products.

Freight and Transportation Services.   To ensure cargo care and frequent service for its customers, MacMillan Bloedel is involved in all aspects of surface transportation including deep-sea shipping and barging, ship brokerage and agency services, stevedoring, freight solicitation, bookings, forwarding, and terminal operations.

MacMillan Bloedel's transportation department takes advantage of opportunities to reduce costs, particularly from deregulation of transportation in the United States. Shipments to overseas markets are made on vessels operated by the company's subsidiary, Canadian Transport Company Limited. This subsidiary operates a fleet of sophisticated forest products vessels and has expertise in damage-free delivery of high-grade paper, pulp, and solid wood products.

With MacMillan Bloedel's reputation for delivering products safely and quickly, the firm has been able to break into the growing market for higher value-added products in the European Economic Community.

DECISIONS ABOUT PRODUCT SOURCING WITHIN NORTH AMERICA AFFECT INTERNATIONAL COMPETITIVENESS

Because MacMillan Bloedel does business in an industry often plagued by excess capacity, which results in low product prices, the company is shifting some of its manufacturing operations toward products with higher productivity and more value-added to help improve its profit margins. The following are some of the crucial decisions made by the firm to enhance its competitiveness.

The mountainous terrain of British Columbia and its remoteness from major markets have forced MacMillan Bloedel to find new forestry methods to offset the high costs of delivering wood to Ontario and Quebec in central Canada, and to the United States. For example, improvements in logging techniques and practices, such as mechanical harvesting and efficient dryland sorting, have helped to improve the quality of logs produced. Intensive reforestation efforts on both Canadian and U.S. lands have insured product quality by increasing the availability of high-quality fiber. New processes have been developed in both pulp and paper and solid-wood converting facilities to increase fiber recovery and reduce end product costs. These improvements in productivity have been the primary reason for a substantial improvement in operating earnings.

Also, MacMillan Bloedel began taking the suggestions of its employees to heart. For example, employees in the Alberni Region made two suggestions that reduced oil consumption. They recommended a modification in power boilers to increase their hog fuel burning efficiency. Then they suggested a change in the method of spraying black liquor, which is a by-product of the pulping process and the lowest-cost fuel available to generate steam. Furthermore, employees at Pine Hill, Alabama, recommended a new method for utilizing a low-cost mix of fuels in producing containerboard. Even the U.S. Bureau of Standards accredited a MacMillan Bloedel laboratory to work with containerboard customers for the purpose of determining the most effective packaging strength.

In 1976, MacMillan Bloedel produced 89 percent standard newsprint and 11 percent specialty grades. Ten years later, standard newsprint comprised only 61 percent, whereas the remainder of newsprint production was in a wide range of specialty groundwood printing papers. The firm also diversified its lumber from construction grade into decorative grades. The latter lumber products are largely made from western red cedar. The company controls over 10 percent of the world's western red cedar market. Since 1980, its range of value-added products from this species has grown from 10 to more than 100.

In 1980, the paper machines in the Alberni Region only produced standard newsprint. By 1985, two of the mill's three paper machines ran lightweight groundwood printing papers in a variety of colors. A crucial product from this specialized printing paper is the yellow telephone directory paper (or "golden pages") that is marketed in the United States, Japan, and elsewhere in the world.

With MacMillan Bloedel's ability to produce yellow telephone directory paper, the Alberni Region mills became one of three foreign suppliers to Japan's Nippon Telephone and Telegraph Company. This gave MacMillan Bloedel a significant boost in its diversification into Japan and improved its chances of making its building materials subsidiary a successful business in Japan.

STRATEGY INSIGHT

International competitiveness comes from integrating suppliers into the sourcing, manufacturing, and distribution practices of the firm.

MacMillan Bloedel has also been successful in its efforts to develop specialty products that can be produced efficiently at each facility or by two or more plants working together. For example, in the containerboard group, preprinted liners are produced at two locations and are converted to finished products at a total of five locations. Display containers are produced at three locations and specialty glued containers are now run at two locations. Specialty products that contribute a higher margin than traditional commodity items are added to plants wherever possible without disrupting operating efficiencies on high-volume corrugated containers.

Finally, the company's earnings (especially those from pulp and paper, which are more dollar-sensitive than those from lumber[22]) and its general world market competitiveness are significantly affected by fluctuations in the U.S. dollar against the yen and the European currencies. Moreover, although the Canadian dollar sometimes shows periods of strength or weakness against the U.S. dollar, the Canadian dollar tends to move in the same direction as the U.S. dollar over very long periods of time. As a consequence, when both dollars are relatively high in the world's currency markets, investments and earnings in the United States are unable to offset those in Canada, and neither Canadian nor the U.S. operations are low-cost producers worldwide.

Thus, when the dollar is high, the North American door is open for low-priced imports (from Scandinavia, South America, and Portugal) to invade both the home North American market and to reduce exports to Europe and Japan.

STRATEGY ANALYSIS OF MacMILLAN BLOEDEL'S INTERNATIONAL BUSINESS PERFORMANCE

The indisputable conclusion is that MacMillan Bloedel passed two of the four tests. In the process of changing itself from a company whose assets are primarily in Canada to a company with one third of its resources in the United States, MacMillan Bloedel is better off today than it was 15 years ago. Moreover, since the recession of the early 1980s, the firm has worked on reducing its Canadian dollar exposure; on keeping both its home and host governments happy; on doing a better job at international integration than its rivals; and on making better decisions about products, sourcing, innovations, and technological improvements. By making all of North America its export platform for Europe and Japan, MacMillan Bloedel has paid off all of its costs of entry into the United States. During the 1980s, MacMillan Bloedel came of age as an international business firm. The firm is ready to do battle with U.S. and Japanese firms for increases in market share, for dominance in the sale of higher value-added products, and for sustainable competitive advantage around the world.

INTERNATIONAL PRODUCT POLICY[23]

MacMillan Bloedel's success in the 1980s in becoming a strong competitor in the forest products, building materials, and fine papers markets is due to the quality of its products; its integrating links among suppliers, manufacturing operations, and customers; and the management of its assets worldwide. These three elements of product sourcing policy were crucial to MacMillan Bloedel's success in overcoming its foreign exchange risk, in minimizing the wrath of its home government, and in becoming an international business firm.

Exhibit 4–A shows the fourth international business decision. MacMillan carried out this decision successfully when it positioned itself in the United States. Exhibit 4–B shows the marketing tactics for rolling out Decision 4. Exhibit 4–C lists the data elements for assessing product sourcing.

INTERNATIONAL MARKETING TACTICS AND DATA ELEMENTS FOR ASSESSING PRODUCT SOURCING

The following provides an explanation of how various firms have used the five tactics listed in Exhibit 4–B for rolling out Decision 4. It also includes an explanation of the data elements listed in Exhibit 4–C for assessing product sourcing.

Tactic: Source Products Offshore

A winning strategy for sourcing products, technology, and other proprietary information includes both national flexibility and global integration in manufacturing and marketing. Many international firms internalize product market opportunities within the firm through corporate and regional headquarters, between parent companies and subsidiaries, and among them with equity and contractual partners, suppliers, and other affiliates. Some subsidiaries are given world product mandates from their parent firms because local governments insist that their countries be export platforms for the markets of North America, Europe, and Japan, or because it is simply good business. Although global integration tends to be a corporate imperative and national flexibility tends to be a government imperative, both must be applied together to keep firms competitive and to keep nation-states con-

EXHIBIT 4–A
International Business Decision 4: Success in Sourcing

Products
Technology
Proprietary information
Licenses
Franchises
Services
Capital
Managerial expertise

Note: Executives must specify decisions to fit the international business problems of the firm. Is it a parts or components problem? Is it a raw materials problem? Is it a distribution services problem?

EXHIBIT 4–B
International Marketing Tactics for Rolling Out Decision 4

Source products offshore
Keep costs down by sourcing offshore
Determine performance characteristics of products
Find out how market uses the product
Adapt products to markets

EXHIBIT 4–C
Data Elements for Assessing Product Sourcing

Market-defying government practices
Firms as national champions
Balancing government and business needs
Integrating external markets (or internalization)
Integrating upstream scale economies
and downstream scope economies
Offshore export platforms

tent about international business. Moreover, firms themselves are encouraging unbundling as their confidence increases in the capabilities of offshore suppliers, distributors, and other affiliate firms. Sourcing raw materials, parts and components, and finished products offshore is the prototype of management in the

1990s as unbundling becomes the norm rather than the exception.

MARKETING INTELLIGENCE

International competitiveness comes from success in managing a network of suppliers.

For example, Cat achieved high levels of international integration through a set of strategic alliances that encouraged intrafirm foreign trade between the U.S. parent, British and Mexican subsidiaries, Japanese and Indian joint venture partners, Canadian and German suppliers, and worldwide distributors to source products from and transfer technology to overseas markets. Also, Cat made a success of its product sourcing decisions by retaining sufficient national flexibility to please both host governments and local customers. Because Cat owns its information system about computerized manufacturing and logistics, parts management, and patents on hydraulic excavators and because it intends never to sell these data (or in the words of economists, Cat intends never to create external markets for its proprietary knowledge), Cat internalizes all of these decisions within the global firm and business network. Unbundling decisions about sourcing are highly dependent on the value of patents, brand names, and copyrights to the international firm, and these choices for unbundling tend to be more favorably received by firms, such as MacMillan Bloedel, whose products are commodities rather than specialized goods.

Tactic: Keep Costs Down by Sourcing Offshore

MacMillan Bloedel sought out forest products with low production and labor costs in the southeastern United States. Komatsu increased its overseas production in the mid-1980s because of the high appreciation of the Japanese yen against the U.S. dollar.

The following is a list of how Komatsu now keeps costs down by sourcing offshore.[24]

1. From Korea, Komatsu buys batteries at a 30 percent lower cost than from Japan.
2. From its Brazilian plant, Komatsu obtains quality casting parts that are 30 percent lower in cost than those from Japan.
3. From its Mexican plant, which makes construction equipment, Komatsu supplies its Chattanooga plant in the United States with plate products at a lower price than those available either in Japan or the United States.

Korea, Brazil, and Mexico are all export platforms for Japanese-owned firms. Japan accounts for 30 percent of worldwide demand for construction equipment, the United States 25 percent, and Europe 20 percent. Komatsu tries to be user-oriented and to rely on marketing teamwork to produce competitive new products. Komatsu's suppliers in Korea, Brazil, Mexico, the United States, and Europe provide technical advice to the team on how to improve quality, redesign products, and keep costs down. In this way, Komatsu matches quality products from its international business network with the national markets, market segments, and market niches of its importers.

MARKETING INTELLIGENCE

International competitiveness comes from adding or subtracting suppliers from networks based on costs, quality performance, and on-time delivery.

Data Element: Offshore Export Platforms

In Japanese, *endaka* means the high yen/low dollar of the period 1986 to 1988. This change in the foreign exchange value of these two national currencies forced Japanese manufacturers to source in the United States so that they could minimize their foreign currency risk. The following list shows some examples:

1. Ricoh photocopiers were sent from Irvine, California, to Europe.
2. Sony color televisions went from San Diego to South America.
3. Honda sent its cars from Marysville, Ohio, to Taiwan.
4. Sumitomo Electric Corporation produced fiber optics in North Carolina 15 percent cheaper than in Japan and shipped them to Japan and Southeast Asia.
5. Sumitomo Rubber Industries Ltd. exported U.S.-made Dunlop tires.
6. Sanyo Industries shipped its U.S.-made fans and vacuum cleaners to South America.[25]

Late in the 1980s, the United States became a crucial manufacturing center for the export of Japanese products to the world. American manufacturers also used foreign countries as export platforms.[26] They joined the Japanese in keeping costs down by producing their products in Taiwan and shipping them to the United States for final sale under U.S. brand names to American customers. The following U.S. companies are examples: General Electric, which is Taiwan's largest exporter; IBM; Hewlett-Packard; General Instrument; Texas Instrument; Digital Equipment; Atari; Wang Laboratories; AOC International; Captertonic; TRW; Mattel; Schwinn; and Wilson Sporting Goods.

For example, Schwinn imports 70 percent of its total sales from Taiwan. The island is a collection of local subcontractors serving the U.S. market with low-cost, technologically sophisticated products. Taiwan is an export platform that serves the markets of Japan, North America, and Europe.

Tactic: Determine Performance Characteristics of Products

Volvo, the Swedish automobile, defines itself as the conservative car whose longevity is legendary.[27] During the 1970s and for the first six years of the 1980s, it made only a few model changes, whereas Japanese cars defined themselves in terms of technological change and U.S. cars in terms of cosmetic changes, both carried out annually for the benefit of U.S. consumers. Even in the mid-1980s, Volvo did not believe it was suffering from the shortening of the product life cycle that was driving many companies to cut the time it took to introduce new products into the market.

MARKETING INTELLIGENCE

International competitiveness comes from making suppliers a part of the marketing team.

In 1987, however, Volvo reorganized its product development team to shorten the time required from idea to finished car, according to its president, Roger Holtback. The key change was to introduce the same approach followed by Honda and Canon, that is, marketing teamwork. Volvo joined product planners, marketing experts, designers, product engineers, manufacturing engineers, and key suppliers in a collaborative project team. The group worked together from start to finish on developing a quality product that matched the needs of customers. In this way, Volvo got better value out of its development efforts, and it could participate more effectively in the growing network of joint ventures and other alliances linking the world's automotive industry.

As a relatively small player in the industry, Volvo could no longer afford to spend between 8 and 10 percent of its revenues on development. This was higher than the industry average of 5 to 6 percent. Volvo had to cut costs through the introduction of the project team for the development of new cars and trucks. Moreover, its cash cow, the 200 Series, was vulnerable to Japanese tactics of double-quick model changes, and its newer 700 series was vulnerable to Japanese tactics of catering to the fashion-conscious segment of the market. Volvo had to redefine the function and need its cars serve in the market or face the question of survival against the Japanese onslaught on the United States and Europe.

Tactic: Find Out How Market Uses the Product

Japanese executives pursue a widely different path from that of Taiwanese exporters toward marketing products in the United States. For the most part, Taiwanese exporters act as subcontractors. They rarely export proprietary products to the United States. American or Japanese executives come in, show the Taiwanese how to make new products, and ship all of the output back to the United States or to Japan. All research on product design, product engineering, product marketing, and product usage is carried out by U.S. or Japanese firms.

On the other hand, Japanese executives design their own products, promote them heavily by developing unique brand names, and carry out a set of international marketing tactics to make these products the dominant ones both at home and abroad. For the most part, the Japanese develop products that are user-oriented and that meet the needs of customers better than competing U.S. and European products.

For example, Sony produces 100 different varieties of its Walkman.[28] For the beach, the Sony Walkman is solar-powered and waterproof. For the tennis court, the Sony Walkman is an ultralight, radio-only model that attaches to a sweatband. To give the customer a concert-hall sound, Sony offers deluxe, oversize headphones with its Walkman.

The following are the conditions for determining market use of products: First, customers must hold favorable perceptions about what the products will accomplish for them. Second, customers must prefer one set of products over a competing group of products. And third, customers must be able to pay for the products. Only by meeting these three tests of market demand will executives match products to markets.

In the case of service marketing,[29] customers are willing to pay a premium price for worldwide package delivery because Federal Express picks up goods in the United States and delivers them in Europe within two days at a price considered reasonable. If you have a Big Mac attack, there are thousands of outlets worldwide that offer fast food and fast service at affordable prices. Waste management, hospital cleaning, insurance, and data management are all export services that U.S. firms provide for their customers.

MARKETING INTELLIGENCE

International competitiveness comes from making distributors part of marketing team.

In summary, successful international marketing executives find out how the market uses their goods, and then they develop products that meet the three tests of market demand: perception, preference, and affordability.

Tactic: Adapt Products to Markets

Product adaptation means changing the services that go with selling the product. These services are based on the perceptions and preferences of customers. For example, to the Japanese, delivery times and after-sales service are two of the most important marketing activities that foreign importers must accomplish if they want repeat orders many years in the future. Although the French machine tool industry is not technologically backward, it has lost export market share because it fails to adapt its export marketing practices (particularly, on-time delivery for inventory and after-sales support services) to the changing competitive conditions forced on them by the Japanese machine tool industry.[30] The Japanese standard in product salesmanship must be adopted by French, British, and U.S. firms or these firms will continue to lose export market share to the Japanese.

MARKETING INTELLIGENCE

International competitiveness comes from making consumers part of marketing team.

Product adaptation is also the ability to change the export product mix to match new market trends. Hong Kong has become the world's leading exporter of toys because of this ability to spot market trends and quickly adapt products to meet demand.[31] The companies involved are Universal Matchbox, Kader (which makes the Cabbage Patch dolls and Smarty Bear for Coleco), Applied Electronics (which makes electronic toys for Fisher Price, Mattel, and Kenner Parker), and Playmates Holdings (the go-it-alone company of the Chan family that makes Cricket, a Chatterbox doll; Corky, her freckled young male friend; and Jill, a doll for girls up to 12 years old). As costs continue to rise in Hong Kong, these toy manufacturers are moving their offshore production sites to China and the Portuguese territory of Macao. Their objective is to adapt their products quickly to new market trends, even from these new locations.

Finally, product adaptation means changing the idea, theme, image, purpose, or mood held about products. Sony did this with its Walkman. More will be said about messages and communication in the discussion of promotion policy in the next chapter.

STRATEGY ANALYSIS OF INTERNATIONAL PRODUCT POLICY

A fourth future already has happened in international business: Product policy remains firmly internalized within the firm unless the foreign exchange value of raw materials, parts, and components or finished goods changes to make offshore sourcing (or farming out) of manufacturing more cost effective. Marketing executives create teams of suppliers, distributors, customers, and consumers to decide on product characteristics and to determine how best to adapt these products to local markets. Although national governments want as much flexibility as possible in the design, use, and service of foreign products, the convergence of consumer preferences worldwide calls for less rather than more flexibility. Overhanging this discussion are several future disputes between governments and international firms about investments, jobs, and exports. One way to minimize these frictions is for nation-states to enter into free trade agreements, customs unions, or common markets that encourage market-conforming rules on trade and investment. Then the market decides between national flexibility and global integration, sometimes to the detriment of regional and national economies that lack a cadre of firms with high levels of technological and marketing skills. The jury is still out on whether Canada will be able to turn its favored position under the U.S.–Canada Free Trade Agreement into strong international competitiveness for its business firms. Canadian-owned firms must do so to maintain their competitive advantage.

CONCLUSIONS FROM THE CASE

The success of MacMillan Bloedel in establishing a global business network of foreign direct investments (mainly in the United States), joint ventures, and distribution offices for worldwide sales has led it to being one of the world's premier providers of wood and allied products. The company's emphasis on developing technology to refine the manufacturing and distribution processes played a major role in positioning MacMillan Bloedel as a low-cost producer in home and host country markets.

MacMillan Bloedel is better off today than it was before 1982. Its international network of saw mills, containerboard operations, building materials service centers, sales subsidiaries, and distributors makes it a stronger North American competitor. Because sales of specialty printing paper are growing in the United States and Japan, and because competition is intense among producers of commodity products, its North American manufacturing operations are being expanded for the company to become a major player in markets outside of North America.

The increase in operating earnings and profits since 1983 shows that MacMillan Bloedel is turning its scale and scope economies into productivity increases, cost savings, and additional assets for investment elsewhere in its international network. Most of these net increases in revenues and profits reflect the lower value of the U.S. and Canadian dollars rather than a permanent change in its worldwide performance.

In the short run, MacMillan Bloedel must continue to do what it is doing in North America (i.e., build up forest product resources, expand downstream investments, and increase specialty products) and expand its export activities into Europe and Japan.

However, in the long run, the company needs to strengthen its hand both in Europe and Japan with additional foreign direct investments. The firm has not made these markets structurally attractive for itself.

MacMillan Bloedel must pay attention to the quality of demand from consumers (such as those in Japan), try to sell to the best customers possible, and decide to compete only against the best competitors both at home and abroad. This is a challenge worthy of MacMillan Bloedel.

Today, MacMillan Bloedel is unable to impose its standards on the forest products industries of Canada and the United States. The company's products are not unique, and therefore it is unable to oust its competitors from these markets. That is the work of tomorrow for the firm.

EXECUTIVE SUMMARY

MacMillan Bloedel is a great case in which to observe the need for international marketing executives to create a set of mutually supported business strategies. Because the firm is a forest resources company, its ability to transform wood, lumber, and pulp into building materials, newsprint, and fine groundwood paper is its most important strategic problem. These conversions must be carried out with the market in mind, hence the emphasis on product market skills as a crucial element in the company's strategy. Moreover, these transformations must be either carried out through the market or internalized within the firm and its global network; therefore, international integration is another key element in the company's overall strategy. Finally, the carrying out of a set of successful strategies depends on management's ability to position its assets wisely at home, in nearest neighbor markets, and on other continents. MacMillan Bloedel has done all of these things very well.

CHAPTER 5

MANAGING CUSTOMER SELECTION WITHOUT U.S.–JAPAN TRADE RECIPROCITY

"What we see, is a blue chip company floating dead in the water."[1] [*Fortune* ranks Kodak 70th among the worst managed companies.[2]]
A Wall Street analyst.

[By 1988,] the thrill of the hunt has begun to permeate the ranks. . . . It's enthusiasm driven by success.[3]
Phillip Samper, *vice-chairman of Kodak.*

COMPETITIVENESS: THE IMPORTANCE OF COMMONLY HELD BELIEFS

In 1982, when an overvalued dollar cruelly exposed Kodak's severe shortcomings in innovation and management, and humbled it before its Japanese competitors, Walter Fallon, then chairman of Eastman Kodak, said, "It's time to make this elephant dance."[4]

Today, Kodak's U.S. corporate headquarters and Japanese regional headquarters are battered and bruised from their enforced dancing lessons. Corporate headquarters no longer believes in technical perfection (i.e., taking decades to develop new technologies) and instead practices market timing. Now, its Japanese subsidiary internalizes Kodak's five new international business values: (1) the endorsement of reciprocal market-conforming trade policies, (2) the use of speed and teamwork to develop technology rapidly, (3) the application of forward pricing to gain large in-

110

creases in market share quickly, (4) the acceptance of a sole-source research mandate, and (5) an enrichment of demand quality among customers. These are neither U.S. nor Japanese values but rather beliefs shared by the world's international management community. Thus, Kodak's U.S. corporate and Japanese regional centers nurture and support worldwide managerial ties whether the firm's executives are American, Japanese, or European.

The globalization of a firm's management culture is never easy, and for Kodak establishing intangible managerial ties worldwide has been especially difficult. Kodak was a paternalistic firm deeply committed to small-town, upstate New York and American free enterprise values with an arrogant lock on the U.S. market. Kodak knew its customers would pay $19.95 (in U.S. dollars) for its Instamatic and Disc amateur cameras, but they would never pay $500 for the new cameras coming out of Japan. The firm was so locked into its own set of beliefs about products and markets that it completely missed the convergence of consumer preferences toward compact, foolproof, high-quality 35mm cameras. Kodak's demise was on the horizon in 1983, when Colby Chandler took over as chairman and CEO. The following are the decisions Chandler made almost immediately: to cut management by 25 percent; to group businesses into five divisions; to raise productivity by 15 percent; to claw back market share; and to slavishly copy Fuji's managerial values, concepts, and practices. Kodak's metamorphosis into a global firm with shared corporate beliefs worldwide is the result of Chandler's work.

The United States Wrangles with Japan over Trade Practices

Like other U.S. firms, Kodak bears the heavy burden of the central country-risk dispute that endangers free trade, international corporate capitalism, and the world's market economy. What will the United States do about its massive trade and capital deficits? Is market-defying government intervention the answer? What can Japan do about its mammoth trade and capital surpluses? Is market-conforming government intervention the answer? Or will these twin problems simply go away once governments devalue the dollar and raise the value of the yen?

As early as 1967, many in the U.S. thought that a little bit of temporary government relief for steel would make this domestic industry competitive once again. In these early days, U.S.–Japan trade disputes were friendly affairs in which each side was solicitous of the other's welfare. No one thought that year after year U.S. steel (and so many other industries) would ask for permanent government protection as the only sure cure for America's balance of trade woes. So when the United States imported too much steel and too many cars from Japan in the late 1970s, these trade dispute proceedings became peevish quarrels over the willingness of the Japanese government to impose "voluntary" export restraints on its international firms.

Throughout the 1980s, Americans brawled loudly in Washington over injury to motorcycles (Harley-Davidson), dumping of zippers (YKK), investment tax credits for numerical control machines (Houdaille), and trading with the enemy (Toshiba). Also, Americans took their petulant bickering to Japan. There they disputed import restrictions on candy, baseball bats, beef, oranges, and many other products; complained noisily about foreign investment restrictions, particularly in the biotechnology and pharmaceutical industries; demanded a less-complicated distribution system; and expressed outrage over the Japanese preference for consensus rather than an adversarial legal system.

Yet by 1989, the Japanese had become the second largest foreign investor in the U.S. because Tennessee, Ohio, and other states did such a good job of convincing Japanese firms to manufacture their products in the United States. Admiration of Japanese success among Americans turned to a belief that the Japanese economy is managed by the Ministry of International Trade and Industry (MITI) to keep foreigners out of domestic markets and to put Japan in control of all overseas markets. This conviction was strengthened once the false god of dollar devaluation was shown to be ineffective in eliminating America's trade deficits.

Today, these loud discordant wrangles bring the Japanese to do something very un-Japanese. They give Americans blunt advice: Do something about budget and trade deficits, short-term time horizons, and preference for financial management over manufacturing. Stop complaining. Follow Kodak's lead. Get on with implementing shared international business values such as reciprocal market-conforming trade policies, speed and teamwork to develop new technology, forward pricing to obtain quick increases in market share, sole-source world product mandates, and market promotions to convince consumers to improve their standards of living.

Mike Mansfield, a Democrat, a former Senator, and Reagan's ambassador to Japan during almost all of these trade disputes, retired with the suggestion that the U.S. and Japan enter into a free trade agreement similar to the one with Canada. The following is his advice: Let markets determine whose products, services, and management are the best. Let firms go after the highest income consumers in each market. Let customers determine whose products enhance life-styles.[5] Mansfield's plea fell on deaf ears because Americans and the Japanese do not have a commonly held set of beliefs about the twin imperatives of government intervention versus business independence. U.S. firms must navigate these rough seas without a joint government map identifying boundary lines, depths of feelings, and safe harbors for doing business in Japan.

American Views of Japan

According to Murray Sayle, an Australian journalist living in Japan,

> There is something at the center of the Japanese system that Americans will never understand or, if they do, will find repulsive and unworkable.[6]

> [MITI is the most] insensitive component of the Japanese government. Its day-to-day policy decisions are made mostly . . . by callow young men in their 30s, swots from the top Japanese universities who know the outside world only from books in Japanese.[7]

Also, Michael Borrus, a professor at the University of California, has concluded from his research on the microelectronics industry that MITI's interventionist strategies encourage "the rapid accrual of production economies in the domestic market . . .

[and these] lead inevitably to export drives to unload product and capture the market share necessary to justify the initial extra investment in capacity."[8]

Moreover, Clyde Prestowitz, a trade negotiator in the Reagan administration, has said that Americans have traded places with the Japanese so that the latter now dominate the international economy in computers and chips, man-made materials and other state-of-the-art products.[9] He is one of the revisionists who believe that

> Japan's economy is basically unlike those of the West. A strong bureaucracy combined with a headless and mostly powerless political system that can do nothing to protect special interests, produces an economy, they argue, that is ruthlessly run to favor producers over consumers, to keep exports higher than imports, to secure Japanese pre-eminence in industries that the bureaucrats have decreed 'strategic'.[10]

Peter Drucker comments on the future by deciding that Americans "will no longer tolerate Japan's adversarial trading methods of recent decades—a wall around the home market to protect social structures and traditions, plus a determined push beyond it for world dominance for selected Japanese industries."[11]

Japanese Views of MITI

According to Daniel Okimoto, a professor at Stanford University, Japan's industrial policy of market-conforming government intervention through MITI slows the entry of foreign goods while Japanese manufacturers get ready for new competition and Japanese distributors find a place for these new foreign goods in their complicated distribution system. This form of government intervention (which came early in the product life cycles of data processing, computer software, and biotechnology and late in the life cycles of iron and steel, paper and pulp, and textiles) is generally considered adversarial by and unacceptable to Americans who believe in an autonomous, rational market economy.[12]

STRATEGY INSIGHT

International competitiveness comes from knowing when to use market-conforming intervention in home and host country markets.

American Successes in Japan

With or without trade reciprocity between the U.S. and Japan, some 4,000 U.S. companies are successful and sell over 50,000 U.S. products in Japan. The market is a large, mass consumer market about one half the size of the U.S. market; quality U.S. products made in Japan appeal to local tastes; and local partners do help U.S. firms enter the Japanese distribution system. But these three factors are not enough. For example, Kodak has among its talent pool Japanese-speaking executives who know the day-to-day management issues of running a business in Japan. Moreover, Kodak's chairman and CEO, Colby Chandler, works hard at developing social relationships with Japanese businesspeople. All of these things will take time, about 10 to 15 years, before Kodak has a position in Japan comparable to its place in the U.S.

Hurried efforts fail in Japan because local managers do not know the shared values of the international firm, have not had the time to internalize the culture of the organization, and cannot translate these effectively into the context of Japanese society. Developing a commonly held set of beliefs is a time-consuming process whether in the U.S., Japan, or both countries. The hard work must be done by CEOs because the government elites of both countries are too far apart to see the wisdom of a free trade pact between the U.S. and Japan.

KODAK AND FUJI COMPETE FOR CUSTOMERS[13]

Kodak is a U.S.-owned firm. Its core business is the manufacture of photographic products (film and paper); these account for about 70 percent of the firm's sales and 90 percent of its pretax operating income. Film and paper products are the company's cash cow.[14] Because over 40 percent of the company's sales are outside the United States, with sales to Japan having begun as early as 1889, Kodak is an international firm that has had a long string of product, customer, and competitive successes.

However, beginning in 1983 with Chandler as the new CEO, continuing in 1984 (the year in which Fuji humiliated Kodak by beating it out as the "official" film of the Los Angeles Summer Olympics), and persisting throughout the 1980s (with Fuji's drive to establish minilabs for processing film in U.S. supermarkets and drugstores), Kodak's dominance in the United States has been seriously threatened by Fuji, a Japanese-owned firm. The following are the penetrating questions Kodak's management had to ask itself before it could claw back market share against Fuji.

Fuji Forces Kodak's Corporate Reorganization

Do the dividing lines between corporate headquarters, functional and business divisions, and overseas subsidiaries nurture and support a coherent cultural unit in the U.S. and Japan? Chandler says no. He has proceeded to put Kodak's U.S. and Japanese businesses through a major corporate reorganization.

As early as 1984, he scrapped Kodak's historic Photographic Division. Before this dramatic change, the film emulsion laboratory used to drop its "silver curtain" and refuse to share new product information with other divisions of Kodak. This attitude resulted in redundant research and an "archaic organization based on functions."[15] Seventeen photographic business units—each with its own general manager and responsibilities for research and development, marketing, and finance—replaced the Photographic Division. These 17 units became entrepreneurial, market-driven businesses and rendered obsolete the image that Kodak was "an aging, paunchy giant."[16]

Kodak's Japanese Regional Center as Coherent Cultural Unit

As part of its reorganization, Kodak also faced the following question: What responsibilities should Kodak's Japanese employees have to forge their cohesiveness as a Kodak cultural unit in Japan? In 1984, Chandler took Kodak's Japanese business out of the Asia, Africa, and Australia regional division and made it into a separate subsidiary. A year later, he replaced local agents and had Kodak take over its long-time (since 1923) distributor, Nagase & Co. Between 1984 and 1987, Kodak's Japanese corporate sales and marketing staff increased by almost six times, from 25 to 140 employees, while its retail staff to sell film, minilab processing, and camera equipment climbed to 3,000 Japanese employees. Throughout this three-year period, Kodak constructed a research and development facility in Yokohama, Japan, and hired 150 Japanese engineers responsible for introducing new products into the Japanese market. Moreover, in 1987, Kodak Japan entered into a joint venture with Imagica, a local film processor, on a 51/49 percent basis and into a joint production agreement with Chinon to produce 35mm cameras in Japan. The devolution of responsibilities for investment, production, research, strategic alliances, and marketing on the regional center gave the firm's Japanese employees a new sense of cohesiveness as a separate, coequal cultural unit of Kodak.

Coordination and Control between the United States and Japan

Another question Kodak faced was the following: What management systems should Kodak put in place to keep its U.S. and Japanese managers within the bounds of a set of commonly held beliefs about Kodak's role in international business? The mission of Kodak's two research and development centers (one in Rochester, New York, and the other in Yokohama) has been to shorten design-to-delivery times for the transfer of technology and new products to both the U.S. and Japanese film and photographic paper markets. Because of their complementary and supporting mission, these two centers were kept separate from the integrated manufacturing and marketing business units in the U.S and Japan.

In these two countries, Kodak integrated its 17 entrepreneurial U.S. businesses with its domestic sales and marketing divisions, and it integrated its Japanese manufacturing operations with its wholly owned distributor and retail sales outlets. Moreover, in Japan, Kodak internalized an external market by taking over its distributor, Nagase, to give Kodak Japan more market power over sales and marketing locally.

Although Kodak U.S. and Kodak Japan carry out their business independently of one another, they are bound together by the technological and new product output of the two global research centers, the worldwide campaign to market Kodak film, and the financial resources of the parent firm. These external boundary lines of the two cultural units are well within the set of commonly held beliefs of Kodak's international executives.

PRODUCT MARKET ANALYSIS

Is the business primarily product or market driven? What do customers really pay a price for? What is the life of the product? Can competitors change the economics of product market segments? Kodak has the following core skills: enormous technical and research capabilities, a powerful distribution network, tremendous financial resources and borrowing power, and a widely recognized brand name. Kodak relied on its technical labor force and its strong research and development efforts to dominate the U.S. market—that is, until 1984, when Der Grosse Fuji blimp flew over the Los Angeles Summer Olympics and Kodak found out that it had a strong international competitor in the United States.

Under Chandler, Kodak introduced Japanese-style quality control in manufacturing and reduced production defect rate from 32 percent in 1985 to 10 percent in 1987. Kodak also reduced from two years to one year the time it takes the company to create a new color print paper line, such as Ektacolor. Time and teamwork pushed U.S. factory productivity up by 20 percent as employee groups isolated and resolved manufacturing problems as early as possible. Kodak's sales per employee jumped from $85,553 in 1984 to $107,000 in 1987, still far behind Fuji, which had sales per employee of $370,000 (in U.S. dollars).

Early on, Kodak realized that Japanese camera users think of

Kodak's film as sleepy, or without sharp and bright images, and so it changed the color balance in its film. Beginning in 1985, Kodak introduced 100 new products; in 1986, it introduced another 20; and in 1987, it introduced VR-G film, which is a direct competitor with Fuji's more vivid color film. Now, Kodacolor film has greater color saturation, improved exposure latitude, and enhanced quality to produce sharper prints, which pleases the Japanese demand for higher quality products.

Currently, Kodak is standardizing its film packaging in the United States, Europe, Japan, and the rest of Asia with its worldwide mark of quality, Kodak Gold. At the 1988 Summer Olympics in South Korea, Kodak spent $10 million (in U.S. dollars) to convey to the world that it had a quality product to sell to all customers irrespective of whether they live in Asia, North America, or Europe.

KODAK'S EIGHT INTERNATIONAL MARKETING TACTICS

- Redesigns world organization by integrating internationally
- Reinvents the Japanese subsidiary as coherent cultural unit
- Makes American and Japanese research laboratories coequal
- Builds up core skills with new products and packaging
- Changes film products to match local customer preferences
- Starts late in retail delivery of products through minilabs
- Promotes film and paper products aggressively
- Acquires brands to diversify product line

FUJI'S FOUR INTERNATIONAL MARKETING TACTICS

- Starts first in retail delivery of products through minilabs
- Obtains first-mover advantage in new cameras and better film
- Promotes film and paper products aggressively
- Adds high-income consumers to its customer base worldwide

DECISIONS ABOUT CUSTOMER PREFERENCES AFFECT INTERNATIONAL BUSINESS PERFORMANCE[17]

Is the film business primarily a convenience activity? How long will consumers wait between picture taking and picture developing? Do consumers put their personal values into film and pictures? Because film ranks second only to birth control pills in terms of consumer anxiety, consumers are insensitive to what they perceive as only a small price differential between Kodak and Fuji. They prefer using a film that has established its brand name and hence demonstrated its quality instead of recording a special event with an off-brand, perhaps inferior film. Moreover, consumers want to see the results of their pictures as quickly as possible. Thus, the heavy promotion of brand names, the intended perception of quality among consumers, and the wide availability of minilabs are high entry barriers in the creation of value within the amateur photographic film market. However, these cues are crucial for film and 35mm cameras to become one of the products necessary to an enriched quality of life.

As discussed earlier, when Kodak began to pay more attention to the demands of Japanese consumers for improved quality in their film, paper, and pictures, it converted its sleepy film into Kodacolor film, which shows sharper and brighter images in developed pictures. Moreover, Kodak began using a different color balance in its film because Japanese customers are not interested in their flesh tones looking too yellow. Instead, they like to look pink. On the other hand, Americans do not like to look too pink; this gives off a beefy flesh tone that is considered an undesirable quality in film in the United States. Therefore, Kodak began to produce two different film qualities to please the tastes of two different sets of customers.

Also, Kodak's American film developers prefer to work in darkrooms. This is not the case in Japan, where local developers prefer to work in subdued yellow lighting. This customer preference comes about because of the limited space available in Japanese print shops. Kodak modified its film in Japan to permit it to be developed in room light rather than in darkrooms.

Fuji was the first to see the strategic importance of shifting some of its developing away from traditional camera and film shops to minilabs. Fuji created a second retail market segment to develop film. These photographic minilabs are made by Fuji; Noritsu, another Japanese firm; and Kis, a French firm. They are small, computer-controlled film processing machines that enable drugstores and photographic outlets to give fast turnaround on developing 35am snapshots at relatively high prices.

In 1986, 10 percent of the 34 billion pictures taken worldwide were developed in these minilabs. In the early 1990s, nearly 25 percent of all color films will be processed in minilabs. These minilabs are considered to be recession-proof by some financial analysts.[18] Unless Kodak is able to establish enough minilab retail outlets, produce or buy the minilab machines inexpensively, and get its film and paper into these stores, most consumers in Japan, Asia and the Pacific Basin, and North America will wind up using Fuji film and paper.

Fuji captured market share in the following Japanese product markets: 35mm camera makers, 35am film and paper producers, and minilabs. On the other hand, Kodak sought to capture market share in only one of these Japanese product markets, namely, 35mm film and paper producers. Fuji had first-mover advantage in these two other product markets, and Kodak was forced to play catch-up ball to regain its footing in Japan. Kodak has had to pay Chinon, a Japanese-owned company, to produce a 35mm camera. Moreover, Kodak has had to pay top dollar to lease or acquire retail sites for minilabs that will use Kodak film and paper exclusively.

Fuji will not be slow in using its dominant incumbent status in Japan. Fuji is already integrating across the three product markets; driving costs down by more product and international diversification; differentiating its products further through additional advertising, more research and development, and better distribution agreements; and doing all things possible to keep Kodak's market share relatively small in Japan.

Fuji is using its strong base in Japan and the lessons it learned in competing against Kodak in Japan to create competitive advantage for itself in the United States. The race between Fuji and Kodak in the United States has just begun. The award at the end of the race is control over the largest film market in the world, with its better customers and improved quality of demand.

Kodak World as Coherent Cultural Unit

Kodak's history: photography begat chemicals begat biotechnology begat drugs.[19] When Kodak acquired U.S.-owned Sterling Drug to complement the recently revived core photographic business, Kodak bought a national distribution system and an array of over-the-counter and prescription drugs. Through Sterling, Kodak acquired Lysol disinfectants and cleaners, d-Con insecticide, Neo-Synephrine nasal decongestants, Stridex skin care items, Bayer aspirin, Phillips' Milk of Magnesia, and Demerol and Midol pain killers.[20] All of these brands fit into Kodak's strategy for product diversification and the creation of market value as a manufacturer of film, chemicals, and drugs.

Again, there are the same penetrating questions but different answers: Does the acquisition of Sterling Drug support coherent cultural units in the United States and Japan? Are customers willing to pay Kodak's high film price for over-the-counter drugs and household products? Do customers have the same income and demand characteristics? The answer is no to all of these questions.

Even though Kodak perceives similarities among customers and markets, the distribution systems for the over-the-counter drugs and household products—drug stores and supermarkets respectively—are different from those for film. The costs, markups, and revenues are also different because over-the-counter drugs and household cleaners need many turns in inventory to make their sales target, whereas film is a high-markup item whose top price is sustained by the perceived value in the Kodak brand name. The chemical business is one cultural unit and the film business is a different cultural unit. By combining the two, the Kodak corporate headquarters has created chaos for its U.S. middle managers instead of managerial simplicity. At least Japanese middle managers have been spared these conflicts of fundamental product market segmentation, inventory turns, and distribution systems. With Sterling Drug, Kodak World is not a coherent cultural unit worldwide.

STRATEGY ANALYSIS OF KODAK'S AND FUJI'S INTERNATIONAL BUSINESS PERFORMANCE

No doubt Kodak is better off today in Japan because of the reorganization and the reinvention of its local business, and because it gave its Japanese subsidiary coequal status with its U.S. film business. Nevertheless, Kodak has been unable to convert its dominant U.S. market position into more than a 15 percent share of the Japanese market.

On the other hand, Fuji remains the dominant firm in Japan. It is converting its Japanese market position into becoming the market leader in Asia and the Pacific. Moreover, Fuji is turning its dominant Japanese market position into becoming a significant challenger in the U.S. market. However, neither Kodak nor Fuji is near becoming the dominant firm in each other's home market.

Although Kodak reinvented its organization, built up its core skills, and matched its quality products with customer preferences, Fuji found other ways to improve the quality of demand for its film and paper, 35mm cameras, and minilab equipment. Right now, Fuji is more expert at seeking out better customers and improving the quality of demand for its film products. This is because Fuji is a more coherent amateur film company than the Kodak-Sterling Drug combination.

STRATEGY INSIGHT

International competitiveness comes from knowing how to create coherent cultural units within regional subsidiaries and between them and the corporate headquarters.

The race for sustainable competitive advantage in the amateur film business continues with no clear winner in sight in the U.S. market and worldwide.

INTERNATIONAL PROMOTION POLICY

The ability of Kodak and Fuji to divide up the amateur film market worldwide comes from their proficiency in capturing their customers' higher incomes, better standards of living, and enriched quality of demand with new cameras and film products. They build up organizations that push new concepts, products, packaging, and retail services into the hands of consumers before consumers know their own minds about what they want and need in cameras, film, and developing services. Both international firms promote their film products through advertising campaigns tied in with the Olympics so that consumers around the world buy their film and reflect in the glory of gold medal winners. Most other film manufacturers have been driven from the world market by aggressive promotion of Kodak Gold and Fuji film.

Exhibit 5–A shows the fifth international business decision. Both Kodak and Fuji carried out this decision successfully when they positioned themselves in each other's home market. Exhibit 5–B shows the marketing tactics for rolling out Decision 5. Exhibit 5–C lists the data elements for assessing customers.

INTERNATIONAL MARKETING TACTICS AND DATA ELEMENTS FOR ASSESSING CUSTOMERS

The following provides an explanation of how various countries used the four tactics listed in Exhibit 5–B for rolling out Decision 5. It also includes an explanation of most of the data elements listed in Exhibit 5–C that are useful in assessing customers.

Tactic: Capture Higher Incomes, Better Standards of Living, and Enriched Quality of Demand

A winning strategy for selling goods around the world includes a keen awareness of national differences, cultural practices, consumer preferences, disposable income, and the quality of products

EXHIBIT 5–A
International Business Decision 5: Success in Selecting Customers

---

Intermediate
Final

Note: Executives must specify decisions to fit international business decision problems. Is it an intermediate customer problem and how does the firm improve its sales to wholesalers and retailers? Is it a final customer problem and how does the firm improve its sales to consumers?

EXHIBIT 5–B
International Marketing Tactics for Rolling Out Decision 5

Capture higher incomes, better standards of living and enriched quality of demand
Assess influence of country of origin on international sales
Know if change in country of origin reduces value of brand name
Use appropriate multicues to convince customers of quality

EXHIBIT 5–C
Data Elements for Assessing Customers

Attitudinal preferences
Quality of life
Latent demand
Upscale markets
Experience effects and similarities in taste
Country of origin
Cognitive dissonance
Status marketing
Promotional cues

---

and services. Through continuous new product development, international firms play an active role in selecting those customers who have higher incomes, improved standards of living, and an enhanced quality of demand. For example, products such as Corona beer, Pampers disposable diapers, and Free Hold mousse define the quality of life in the United States as well as in Mexico, Japan, and France. Improvements in the products, their packaging, and the after-market services offer consumers the opportunity to believe they are enjoying a better standard of living. Therefore, Procter & Gamble, L'Oréal, Kodak, Fuji, and others use all possible marketing strategies to target customers who can afford to pay for these product market improvements.

As the quality of demand improves for all products, international firms compete with more high-valued products for customers who are better off, know what they want out of life, and desire to improve their standard of living. The ability of customers to choose from among competing products is how marketing transforms cultural practices into consumer preferences, and the latter into product market decisions. A well-thought-out strategy of customer selection by international firms helps to enhance the quality of demand in home and host country markets.

Data Element: Attitudinal Preferences
When U.S. yuppies changed their image of the good life from Canadian winters to Mexican summers, they switched to drinking Corona beer to give them the quality of life they seek from imported beer. Their attitudinal preferences were confirmed by the advertising and promotional cues employed by the Mexican company. Corona defined their leisure life, and their way of living defined what Corona was in the U.S. market against Molson.

Data Element: Quality of Life
The two-way link between local culture and global marketing was uncoupled in the case of Pampers. When P&G sought to convince Japanese mothers to change their view about how often to diaper their babies, Japanese women refused to accept the promotional campaign to change Japanese cultural norms. Instead, these customers bought competing disposable diapers from Kao and UniCharm, local firms that understood the close link among cultural preferences, promotional strategy, and quality of demand. Pampers did not define the Japanese nurturing life, and the Japanese way of living did not define what Pampers was in the market against its local competitors.

Data Element: Latent Demand
L'Oréal accomplished the most difficult task of all. First, it found out what consumers wanted in hair care products. Then

it set about creating, testing, and marketing these new, higher value-added products. In the process, L'Oréal changed the cultural preferences of Americans, modified its worldwide marketing strategies, and upgraded the quality of life for all of its customers.

Data Element: Upscale Markets

For marketing executives, products have no meaning unless they are sold in markets. Products and markets mirror one another. When products do not quite match up to consumer preferences, such as Molson after 1986 in the United States, or when goods fail to perform as expected for customers, such as Pampers in Japan, these goods show a distorted market image. When the match between products and markets is nearly perfect, such as film with sharper images in Japan, the goods reflect exactly what is demanded in markets. Within limits, the price is irrelevent to customers. They want products that reflect their enhanced, upscale quality of demand.

Data Element: Experience Effects[21] and Similarities in Taste[22]

A winning strategy for selling goods worldwide includes providing products to customers who have similar tastes in beverages, packaged foods, automobiles, and consumer products. New products are designed and developed for the home market and quickly appear in host markets with similar cultural and economic conditions. Most of the pricing, promotion and distribution strategies, product design, packaging, and manufacturing technology are easily transferable among markets with similar tastes. The following are several examples of how what is learned in the home market, or so-called experience effects, is transferred to a host market in which the similarities in tastes between the two markets (e.g., the United States and Japan[23]) creates sustainable competitive advantage.

1. The Japanese drink more Coca-Cola per capita than anyone else in the world after Americans, Mexicans, and Australians. Coke produces over 60 percent of the carbonated beverages sold in Japan.

2. IBM is the third largest computer company in Japan (behind Fujitsu and Nippon Electric Company).
3. McDonald's has over 500 stores in Japan that cater to the same demand for fast foods as found in the United States.
4. Johnson & Johnson manufactures Band-Aids, baby oil, and other bathroom products, and Johnson Wax Japan produces wax, polish, glass cleaner, and air fresheners in Japan similar to those they produce in the United States.

MARKETING INTELLIGENCE

International competitiveness comes from success in selecting customers with an enhanced quality of demand.

International firms must capture higher incomes, improved standards of living, and an enhanced quality of demand with new products or they will lose the continuing battle for international competitiveness.

Tactic: Assess Influence of Country of Origin on International Sales

Does knowledge about country of origin affect purchase decisions of customers? The answer depends on the following: (1) the international similarities and differences in consumer preferences; (2) the importance national customers attach to specific quality attributes of domestic and foreign products; and (3) to what extent these product advantages are promoted locally by domestic and foreign firms.

Clearly, U.S. customers attach Canadian winters to Molson and Mexican summers to Corona. Country of origin is important to U.S. consumers irrespective of the similar physical product characteristics of the two imported beers. Corona does very well promoting its country of origin at the expense of Molson.

MARKETING INTELLIGENCE

International competitiveness comes from success in using the influence of country of origin to enhance the quality of demand among customers.

If Japanese consumers in Japan know that a roll of Kodak film is manufactured in the United States, would they buy this roll of Kodak film instead of an equivalent roll of Fuji film that is manufactured in Japan? Definitely not—hence, Kodak's decision to manufacture film in Japan according to the preferences among Japanese for flesh tones in color prints looking pink rather than yellow. The phrase *Made in Japan* must be prominently displayed on the gold Kodak package or the sale is lost in Japan. The influence of country of origin permeates market decisions of even very large international firms whose products outwardly look the same.

Tactic: Know if Change in Country of Origin Reduces Value of Brand Name

Does knowledge about a change in the country of origin affect customer decisions? Sometimes it does. Currently, Japanese firms are manufacturing their automobiles in the United States, and Honda is selling some of its U.S.-made cars back home in Japan. To date, Japanese customers have not boycotted U.S.-made Hondas even though a perception exists among the Japanese and Americans that the quality of manufacturing in the U.S. has slipped behind Japan's ability to produce quality cars.

Nevertheless, changing the country of origin is fraught with danger for many manufacturers. For example, in 1984, Chrysler made two-door K cars—the Plymouth Reliant and the Dodge Aries models—at its Toluca, Mexico, plant.[24] The automobiles looked the same on the outside and, except for engine serial numbers, the cars were the same on the inside as well. Because Chrysler's manufacturing costs were lower in Toluca and the firm had excess capacity there, it decided to export Mexican-made K cars to the United States.

The problem for Chrysler was one of image about Mexico as a country of origin for manufactured goods. Americans think of Mexico as a vacation destination, a country that makes good beer (e. g., Corona, Dos Equis, Tecate, and others), but as an underdeveloped industrial economy. Americans do not think Mexico has enough skilled workers and technology to build high-quality, technically sophisticated products such as automobiles.

Irrespective of the facts about product quality and product performance, Mexican-made cars, even with the Chrysler brand name, are thought to be of poor quality. Consequently, U.S. consumers who knew they were being offered Mexican-made Chrysler cars decided against buying these Plymouths and Dodges unless they were offered a substantial discount by Chrysler's U.S. dealers. So, some dealers refused to accept delivery of these cars, others ripped off the bright green stickers showing Mexico as the country of origin, and Chrysler stopped shipping its Mexican-made cars to the United States.

This willingness to buy brand name goods that are made in the United States and this unwillingness to buy the same brand name goods that are made in Mexico is called cognitive dissonance. When consumers perceive differences between the goods of two countries, when the differences show a substantially negative view of one set of national goods, and when these negative perceptions influence consumer decisions about which goods to purchase, a change in the country of origin for imported products is a risk for international firms. Over time, with consistent manufacturing quality and after-sales service, the country of origin issue could fade for Chrysler as U.S. consumers learn to like Plymouths and Dodges whether they are made in Canada, the United States, or Mexico.

Data Element: Cognitive Dissonance

Cognitive dissonance occurs in international marketing when customers have a favorable perception about the quality of products from one country and an unfavorable perception about the quality of products from another country. Also, cognitive dissonance occurs in international marketing when customers prefer products from the country with positive images and refuse to purchase products from the country with negative images. Moreover, cognitive dissonance occurs in international marketing when customers can afford to buy the products from the country with positive images and cannot afford to buy equivalent products from the country with negative images.

In response to customer perceptions, preferences, and affordability, marketing executives import products from those countries with positive images and do not import products from those countries with negative images. When international marketing executives import products from countries with negative perceptions among consumers, they are tempting fate; over time, these goods will move downward in market status and the brand names associated with them will be devalued. These are the dangers of cognitive dissonance in international marketing, and these were the dangers faced by Chrysler when it imported Mexican-made cars into the United States. No amount of promotion could change the view held by Americans about Mexican-built cars.

MARKETING INTELLIGENCE

International competitiveness comes from success in changing the country of origin to enhance status marketing among up-market consumers.

Data Element: Status Marketing[25]

In general, products from the industrial countries such as Japan, the United States, and countries in Europe, carry with them a higher status than similar products with the same brand name from the newly industrialized countries. Thus, a change in the country of origin affects what image is conveyed about the product through its brand name.

Goods from industrial countries convey the following product attributes: reliability, good workmanship, durability, high quality, high performance, reasonable price, innovation, economical operation, low service costs, exclusiveness, the ability to create pride of ownership, and stylishness. However, goods with the same brand name from less-developed countries do not convey these product attributes.

Therefore, a change in the country of origin of a product forces international marketing executives to either reposition the brand name or change it to a new name. In the latter case, they may not want to use a valuable brand name on a product that customers will perceive as a cheap import because to do so would cause irreparable damage to the value of the brand name worldwide. In the former case, these marketing executives will choose a new promotional campaign that offers customers the best features in terms of price and quality attributes from the new country of origin.

Tactic: Use Appropriate Multicues to Convince Customers of Quality

For many products, country of origin is only one reason why customers buy imported goods. There are other reasons (or multicues) for purchasing film manufactured in Japan and the United States, such as the physical characteristics of the film and its associated retail services.

In the case of automobiles manufactured in the United States, Japan, and Germany,[26] U.S. customers buy high-performance cars manufactured in three different industrial countries for the following 13 reasons (or multicues): price, handling, horsepower, acceleration, gas mileage, safety, driving comfort, passenger comfort, reliability, durability, workmanship, styling, and color selection. Consumers rate U.S., Japanese, and German cars higher overall when their gas mileage, handling, horsepower, driving comfort, reliability, and styling are rated higher. These multicues suggest that high performance rather than country of origin is the primary reason for buying these cars. Moreover, no differences in images (either positive or negative) are associated with high-performance cars imported from Japan or Germany, or manufactured in the United States.

MARKETING INTELLIGENCE

International competitiveness comes from selecting the right set of promotional cues to capture consumers with higher incomes, improved standards of living, and an enhanced quality of demand.

Although many automobiles that are manufactured in the developed industrial countries include a large portion of parts and components from less-developed countries, nothing should be said in the promotional campaign about these parts and components from the newly industrialized countries of Asia and Latin America. This will introduce a negative cue for potential customers among a sea of positive images about U.S., Japanese, and German cars.

Therefore, international marketing executives should use a promotional campaign for the U.S. that is built on the high performance of automobiles manufactured in Japan and Germany. If country of origin is also used in the advertising campaign, it should reinforce the positive image already held about the cars and their high performance by potential U.S. consumers.

STRATEGY ANALYSIS OF INTERNATIONAL PROMOTION POLICY

A fifth future has already happened in international business: Promotion policy remains firmly tied to corporate culture unless executives violate some national culture norms through the improper use of cues, such as Chrysler's use of Mexican country of origin in the United States, or P&G's lack of attention to the nurturing of babies in Japan. Americans and Japanese have strong beliefs about each other's government policies on trade and investment, manufacturing quality, and recipes for competitive success. Some of these are good cues and others are bad cues. Irrespective of the simmering disputes between the U. S. and Japan, large-scale international firms raise returns on sales in both countries through innovative product designs that capture the fancy of upmarket consumer segments for 35mm cameras, slow-speed film, and other products. Even without free trade with the United States, Japanese firms are strong competitors of American firms both at home and abroad. Similar to Fuji, many Japanese firms use their new products to enhance the quality of demand among their best customers throughout the world to maintain competitive advantage.

CONCLUSIONS FROM THE CASES

The success of Kodak and Fuji in establishing strong market positions in each other's home territory has led them each to dream of becoming the dominant firm in the other's home country market. Their emphasis on contesting markets through foreign direct investments leads them to finding better customers for their higher value-added products. Film defines the quality of life in Japan, the United States, and Europe, and their similar standards of living encourage improvements in film products for the benefit of countries in both the developed and less-developed parts of the world. Such emphasis on the quality of demand has stood Kodak and Fuji in good stead as they have become the classic U.S. and Japanese examples of successful international business firms.

Both Kodak and Fuji are better off today than they were before their competition began in the 1970s. Their international business networks of parent firms, subsidiaries, research centers, and retail distribution outlets have made them stronger world competitors. Because sales of cameras, film, and other photographic equipment are growing in Japan, the United States, and elsewhere in the world, they are now the two most important firms in their industry.

Kodak and Fuji have derived sufficient cash flow from pretax operating income to pay back their investments and to make new ones at home and abroad. The products they sell have high margins, high sales, and high profits. Nothing hinders them financially from making other investments in Europe, southeast Asia, and the rest of the world.

Although both Kodak and Fuji dominate their home markets, neither has been successful in restructuring the other's home market. Each is still in second place when it comes to competing with the other at home.

EXECUTIVE SUMMARY

Kodak and Fuji are good cases in which to observe how firms work on improving the quality of demand. They have redesigned their worldwide organizations, reorganized their foreign subsidiaries, reinvented their products, rehabilitated their packages, and reestablished their retailing businesses. These two international firms seek to continue doing what they always have done, but to do their marketing jobs better every day so that they stay one step ahead of their competitors. Sometimes they come up with new products that they promote to their customers as improvements in the quality of life. If consumers accept these improvements (i.e., if they believe in the multicues used to promote these products), then these international firms have a good product market match both in home and host country markets. That is the essence of the Kodak and Fuji cases.

CHAPTER 6

MANAGING VALUE CREATION WITH ONE NORTH ATLANTIC GROUP FOR THE UNITED STATES AND EUROPE

Demographics are revolutionizing our strategies for the world's consumer goods markets. We are big brand people [on both sides of the North Atlantic. However,] if we forget the importance of local selling and marketing we will rue the day,[1]
  Mike Heron, *European regional director of Unilever.*

We are aiming at focused, flexible production units. The old national organisation of Unilever companies omnipotent in their own markets is going to have to change. They will no longer necessarily control their sources of supply.[2]
  Michael Angus, *chairman and CEO of Unilever.*

We will beg, borrow, and steal every bit of Unilever expertise from round the world to get into hair, deodorants, and other core categories of personal care products.[3]
  Robert Phillips, *president of Chesebrough-Pond's, one of Unilever's U.S. subsidiaries.*

COMPETITIVENESS: THE IMPORTANCE OF BUILDING A DOMINANT POSITION

Unilever, which is equally owned by the Dutch and the British, grew large by building dominant positions in several lines of business: food and drinks (margarine, fats and oils, frozen foods and ice cream, tea, soups, dressings, and meats); detergents; and personal care products. Unilever is 80 percent big brands and hence largely monocultural in North American and European consumer markets.

Within Unilever, specialty chemicals and agribusiness items are separate stories. They succeed because the firm gives them the freedom to have their own accounting systems, planning horizons, price strategies, distribution tactics, and so on. These two businesses are different cultural units, but their goal is the same: to build a dominant position in key world markets. When they cannot accomplish this assignment, Unilever sells them—such as it sold Stauffer Chemicals to ICI, and Prince tennis racquets and Bass shoes to other firms.

In the United States, Unilever's personal care products subsidiary, Chesebrough-Pond's, flourishes because the market forces that influence middle managers in North America are similar to those that influence middle managers in Europe. These executives and their bicontinental product markets are managed jointly through a high-level North Atlantic Group within the corporate structure of Unilever.

STRATEGY INSIGHT

International competitiveness comes from managing foreign investments through high-level product market groups with responsibility for subsidiaries on several continents.

The following market forces foster the development of one group product manager of big brands for both Europe and the United States:

1. Customers pay a price for big brands, such as Vaseline and Pond's, that represents their view of the products' inherent value.
2. Products are manufactured by batch processing.
3. Distribution costs are relatively low for high-value, low-weight products.

4. Raw materials, food ingredients, packaging, and equipment are bought in bulk.
5. Brands earn a return in two or three years if they are successful, and the life of successful brands is long.

Unilever's market position in Europe is overwhelming. The firm is the single most important buyer of oil in Europe, and it transports more products throughout the continent than any other company. From this market position has come higher levels of international integration with North America, greater scale economies in research and marketing, increased market share in the detergent and personal care products industries, and improved profitability throughout the world. Through the North Atlantic Group, Unilever hopes to make its businesses in North America as successful as those in Europe.

Europe's Common Internal Market

By 1992, the European Economic Community's common internal market among its 12 member nations is to be a fact for all business executives. This means no production, trade, or transport barriers among a market of 325 million people. Because 60 percent of Unilever's sales come from the EEC, Unilever has been casting about for a way to strengthen its competitive position within the EEC, the European Free Trade Association, and the North Atlantic region that stretches from California to the Elbe River (the frontier between East and West Germany). Therefore, Unilever decided to set up its single North Atlantic Group to manage all big brands for sale to some 700 million consumers on both sides of the Atlantic Ocean.

Within this two-continent region, the market conditions for the food business are in a state of flux. The population is aging, demand is switching from processed products to convenience foods, mass markets are fragmenting, and distribution is moving toward powerful retailer concentrations.[4] Are the changes in the demand for microwavable food that are coming about because of the fast rise in single households in the U.S. going to be repeated in Europe as well? Unilever's answer is yes, and its North Atlantic Group is its managerial organization through which Europe will be ready for the next wave of changes in the food business.

The Rest of Europe

How does Unilever count who is European? When 50 million Turkish consumers were declared sufficiently European in tastes—they want Western-style products rather than those more common to the Middle East[5]—the firm shifted the managerial oversight of Turkey's markets from its overseas directorate to its European regional directorate, which is under the control of the North Atlantic Group.

As market economies emerge in central, eastern, and Soviet Europe, they too will be shifted from overseas countertrade units to the European directorate and North Atlantic Group. Unilever is in the forefront of extending the reach of the EEC to Poland, Czechoslovakia, Hungary, and other countries in transition from socialism to capitalism. With that come the benefits of an American lifestyle within a European context, or the convergence of tastes, preferences and demand on both sides of the Atlantic Ocean.

Euro-Production

Because the EEC is to become one large market, Unilever has cut its 13 toilet soap factories scattered throughout the continent to 3 within the EEC. Moreover, it has standardized the bottle for its Timotei shampoo while varying the ingredients to suit differences in climates and hair types. People's habits and preferences do vary a bit between Scotland and Sicily, and Unilever wants to be sure customers get what they want. Yet the former omnipotence of the national companies within Unilever is changing. This is because the EEC is to become one common internal market, the other European countries are climbing on the EEC's bandwagon, and North America and Europe are recognizing that their similarities in consumer tastes and preferences are greater than their differences.

Euro-Consumers

Although Unilever is in the business of creating consumers, the firm is careful not to practice the notion that all European (and

American) consumers are the same. Unilever's products are not those with international snob appeal, such as Rolex watches or Gucci shoes for only the very rich, nor those for which a "one sight, one sound, one sell" marketing strategy makes sense, such as Coca-Cola or Marlboro cigarettes.

Instead, Unilever plans globally, and acts locally, that is, it tailors its products to narrow markets. Promotional strategies for Impulse, a body spray, show a young man in Great Britain giving a woman a bunch of flowers, whereas in Spain he offers only one rose.[6] Unilever practices micromarketing and segments its markets by geographical, ethnic, and other lines. Several marketing strategies used in Spain fit neatly into the U.S. Hispanic market whereas others do not. In this way, Unilever seeks to gain its fair share of the Euro-consumer's dollar, which is about 97 percent of what Americans spend on similar personal and home care products.

Research Connections within the North Atlantic Group

Unilever has four central research laboratories, three in Europe and one in Edgewater, New Jersey. Through cross-fertilization research on both sides of the Atlantic, variants on British Colworth's Cornetto cone and Vienetta dessert were used by Good Humor, a U.S. subsidiary, to give it sound profits for the first time in 30 years.[7] These research groups also stopped the head of a Yogi Bear ice cream cone from falling off at the first bite. Now, ice cream concoctions are booming in both Europe and the U.S. for all Unilever subsidiaries.

STRATEGY INSIGHT

International competitiveness comes from knowing when to jump into common markets with rationalization, specialization, and flexible manufacturing.

Taste Barriers Will Stay High

According to David Stout of Unilever, "local tastes are far more firmly entrenched when it comes to what we eat than what we wear, [how we clean our homes], what we watch, or the music we listen to.[8]Nevertheless, increased travel is spreading the taste for regional dishes across the Atlantic, and Europe is following America's concern for more nutritional and healthier foods. On the other hand, U.S. is learning from Europe about sterile packaged convenience goods with long shelf life and lower distribution costs.

As the common internal market comes into force, the 12 member states and other European countries will give mutual recognition to national standards and regulations, and frontier-free transportation and warehousing will lower the costs of distribution. Unilever plans to cut the number of its 200 European factories by one fourth within four to five years while other North Atlantic food firms go through a similar process of rationalization, specialization, and flexible manufacturing.

Many of the changes going on in Europe have a transitional feel about them because the opportunities for success are great, but not everyone is clear about what the appropriate risks are, given the potential benefits. Unilever's search for a long-term commercial sense within Europe and with North America led it to form its North Atlantic Group to manage product development, new technologies, component purchasing, consumer demand, and retail outlets. The firm's response to 1992, the collapse of socialism, and demand convergence is to act locally while trying to reap the benefits of being global. It is a tall order but one that Unilever is trying to implement both within the North Atlantic Group and all over the world.

UNILEVER AND THE ACQUISITION OF CHESEBROUGH-POND'S[9]

Throughout its history, Unilever has been a decentralized federation of 500 national companies. Today, their freedom to make independent decisions about manufacturing, distribution, and marketing within Europe and North America is being curtailed as the North Atlantic Group makes more judgments centrally about factory runs, warehousing, and packaging. In the United States, the firm's companies operate under their own names, such as Chesebrough-Pond's, Lever Bros., Lipton Tea, and National Starch. Each is different from another in terms of brand management, pricing policy, and retail support services. Although Unilever believes its corporate culture of decentralization breeds a quick reaction to changes in the market, innovations in research and development, and the development of entrepreneurial skills among local management,[10] Unilever is doing what other transnational firms (e.g., Gillette) have done: regrouping its commercial activities for Europe and North America under one common managerial roof. In this way, Unilever is turning Europe 1992, the European Free Trade Association, the U.S.–Canada Free Trade Agreement, and the convergence of demand among European and American consumers to its own advantage.

AMERICAN FAILURE FORCES EUROPEAN MANAGEMENT INVASION

In 1980, Michael Angus, a burly Scot and head of Unilever's chemicals division, was sent to the United States "to prevent Lever Bros. from collapsing under the drubbing being handed out by Procter & Gamble and Colgate Palmolive.[11] Angus brought in teams of European experts in engineering, manufacturing, marketing, and product quality. They found brands underpromoted because when volume fell, spending on promotion, advertising, and research was curtailed. During his four years in the United States, Angus gave Lever Bros. an international style of management, one not so dependent on U.S. corporate habits.

Through the 1984 acquisition of Shedd's, a margarine manufacturer from Beatrice Foods, Lever Bros. was able within two years to raise its market share from 7 percent to 30 percent. During the Angus years, Lever Bros. also was able to rebuild its soap and detergent businesses, invest in research and development, and become a more efficient manufacturer.

However, Lever Bros.'s personal care products division remained beset with problems. Aim toothpaste stayed a distant fourth against P&G's Crest and Colgate. Signal mouthwash was far behind P&G's Scope. Dimension shampoo was never heard of in the United States.[12] And good household products' brand names—such as Sunlight automatic dishwashing powder, Surf laundry detergent, and Snuggle fabric softener, which captured 15 to 20 percent market shares—were driven back by P&G's frontal attack with Liquid Tide. Lever Bros. lost $39 million (in U.S. dollars) on Surf alone between 1982 and 1985.[13]

By the time Angus became chairman of British Unilever PLC in 1986, the coequal partner of this Anglo-Dutch concern, Lever Bros. had failed in its attempt to acquire Richardson Vicks, a personal care products firm, and was still without this important line of business in the United States. Yet the die was cast, for later on the company did position itself both in the U.S. and Europe through a wide range of acquisitions, totaling about $8 billion.

ACQUISITION STRATEGY

Shortly after the failure to acquire Richardson Vicks, Unilever purchased Chesebrough-Pond's for $3.1 billion. This 1987 acquisition was the start of something new and different for Unilever in the United States.

Whenever world markets are studied by consumer products companies, the United States turns out to be about 40 percent of the total world market.[14] This is especially true in the personal care products business. For example, in France, annual deodorant consumption is just one bottle per capita versus almost three in the United States; in Belgium, annual toothpaste consumption is one fourth of that in the United States.[15] So Unilever felt it had to be in the United States at whatever the cost.

Through the acquisition of Chesebrough-Pond's, Unilever now controls 25 percent of the U.S. hand and body lotion market. For the company, this translates into a 50 percent increase in personal care products worldwide and a 20 percent increase in Great Britain for the company's subsidiary, Elida Gibbs. For Chesebrough-Pond's, the acquisition made it a consumer-driven company, according to Robert Phillips, its president.

PHILLIPS ON BEING A CONSUMER-DRIVEN COMPANY[16]

- Chesebrough-Pond's is now a consumer-driven company and means it. Most public companies' plans in the United States pivot around earnings per share figures for the next eight quarters.
- Long-range thinking now is devoted solely to the market. We have plans and we will stick to them despite the ripples.
- We are going to pour hot oil on the competition in skin care.

Phillips is the first to admit that Chesebrough-Pond's is "not in hair and . . . deodorants. But these are core categories for which we have new initiatives. We will beg, borrow and steal every bit of Unilever expertise from round the world to get in there."[17] Mike Heron, Unilever's European regional director, has said, "Almost all our failures [in the United States] have been the result of Americanising international concepts. Things have been modified unsuccessfully. We don't ask them to mimic the UK or German way of handling a product, and we don't want them to ape fashions in the domestic U.S. market.

"We ask: 'are you sure you understand the concept' ?"[18]

For example, Timotei shampoo is widely successful in Europe, Canada, and worldwide based on the concepts of youth, protectiveness, and purity. Heron argues that Chesebrough-Pond's tried to Americanize the concept and therefore the product flopped in the United States. Heron wants Phillips to recognize that these concept intangibles are universally desirable. The North Atlantic Group insists that Chesebrough-Pond's vary only the means of expressing these universally desirable intangibles in their advertising and point-of-purchase selling activities.[19] But Chesebrough-Pond's is not to change the concept itself.

To get the concept right, Mike Perry, the Unilever main board director responsible for global personal product operations, meets with Phillips and his coequals from Great Britain, West Germany, France, and Italy every six weeks. They work on common issues for the North Atlantic Group and are developing the habit

of transferring the best ideas among themselves. Timotei originally came from Finland, and Impulse from South Africa. "The
greatest benefits . . . accrue not from production economies of
scale . . . but from the steady refinement which comes as the
[brand] concept is passed from country to country."[20]

Unilever's acquisition of Chesebrough-Pond's has been quite
successful so far because Robert Phillips has worked very hard at
making his U.S. subsidiary accept the commonly held beliefs of
Unilever. The latter wants to take the former's dominant position
in skin care and convert it into a dominant position in all personal
care products. When this is actually accomplished, Unilever will
become what it thought it would be when it acquired
Chesebrough-Pond's—a contender for the dominant position in
all personal care product categories within the United States.

DECISIONS ABOUT BRANDS AFFECT
INTERNATIONAL BUSINESS PERFORMANCE

The Chesebrough-Pond's acquisition also gives Unilever a
strengthened capability to fight P&G and Colgate for vital retail
shelf space in the United States. For example, Unilever gained
Pond's face cream, Vaseline petroleum jelly, Vaseline Intensive
Care, Q-Tips, Cutex, and Prince Matchabelli, and thus it leap-
frogged from sixth to second place in the world league of personal
care products manufacturers. Pond's is number two behind Nox-
ema, and Vaseline is number one in all its markets.

Through Chesebrough-Pond's success, Unilever gained more
shelf space for all of its products, and it has begun to close the gap
in pretax earnings between itself and P&G. In 1985, Unilever
earned a meager 5 percent pretax in Europe while P&G earned
22.5 percent pretax in the United States.[21] With these funds, P&G
was able to outbid Unilever in the contest over Richardson Vicks.

The next time around, Unilever used its stronger earnings
base from Chesebrough-Pond's to acquire more brands for its
worldwide markets.[22] For example, in 1989 Unilever bought Fabergé. Its Elizabeth Arden skin creams and lotions for the face
and body (which are for the high-income end of the market) complement Pond's face cream and Vaseline hand lotion (which are

for the middle part of the market). These two acquisitions permit Unilever to take advantage of booming skin care sales to the aging populations in Europe, North America, and Japan. To do this successfully, Unilever must compete against L'Oréal of France, the top firm in the industry, Shiseido and Kao from Japan, and P&G and other U.S. firms.

Through the Chesebrough-Pond's acquisition, Unilever initiated a new subsidiary, Parfums International, to sell high-class perfume. Its first venture was to distribute Elizabeth Taylor's Passion, a high-priced florid fragrance that was the most successful new introduction on record in the United States.[23] This perfume was later introduced into Great Britain, France, Italy, and West Germany. Through the Fabergé acquisition, Unilever obtained Fendi, Chloe, Lagerfeld, KL, and Brut. All of these upmarket perfumes have been added to Unilever's existing Denim and Bizarre lines of scents. It is from their steady refinement as they have been passed from country to country that these brands have given their greatest benefits to Unilever worldwide.

For Unilever to create value with these higher priced facial creams and scents, it will have to provide sales staff and point-of-sale equipment in department stores. This is a significant change in the way in which it carries out its retail business by bulk deliveries to the distribution centers of the retail chains. It means the development of a new cultural unit with a set of commonly held beliefs different from those held by executives in the skin and face cream business. Within Unilever, both share the common culture of big brands and the drive for a dominant position in all product categories.

UNILEVER'S FIVE INTERNATIONAL MARKETING TACTICS

- Saves U.S. business by transferring core international management skills
- Builds up U.S. market position through brand acquisitions
- Sets up North Atlantic Group to manage Europe and North America

- Transfers concepts, products, and brands among national companies
- Reconfigures Unilever world: United States, Europe, and Japan

Asia and the Pacific as Separate Units within Unilever World

East Asia and the Pacific, which accounted for 18 percent of the free world's gross domestic product (GDP) in 1970, are reaching for 31 percent of GDP in the year 2000. Japan, as well as other countries in the region, is the main driving force of Unilever's expansion in the region. However, because this region is hedged in by punitive national border tariffs and demands for foreign exchange earnings in return for manufacturing rights, capital expenditure demands are burdensome. Plants must be built for each local national market. Nevertheless, in some countries, such as Malaysia, Thailand, Indonesia, and the Philippines, Unilever's sales are three times greater than those of P&G and Colgate, and nine times greater than those of Lion, the rival Japanese group.

Unilever ranks sixth in the league of the largest foreign companies operating in Japan, way behind Nestlé and far ahead of P&G. Nippon Lever built itself up in margarine and black tea. Then it organized joint ventures between its National Starch subsidiary and Kanebo and Oji in specialty chemicals. From this market position, Nippon Lever won second place in the fabric softener sector with its brand name FaFa. Moreover, within seven years, it took number one position in the shampoo business away from Kao and built a 60 percent market share with its brand Timotei. The rewards have been high in Japan because net margins and profits are greater there than in either Europe or the United States.[24]

STRATEGY ANALYSIS OF UNILEVER'S INTERNATIONAL BUSINESS PERFORMANCE

Unilever remains the dominant firm in Great Britain and in the rest of Europe. Except in the tea and starch businesses, it has been unable to convert its European market position into market leadership in the United States. Its U.S. rivals have been able to keep it at bay.

On the other hand, Unilever has been able to challenge its Japanese rivals in their home market and to take the number one market position in several important personal care product categories. Their U.S rivals have been kept at bay in Japan.

STRATEGY INSIGHT

International competitiveness comes from knowing how to create appropriate cultural units for all subsidiaries.

Unilever is strengthening its competitive connections between Europe and the United States through its North Atlantic Group. Nevertheless, the race for sustainable competitive advantage continues with Unilever not sure it will remain the champion in Europe yet trying to be a serious contender in both Japan and the United States.

INTERNATIONAL BRAND MANAGEMENT POLICY

Unilever took over Shedd's, Chesebrough-Pond's and Fabergé to acquire Pond's, Vaseline, Q-Tips, Cutex, Elizabeth Arden, and Brut. These brands create value in the minds of consumers. If such images are favorable, they give international firms market position, market share, scope economies, and profits. Unilever's new brands must be managed better than they were under their previous owners so that the parent firm can recover its acquisition (or entry) costs. Also, these brands must outsell their competitors in the United States so that the U.S. subsidiary is doing better today in terms of market share and profitability than it was yesterday. Moreover, these brands must become the dominant brands in the United States, Europe, Japan, and elsewhere in the world so that they increase Unilever's pretax earnings and make Chesebrough-Pond's and Fabergé the dominant firms in the personal care products industry.

Exhibit 6–A shows the sixth international business decision. All big-brand companies, including Unilever, carry out this decision successfully when they sustain themselves in each other's personal care products home market. Exhibit 6–B shows the marketing tactics for rolling out Decision 6. Exhibit 6–C lists the data elements for assessing value creation that are discussed throughout this chapter.

INTERNATIONAL MARKETING TACTICS AND DATA ELEMENTS FOR ASSESSING VALUE CREATION

The following provides an explanation of how various companies used the three tactics listed in Exhibit 6–B for rolling out Decision 6.

Tactic: Acquire Brands, Trademarks, and Other Intellectual Property

Chapters 1 through 5, explained how Molson, Corona, P&G, L'Oréal, Caterpillar, Komatsu, MacMillan Bloedel, Kodak, and Fuji built up their brand positions through organic growth. Their products were developed internally and given a brand name or trade logo (such as CAT) to establish their image and place in the market. On the other hand, Unilever bought established brand names as a quick way to become a major player in the personal care products market. To make the Chesebrough-Pond's and Fabergé acquisitions successful, Unilever also must do well in carrying out the following tactics.

MARKETING INTELLIGENCE

International competitiveness comes from success in acquiring and enhancing the value of brands, products, and other intellectual property.

EXHIBIT 6–A
International Business Decision 6: Success in Creating Value for Customers
with High-Quality Demand

Product attributes
Brand management
Acquisitions
Organizational design
Executive performance

Note: Executives must specify decisions to fit international business problems. Is value
created through the acquisition of brands? Is value created through a change in
organizational design?

EXHIBIT 6–B
International Marketing Tactics for Rolling Out Decision 6

Acquire brands, trademarks, and other intellectual property
Measure actual movement of brand name products through channel
Create promotional campaigns to pull products through channel

EXHIBIT 6–C
Data Elements for Assessing Value Creation

Acquisitions
Brands, trademarks, copyrights, and patents
Strategic alliances
Greenfield investments
Unit share volume
Dollar share sales
Inventory levels
Shipments to agents, distributors, and other middlemen

Tactic: Measure Actual Movement of
Brand Name Products through Channel

Whether brands are created internally or acquired from other
firms, another crucial product attribute (along with quality, performance, and country of origin) is the familiarity of importers,
wholesale and retail distributors, and final customers with the

product concept and brand name itself. Do they have a brand preference? Do their purchase patterns reflect this brand preference? Are they changing their brand preference? Why are they changing their brand preference?

Such interest in the product can be tracked on a daily, weekly, or monthly basis through audit procedures of product movement through the channel of distribution.[25] In the case of the U.S. launch of Timotei shampoo, it was clear almost immediately that the product was not moving off retail shelves and that stock was sitting in warehouses and other distribution centers. Yet Chesebrough-Pond's failed to pay attention to information from the following reports:

1. Sales and distribution coverage reports by retail outlet.
2. Product movement reports.
3. Shipments from offshore plant to ocean or air carrier, to customs broker, to wholesaler, and to retailer.
4. Levels of inventory maintained at offshore plant, at warehouse of port of embarkation, in a bonded warehouse of importing nation, at wholesaler, and at retailer.
5. Sales and shipment statistics of competitors.

These data reflect customer intentions, perceptions, and expectations about the brand name product; they tell international marketing executives when, where, and how the products will be used; and they show the purchase decisions of customers. By not paying attention to this information, Timotei became one of the worst marketing launch disasters in the United States.

MARKETING INTELLIGENCE

International competitiveness comes from success in knowing specific marketing information about sales, inventory turns, and customer preferences.

In 1990, a second launch of Timotei is being tried in California. This time, Chesebrough-Pond's is talking to retailers about the product concept and measuring the movement of the product at each stage in the channel of distribution. Time will tell whether or not the successes in Canada and Europe can be repeated in the United States.

Tactic: Create Promotional Campaign to Pull Products through Channel

One of the most important international marketing tasks is to retain customer loyalty for brand name products over long periods of time. This loyalty must be maintained even when familiar brand names, such as Vaseline and Pond's, are acquired by foreign-owned firms.

International marketing executives must create a promotional campaign that convinces customers to continue demanding the product even though there has been a change in ownership, country of origin, or other crucial product attributes. The international marketing strategy is to make the costs of switching from one brand name product to another so expensive to current customers that they will accept a change in the country of origin rather than give up the perceived value of the brand name product.

Throughout the world, a few brand name products carry with them such strong customer preferences that they truly are global brands. The country of origin is completely immaterial to customers of Marlboro cigarettes, Coca-Cola, Levi's jeans, and McDonald's hamburgers. Their customers are so loyal that they cannot switch to competing products. Because of this strong commitment to the brand name products, these international firms promote them worldwide with a "one-sight, one-sound" global advertising campaign.[26]

Other products, such as Canon cameras, tailor their promotional messages for specific national audiences. For example, sports stars are used in the United States and movie stars are used in France to remind customers that Japanese-made Canon cameras are the best for the money. The country of origin is mentioned because it does matter to customers of high-tech equipment that the product is manufactured in Japan rather than in the United States.

MARKETING INTELLIGENCE

International competitiveness comes from success in promoting the product concept, its desirable intangible benefits, and the brand with a clear understanding of convergence or divergence in demand.

Once a brand name is established in the minds of consumers, their product preferences can be reinforced through either one-sight, one-sound or tailored promotional campaigns. Advertising campaigns by P&G, Colgate, and others inhibited U.S. consumers from switching to Timotei, a competing brand name shampoo; instead, they encouraged consumers to pull the preferred, established products through the channel of distribution. Such a tight relationship between promotional campaigns and the flow of products from factories to markets in Europe, the United States, and Japan is part of the value acquired when brands, trademarks, and other intellectual property are taken over by international firms. Information about this brand management relationship is crucial in the continuing battle for competitive advantage worldwide.

STRATEGY ANALYSIS OF INTERNATIONAL BRAND MANAGEMENT POLICY

A sixth future has already happened in international business: Brands and service marks are becoming so valuable to firms that firms prefer to acquire these properties rather than create new ones. These firms promote them to the fullest so that all customers, whether they are in Europe, the United States, or Japan, demand goods and services without substantial change from one country to the next. An international life-style calls for international marketing executives to pay attention to the details of unit share volumes, dollar sales, distribution problems, and inventory levels. These are good indicators of customer satisfaction with world-renowned brand names. If these data are used properly, they help firms maintain competitive advantage.

CONCLUSIONS FROM THE CASE

The success of Unilever in acquiring valuable brand name products in the United States through its acquisition of Chesebrough-Pond's and Fabergé has led this British-Dutch international firm to dream of displacing Procter & Gamble and Colgate Palmolive from first and second place, respectively, in the U.S. personal care products market. Such emphasis on value creation through international brand management is how consumer products firms wage their continuing battle for competitive advantage.

Unilever is better off today than it was before it made its U.S. acquisitions. It now has strong brand names. They provide clear images of what personal care products should be for U.S. consumers. Can Unilever transfer these brands, images, and product attributes overseas? Will they tailor them for specific national markets or use global brand management? These are questions for the future.

Unilever paid off its U.S. acquisitions by selling off assets of the acquired companies and by improving its cash flow from pretax earnings. However, Unilever has a long way to go before its pretax operating income is equal to that earned by P&G.

Although Unilever dominates the British and European markets, and although it does better than its two U.S. rivals in key Asian markets, Unilever has not been successful in restructuring the U.S. market. It is still number three in personal care products and even further behind in household detergents. If Unilever wants to be the dominant firm in the United States, it must build up brand loyalty through promotional campaigns, effective distribution policies, and investments over a very long time. Unilever will probably have greater success taking U.S. brands abroad than it will have ousting P&G from its preeminent role in the U.S. market.

Unless Unilever becomes a much stronger competitor in the U.S. and Japanese markets, it will have trouble sustaining its competitive lead in Europe. In the 1990s, international firms must connect research and marketing among Europe, the United States, and Japan so that each gives its best to all other areas of the world.

EXECUTIVE SUMMARY

Unilever is a good case in which to observe how international firms work on creating value through the acquisitions of brands, products, and other intellectual property. It reinforced its core skill of international management by taking a more active role in the future of its U.S. subsidiary, Lever Bros. This led to the spate of acquisitions that created value in margarine (Shedd's) and personal care products (Chesebrough-Pond's and Fabergé). Unilever has not yet been able to create value in household detergents within the U.S. market. For Unilever, the U.S. is only one of three important world markets. If consumer preferences continue to converge worldwide, perhaps some of the successes in Europe and Japan will turn the U.S. household detergents market around for Unilever. Its success in building competitive research and marketing connections in ice cream between Europe and the U. S. is an example of what Unilever can do in its continuing battle for competitive advantage in the United States. That success in creating value is the essence of the Unilever case.

STRATEGY ANALYSIS OF MARKETING MANAGEMENT AND INTERNATIONAL BUSINESS: THE INTERNATIONAL MARKETING FORECAST

Throughout Part II (Chapters 4, 5, and 6), the themes of product sourcing, customer selection, and value creation have been paramount for international marketing executives. Executives must be prepared to make these ideas operational so that their middle managers can build up and strengthen markets in all product categories either at home or abroad. The following list provides the information needed to make a good international marketing forecast:[27]

1. Sales forecasts are forecasts of gross sales for a given level of marketing effort, a given period of time (e.g, one year, three years, and five years), and a specific marketing plan. Sales forecasts answer this question: What are the opportunities for next year and the years thereafter?

2. Sales quotas are motivational targets to stimulate sales efforts among the sales force. Usually, they are set higher than the sales forecasts and reflect the desire of international marketing executives to grow new markets through global brand name products and an expanded product line.

3. Sales budgets are estimated revenues from sales, used in planning cash flow.

4. Inventory levels, sales turnover, and movement of products through channel are forms of information that help international marketing executives know how well actual sales are conforming to the sales forecast, sales quotas, and sales budget.

5. Actual sales of competitors are data from the previous year that alert marketing executives to the strength of their competition and the problems they will have to contend with in the current year.

6. Market potentials are estimates of how much the market can absorb when the sales force of the international firm and its competitors are highly motivated to achieve the sales quotas set by marketing executives.

7. Promotion potentials are estimates of how fast the market can grow when a new advertising campaign is introduced to emphasize the appropriate attributes of the product and to target national markets with a global brand name and product line.

An international marketing forecast must provide answers to these following questions: What do we know already about sales, product acceptability, and market penetration? What additional information do we need to collect? Where can we get this information? What are our opportunities for increasing market share and growing in the market? What results should we expect in one year, three years, and five years?

Does the international marketing forecast help us prepare pro forma statements about next year's sales revenues, profits, and cash flow that we can expect from our international business network? Does the forecast help us prepare an international marketing plan and the accompanying appropriate international marketing strategies? Does the forecast help us carry out the practice of international marketing successfully by selling appropriate products to our best customers? Does the international marketing forecast help us create value in all potential markets worldwide?

Such international marketing forecasts help firms become insiders, develop a set of commonly held beliefs, and build dominant positions in all crucial markets of the world. Thus, these firms are able to maintain competitive advantage whether they are owned by the Japanese, Europeans, or Americans.

PART III

ORGANIZATIONAL LEARNING AND INTERNATIONAL BUSINESS

How to Sustain Competitive Advantage

Market Information
Assets
National Differences

CHAPTER 7

INFORMATION REQUIRED
ABOUT ALTERNATIVE FUTURES

[Although the company wants to increase production after 1991, it is a question of] looking at our physical and human resources. We have to work very closely with our suppliers to see that they can step up production while still meeting schedule and quality standards.[1]
   Frank Shrontz, *president of the Boeing Company.*

You have to generate management information so that you can actually influence decisions and not be constantly looking back at the past.[2]
   Bob Smith, *finance director of the European Airbus consortium.*

Today one predicts the price of anything at one's peril for 1990, let alone 2015. . . . Stir in new technologies that are altering the fundamentals of design, manufacture, distribution and organization alike, and you induce even fiercer volatility. . . . None of management's tools—basic accounting practices, patterns of organization, formulation of strategy or workforce care—can cope with the new rates of change.[3]
   Tom Peters, *the guru of excellence in management.*

COMPETITIVENESS: THE IMPORTANCE OF GETTING THE ANSWERS RIGHT

The following explains how Boeing is seeking to get the answers right during a period of rapid change in the airline industry:

   Boeing . . . believes that, over the next 15 years, a total of [9,935] new jets of all types from all manufacturers will be added to the world fleet . . . compared with its forecast of only a year ago of some 6,908 new jets. . . . Of the overall Boeing figure, a substantial element will be accounted for by the replacement of existing aging and fuel-inefficient fleets; but by far the greatest part . . . will represent aircraft purchases to meet traffic growth. . . . This forecast is broadly in line with those of other major jet airliner manufacturers; and, as a result, . . . they are already increasing their production rates to meet the expected demand.[4]

STRATEGY INSIGHT

International competitiveness comes from knowing how to use information about possible alternative futures to reinvent the firm.

When executives of Boeing and Airbus interact with new planning assumptions about expected demand and future traffic growth, they stop asking "What if. . . ?" and begin asking "How should we react to. . . ?"[5] Their conclusion is to build bigger planes to overcome airport congestion and gain cheaper operating costs per seat-mile.[6]

Nevertheless, a worst-case scenario is not far from their minds—the world economy turns sour; airline customers cancel planes already on order but not yet built; well-trained personnel are laid off; and quality standards fall.[7] If that happens, Boeing will be unable to make the "cultural transition from hire-and-fire to a Japanese style of [long-term employment and] management lifted straight from Deming."[8] This refers to W. Edwards Deming, the guru of quality control. Also, Frank Shrontz will be unable to reinvent Boeing and its suppliers as a total-quality company. Thus there is a need for Boeing, its suppliers, and Shrontz to get the answers right to the following problems of the 1990s: expected passenger demand and traffic growth, airport congestion and landing fees, air and noise pollution, operating costs per seat-mile, electronic cockpits and flying by the wire, and the competition from Airbus.

BOEING VERSUS AIRBUS[9]

Once before, Boeing failed to get the answers right. Between 1974 and 1988, Boeing's share of the global commercial airline market fell from 70 percent to 55 percent, while Airbus (the European consortium) and McDonnell Douglas grabbed 29 percent and 16 percent, respectively.[10] Because Boeing failed to pay attention to the competitive threat of Airbus, Boeing's crucial managerial problem for the 1990s is its decline in market share worldwide.

Boeing's Penalty for Getting the Answer Wrong: Airbus

Previously, the airframe manufacturers acted independently of one another. Now, with the emergence of high fixed costs in new product development, they are becoming more interested in cooperative alliances and even joint venture partnerships. Moreover, because many of those who buy planes are government agencies, the European governments especially demand that parts and components be sourced locally, more flexible financing be offered, and bigger contract cancellation loopholes be granted. This is easier for Airbus than for Boeing because Airbus is owned, financed, and supported by Aerospatiale (France) and Messerschmitt-Boelkow-Blohm (MBB, West Germany) with 37.9 percent each; British Aerospace (Great Britain) with 20 percent, and CASA (Spain) with 4.2 percent, all members of the EEC, and supported in whole or part by member governments.[11]

Airbus entered the commercial aircraft industry in 1974 to carry out the industrial policy of the EEC. The governments of France, Germany, Great Britain, and Spain made loans to Airbus that would be paid back when planes were sold to commercial users. The fuselages, wings, and tail sections are manufactured by MBB, British Aerospace, and CASA, whereas Aerospatiale makes the cockpits and hose sections, and assembles the planes.

Between 1974 and 1983, Airbus only took market share away from McDonnell Douglas and Lockheed. After these early years, Airbus also was taking market share away from the dominant firm, Boeing.[12]

However, debt continues to mount for Airbus, particularly when the dollar goes down in value in terms of the yen or the deutsche mark. For example, Airbus loses about $7 million (in U.S. dollars) on each aircraft sold to Northwest Airlines and other U.S.-owned airline firms.[13] Because of this foreign exchange risk, Airbus is changing its dollar-denominated sales contracts to those denominated 25 percent each in francs, deutsche marks, pounds sterling, and U.S. dollars.[14] Airbus expects to break even in the 1990s when it gains a 30 percent market share, mostly at the expense of Boeing.[15]

Airbus's Strategy for Overcoming High Entry Barriers Raised by Boeing

Huge fixed costs are part and parcel of the commercial aircraft industry. These include high capital investment, intensive research and development, and a small number of customers. Throughout the post-World War II period, Boeing has been the dominant firm and thus able to run these costs down through mass production. Moreover, because of the buildup of U.S. military aircraft and aerospace vehicles, Boeing acquired substantial technical advantages over its rivals. Finally, Boeing aircraft, such as the 747 and others, is simply better known by its customers than products from Airbus.

To overcome these high entry barriers, four European governments and their commercial aviation firms formed a strategic alliance to pool their financial and technical resources and to guarantee a certain volume of sales in the future. In 1974, Airbus first introduced a plane, the A300, that was for the intermediate-range market segment and that had lower average maintenance costs than equivalent Boeing aircraft. This was niche marketing at its best. According to Herbert Flosdorf, Airbus's general manager, the success of the A300 was due to "chinks in the American armor . . . [and having] the right size airplane at the right time, oriented towards customer needs and offering superior economics at a time when all other contenders did not."[16]

Four years later, Airbus extended its product line by adding the A320 to compete in the short-to-medium-range market segment. In 1987, Airbus introduced the A330 and the A340 to compete in the long-range market segment. These new planes were added because of market opportunities in Europe, the United States, and Japan. "Nobody questions that [Airbus] makes fabulous airplanes. . . . They have set new standards in civil aviation technology."[17]

Ever since Airbus began, it has been challenging Boeing's precedent of maintaining quasi-permanent prices for a class of planes in the short-, medium -, and long-range market segments. Airbus has lowered its prices by requiring smaller down payments, lower cancellation fees, and less-than-market-rate loans from the four European governments involved in the consortium.[18]

Still today, Airbus uses government subsidies to overcome the entry barriers raised by Boeing, to create a spider's web of strategic alliances among its partners, and to manufacture aircraft that adds value to its customers.[19] Notwithstanding these strategic decisions, Airbus cannot make money on the planes it sells to European and U.S. airline firms. Bob Smith, Airbus's new finance director, hopes to turn losses into profits sometime in the 1990s.

Boeing's Strategy as the Dominant Firm in the Airframe Industry

Since the early 1950s, Boeing has been the dominant firm in its industry. All of Boeing's production, research and development, quality control, and assembly facilities are centralized in the state of Washington—and all coordination of pricing, sales, and marketing strategies for the United States, Europe, and Japan comes from Seattle. Yet service, maintenance, and procurement are dispersed in customer markets throughout the world to reassure both customers and governments about Boeing's commitment to them in the face of competition from Airbus.

Boeing has sought to keep out all foreign competitors from its home market, the United States. This still is its largest market for commercial aircraft. When Boeing realized that France, Great Britain, and Germany were manufacturing aircraft for themselves rather than for the growing European market, Boeing targeted the EEC as a high-growth market opportunity. Until 1974, Boeing (together with McDonnell Douglas and Lockheed) had this market to itself. And Boeing was very successful. Europe and the U.S. are similar in many ways: population, income levels, and trends in air travel. Europe is America's nearest neighbor both in terms of geographic and cultural distance, and this contributed to Boeing's success.

Boeing is a technology-driven company, whereas Airbus is a market-driven company with a more innovative approach toward sales financing and the cancellation of contracts. As mentioned earlier, Boeing centralizes its research and development and production in, and coordinates its logistics, sales, and marketing efforts from, the state of Washington. Given the growing importance of governments and customers in the demand for commercial aircraft, Boeing has set up procurement operations for parts and components throughout Europe, Japan, and elsewhere in the world. Nevertheless, product development in new commercial aircraft is a five-to-seven-year process, so technical and market information flow to the state of Washington, where it is turned into better performing, higher quality commercial aircraft for the world.

Although Boeing sees Airbus as its major competitive threat, Boeing still places its bets on spending more money on research and development, upgrading technology, and introducing new, more comfortable, more fuel-efficient planes. Because Boeing continues to be the dominant firm in the industry, its emphasis on a technology-driven strategy over a market-driven strategy is still working to its advantage in the U.S. and Japan.

Today, things are somewhat different because Airbus is Europe's challenger to Boeing. Also, airline deregulation is not as far along in Europe as it is in the United States and will not be completed until the mid-1990s. Moreover, the EEC is putting a great deal of stress on the expansion of the intercity rail system among its 12 member countries and on the construction of the rail/passenger car tunnel under the English Channel between Great Britain and France. Therefore, the trends in air travel will be different in Europe, and Boeing will have to fight for its market share against an entrenched, government-subsidized competitor.

With the potential threat to Boeing's home market, the real threat to Boeing's European market, and the expansion of America's trade and investment relationships in Asia and the Pacific, Boeing sees these markets as its competitive challenge for the future. But so does Airbus.

Boeing's Ongoing Problems as an Exporter to Europe

Like most U.S. companies, Boeing has to wonder whether the coming of the common internal market for Europe in 1992 will result in increased trade barriers for non-European companies that prefer to export to the EEC rather than to invest within it. Because many commercial airlines are owned by European governments, Boeing has to face the fact that Airbus will be favored over U.S. firms. This is a substantial risk to Boeing's position in Europe.

Since 1987, Boeing has threatened antidumping action against Airbus for aircraft sold below cost. The question turns on what subsidies are legal under the General Agreement on Tariffs and Trade (GATT).

Boeing contends that when European governments provide less-than-market-rate financing they are subsidizing the cost of manufacturing planes that would be unprofitable without these cheap loans. Airbus has received about $14 billion in European government funds while losing an estimated $15 billion (in U.S. dollars) over the first 14 years of its life.[20] Moreover, West Germany has written off $1.7 billion of the debt owed by Airbus, and France has received back only about 14 percent of the funds it lent to Airbus.[21] Significant case law exists under the GATT to declare these a series of *illegal* subsidies.

Airbus says that these subsidies are to counter Boeing's receipt of tax credits for research and development from the U.S. government. Again, significant case law exists under the GATT to declare these a series of *legal* subsidies.

The U.S. legal question turns on how the support is provided and whether or not the results cause injury (i.e., loss of market share, sales, profits, employment levels, procurement alliances, and service and maintenance contracts) to American competitors. Boeing's challenge under the subsidies code of the GATT and Super 301 of the 1988 Omnibus Trade and Competitiveness Act is still pending.[22]

When the U.S. dollar is weak, Boeing's exposure to export currency risk rises. Although Airbus is moving toward multicurrency contracts, Boeing still prefers all of its contracts to be denominated in U.S. dollars. Such a move will help Boeing in its competition with Airbus. The major risk facing Boeing is the link between European governments, their commercial airlines, and Airbus. Boeing is still working on a solution to this important problem.

To overcome Airbus's links with European governments and their airlines, Boeing entered into strategic alliances with 200 European subcontractors. They were given Boeing's less significant proprietary knowledge and training in quality control to manufacture components for Boeing aircraft. Such local sourcing also goes lockstep with foreign governments' purchasing of a fleet of commercial aircraft from Boeing.[23]

Today, Boeing sees Airbus as its major challenger, as the key threat to its position as the dominant firm in the commercial aircraft industry. Boeing's sales of commercial aircraft within Europe are not rising as fast as they did in the past. Moreover, Boeing is losing market share in Europe (and worldwide) to Airbus. Boeing's management has only been modestly successful.

DECISIONS ABOUT SUPPLIERS AFFECT INTERNATIONAL BUSINESS PERFORMANCE

Boeing offers a classic example of the broad view of internalization. The firm is more than its manufacturing operations in the state of Washington. The firm works with its parts and component suppliers to co-develop new innovative aircraft designs and to co-deliver higher levels of quality. Because of demands by the EEC, more nonproprietary, subassembly parts are being sourced from British, French, German, and Spanish suppliers. Moreover, Boeing works closely with the airlines and their unions to ensure that repair, service, and maintenance are carried out at the highest levels of quality possible. These strategic alliances may ensure that Boeing has continued, unimpeded access to the EEC after 1992.

BOEING'S INTERNATIONAL MARKETING TACTICS

* Positions assets to take advantage of international opportunities
* Expands technical market information and product market skills
* Strengthens alliances with suppliers to create international network
* Becomes dominant firm in the airframe industry
* Exports planes to all overseas markets
* Pays penalty for inadequate international information

Boeing continues to expand its capital expenditures in and sales revenue from Europe. These data show the expansion of its foreign sourcing efforts as well as the fact that it is doing a better job in making its European alliances a more productive part of its international business network.

STRATEGY ANALYSIS OF BOEING'S INTERNATIONAL BUSINESS PERFORMANCE

Boeing has done very well. Is has more revenues and deliveries today than it had before. It is better off, but it has a major problem with Airbus, particularly in Europe. Boeing must take corrective actions soon or find itself no longer dominating its industry.

Boeing needs to pursue a cooperative alliance, a joint venture partnership, or both with Airbus or another European airframe manufacturer, such as Fokker. By integrating a European airframe firm into Boeing's international business network, Boeing would protect its revenue stream (about 15 percent of its total revenues) from Europe. Moreover, Boeing would become a European firm for purposes of the EEC and the latter's drive to complete the common internal market by 1992. Through such an alliance, Boeing would reduce its foreign currency exposure in U.S. dollars, and Airbus (or another) would find a new source of funds to share the high fixed costs of developing a new fleet of planes for the mid- and late 1990s.

STRATEGY INSIGHT

International competitiveness comes from knowing how to create
strategic alliances with suppliers, distributors, and competitors.

To make a joint venture partnership successful, both Boeing
and Airbus must give up the planned production of competing
commercial aircraft and end their bickering over what are legal
and illegal subsidies under GATT, Super 301, and EEC trade law.
In summary, Boeing cannot afford to give up its European market
and remain a dominant firm in its industry. Boeing must find an
accommodation with Airbus and the governments that support
this firm, or make a deal with another European firm. A formal
joint venture partnership will help Boeing accomplish many of its
goals for the next decade.

INTERNATIONAL MARKET EXPANSION
POLICY

Boeing has used its control over proprietary information to
build up a dominant position in the commercial aircraft industry and to sustain its competitive advantage. When its dominance was threatened, Boeing tied its suppliers and customers
into a spider's web of alliances based on new information concerning product design, repair, service and maintenance practices, and sales and marketing strategies. Exhibit 7–A shows
the seventh international business decision. Exhibit 7–B
shows the international marketing tactics for rolling out Decision 7. Exhibit 7–C lists the data elements for assessing rates of
change in international business that are discussed throughout this chapter.

INTERNATIONAL MARKETING TACTICS AND DATA
ELEMENTS FOR ASSESSING RATE OF CHANGE

The following provides an explanation of how various firms have
used the seven tactics listed in Exhibit 7–B for rolling out Deci-

EXHIBIT 7–A
International Business Decision 7: Success in Using Information to Cope with Rapid Rate of Change in International Business

Technical
Market
Financial

Note: Executives must specify decisions to fit international business problems. Is there an environmental problem? Or is it only a design change? Or are the fundamental socioeconomic forces changing?

EXHIBIT 7–B
International Marketing Tactics for Rolling Out Decision 7

Use technical and market information
Identify similar markets with high growth potential
Scan limited number of markets
Calculate cost of additional market penetration
Tie products to end use in markets
Convert luxuries into necessities and fashionable products
Decide on market expansion strategy

EXHIBIT 7–C
Data Elements for Assessing Rates of Change

Hunches, intuition, or guesses
Political, economic, and cultural changes
Technological and managerial change
Convergence of demand
Footloose business opportunities
Supply- and demand-related effects
Seasonal market uncertainty
Government support programs for new contenders
Business strategies of concentration and diversification
Pro forma sales statements
Alternative futures

sion 7. It also provides an explanation of four strategies for market expansion.

Tactic: Use Technical and Market Information

Information-based technology gives executives speed, responsiveness, adaptiveness, and feedback on the value of proprietary and market information. The international firm and its network of alliances can now make information available to all subsidiaries, affiliates, partners, licensees, and customers as quickly as possible. As information accumulates, it begins to show patterns, shapes, and models. From this conversion of intuition into data and finally into recommendations, a clear picture of what Boeing can become in the future emerges for its executives.

MARKETING INTELLIGENCE

International competitiveness comes from using appropriate information to explain rate of change in international business.

Tactic: Identify Similar Markets with High Growth Potential

A careful review of the cases discussed so far shows that many firms select new markets for their exports and investments on the basis of similarity with their existing markets. Molson and John Labatt of Canada went to the United States. P&G, Caterpillar, and Kodak entered Japan. MacMillan Bloedel, Komatsu, Fuji, and Unilever gained market share in the United States. Boeing saw Europe, the United States, and Japan as its primary markets for expansion. This is not simply a matter of using the nearest-neighbor approach to international marketing but involves other managerial issues as well.

MARKETING INTELLIGENCE

International competitiveness comes from selling products in similar markets worldwide.

First, examine the supply-related effects. Can the costs of delivering products and services to customers be reduced by standardizing marketing operations and concentrating them in similar markets? Boeing's repair, service, and maintenance are the same for all customers.

In the case of Airbus, the 17-week strike at British Aerospace

> cost Airbus the loss of about 30 aircraft in 1990 or about US $1.5 billion in lost aircraft sales. . . . Aerospatiale (the French partner) claims that British Aerospace mismanaged the strike . . . and [the former wants the latter] to pay 40% of the costs incurred by the Airbus consortium as a result of the strike. . . . British Aerospace, for its part, claims that the strike was out of control and a case of "force majeure". . . . [The result is that in the future] production [will be] based on industrial efficiency rather than on national interests.[24]

Because of the strike, Airbus will not be able to treat all customers equally unless the European airlines give up their place in line to U.S. and Japanese companies.

Second, look at the demand-related effects. Can sales be increased quickly by offering products and services in overseas markets whose consumers have tastes and habits similar to those in the home market? Boeing's product design, quality image, and advertising are the same for all customers.

Study the effect of market uncertainty. Boeing confronted new thinking about cash flow, fixed costs, foreign exchange, competition, technology, and markets when it ran up against Airbus. Although Boeing was better off after its confrontation with market uncertainty, it was unable to restructure the industry in its favor because one area of market uncertainty—government subsidies—remains beyond its reach until it negotiates a strategic alliance with Fokker or another European airframe manufacturer.

Tactic: Scan Limited Number of Markets

Boeing has always kept its attention directly on its home market, the United States. Neither McDonnell Douglas nor Airbus is permitted to preempt Boeing at home. Boeing saw that the main threat to its revenues and cash flow comes from loss of market share in Europe. It expanded its procurement of parts and components from European sources to limit the damage to its market share from Airbus. This accumulation of experience with government support programs helped Boeing refine its strategies for entering the Japanese and other Asian markets.

MARKETING INTELLIGENCE

International competitiveness comes from being successful in leading markets of the world.

Boeing found that it had to go the extra mile in lower fees for deposits and cancellations or find Europeans, Japanese, other Asians, and even Americans buying commercial aircraft from Airbus. Boeing has learned a great deal from its European competitor while focusing its attention on the one high-growth market whose loss could do irreparable damage to Boeing as an international firm.

Tactic: Calculate Cost of Additional Market Penetration

Boeing has no choice but to pay the up-front procurement costs among European suppliers to gain increased market penetration in the EEC. No doubt Boeing will do the same through a joint venture partnership with Fokker or some other European airframe manufacturer so that Boeing can continue to sell its new aircraft to European commercial airlines in the 1990s.

Tactic: Tie Products to End Use in Markets

Boeing let Airbus get ahead in the race for a midrange commercial aircraft. Boeing failed to pay attention to the difference in local preferences between Europeans and Americans that exists because distances are a great deal shorter in Europe than they are in the United States. With Boeing's mistake in the use of market information, Airbus was able to become a contender in the continuing battle for competitive advantage.

Tactic: Convert Luxuries into Necessities and Fashionable Products

Boeing, along with its U.S. and European competitors and customers, has turned long-distance air travel into a necessity for businesspeople and a fashionable product for any middle- and upper-income persons who have the money to travel. By building up demand for its aircraft, Boeing created and dominated its industry for some 40 years. Now, no substitute exists for air travel when people want to travel quickly within most countries, across continents, and among two or more continents. Boeing and others used technical, market, and financial information to its fullest advantage.

Tactic: Decide on Market Expansion Strategy

Recall the discussion in Chapter 6 on the international marketing forecast. Executives need to make sales forecasts, sales quotas, and sales budgets; to determine movement of products through the channel; and to know actual sales of competitors, market potentials, and promotion potentials. From these come pro forma statements about market expansion.

Executives must select a rate of market expansion they prefer so that they can allocate their sales management effort among countries, industries, and market segments. They can choose a gradual rate of growth in similar markets (or market concentration), a fast rate of growth in dissimilar markets (or market diversification), or some combination in between. The following are four typical choices made by international marketing executives.[25]

Market Expansion Strategy 1

Executives concentrate on specific market segments in a few countries, and they increase the number of markets served gradually. This is dual concentration in market segments and national markets. Customers are similar in different countries. However, the costs of market penetration are substantial and above the resources of many international firms. The successful use of this strategy depends on market segments that are both large and stable. Boeing and Molson are examples of firms that have used this strategy successfully.

Market Expansion Strategy 2

Executives concentrate on specific countries but appeal to diverse market segments in these countries. This strategy requires a product line that can appeal to these diverse market segments. Moreover, the costs of advertising must be distributed across the product line so that the international firm gains economies of scale in promotion. The sales potential of the home and host country markets must be large. Kodak and Fuji are examples of firms that have used this strategy successfully.

Market Expansion Strategy 3

Executives diversify the markets they serve but concentrate on specific market segments. This strategy requires a specialized product line, a similar promotion and distribution effort in all markets, and potential customers in many countries. The costs of entry into individual national markets must be low relative to resources available to the international firm. Caterpillar and Komatsu are examples of firms that have used this strategy successfully.

Market Expansion Strategy 4

Executives diversify both the national markets and the market segments within these countries that they serve. This is dual diversification in market segments and national markets. It is an aggressive strategy for an international firm with a product line appealing to many segments, and with sufficient resources to gain a fast entry into many markets of the world. P&G and Unilever are examples of firms that have used this strategy successfully.

International marketing executives must specify their rate of market expansion from gradual to fast. They can choose one of four market expansion strategies. Such a choice asks them to decide on the number of countries and the number of market segments their firms will serve. Although many similar markets may be uncovered, executives must be realistic about the time it takes to expand overseas and the costs involved in serving markets all over the world.

MARKETING INTELLIGENCE

International competitiveness comes from making products useful and fashionable to end users so that a carefully crafted market expansion strategy can be employed successfully at home and abroad.

Expansion overseas is an incremental process fraught with many uncertainties. A series of sequential decisions about choosing an appropriate market expansion strategy gives executives the opportunity to make a go or no-go decision at each crucial step in the market expansion process. Their strategic commitment will be based on information about market similarity correctly transmitted among the firm, its suppliers, and its customers—hence the need for information worth using about alternative futures.

STRATEGY ANALYSIS OF INTERNATIONAL MARKET EXPANSION POLICY

A seventh future has already happened in international business: Information is crucial to managing successfully the rapid rate of change occurring in the world's markets. Firms must change their production, financial, accounting, and marketing systems and alter their market expansion strategies accordingly. Nowhere is the impact of rapid technological, financial, and marketing change more evident than in the airframe industry; today's European and U.S. competition soon will be joined by Japanese competition. The airframe firms must deal effectively with this rapid rate of change to sustain their competitive advantage.

CONCLUSIONS FROM THE CASES

The success of Boeing in using technical and market information throughout the world must be weighed against its failure to pay attention to the growth of Airbus in Europe during the 1980s. Boeing is better off today and long ago absorbed all the costs of entry and carrying out its business. For many years, Boeing's technology dominated the industry. It continues to sustain its competitive advantage with new planes whose electronic cockpits and other technologies lead the world in their sophistication. However, Airbus is there, waiting in the wings, hopeful that Boeing will make another misstep.

EXECUTIVE SUMMARY

Boeing employed the international marketing tactics discussed earlier to carry out Decision 7, success in using information. This important decision needs to be considered in concert with Boeing's expansion of its core product market skills, that is, technical competence, quality, and new planes.

Together with the positioning of assets worldwide to expand market opportunities and the emerging importance of strategic alliances, especially with European suppliers, a clearer picture emerges of how Boeing became successful and stayed on top for so long in the commercial aircraft market. That success in using information to improve its productivity both inside and outside the firm is the essence of the Boeing case.

CHAPTER 8

ASSETS NEEDED
TO FINANCE
MARKET EXPANSION

We're not in [the pharmaceutical] business for charity. Our whole industry is guilty of letting research projects go on too long,[1]

Stanley Fidelman, *head of research planning for Merck.*

We have as strong a capability as any pure biotechnology company. . . . If we could double our market share, then we would have the revenue stream that will allow us to work in all the interesting fields at once.[2]

Dr. P. Roy Vagelos, *Merck's CEO.*

When Merck puts its mind to something, its resources—its money—can bury everyone else.[3]

Samuel Isaly, *a leading Wall Street pharmaceuticals analyst.*

COMPETITIVENESS: THE IMPORTANCE OF STAYING POWER

Merck is given the highest marks by the pharmaceutical industry and the financial community for managing its $650 million-a-year (in U.S. dollars)research effort tightly and tying it closely to the marketing of drugs.[4] Because it often takes 10 years and $100 million to bring a new drug through the necessary safety trials to market, "There are continuous meetings between scientists working on a new product and the people who will eventually sell it. This ensures that when the drug comes to market it will meet a real need,"[5] according to John Lloyd Huck, retired chairman of Merck.

But Merck does not simply throw cash at discoveries. It hires top drug researchers, directs them to cure particular ailments, and gives them ample opportunity to make new scientific breakthroughs. The following are some examples: ivermectin treats cattle for parasites; mevacor reduces the buildup of cholesterol in arteries; vasotec keeps high blood pressure under control; and primaxin combats enlarged prostrate glands in men. "The company doesn't meddle with the day-to-day research work. But it is good at setting priorities and communicating to researchers what those are,"[6] according to Dr. Eugene Cortes, who was a research vice president at Merck before becoming the research director at Sterling Drug, the Kodak subsidiary.

STRATEGY INSIGHT

International competitiveness comes from knowing how to use assets effectively to reinvent the firm.

When Dr. P. Roy Vagelos was Merck's research director, he pioneered "tailored drug design," the process of identifying key steps in the progress of an illness and then designing a drug to break the chain. "We undertook to change [the direction of] research entirely . . . . It was a fantastic risk for the company,"[7] Vagelos has said. This underscores the essential element of Merck's competitiveness: its technical, financial, and marketing staying power. "My dream [as chairman]," Vagelos has said "is to be like Bell Laboratories in its heyday. It was so large and could work on so many things that would not pay off for years. I'm talking about the absolute strike, like the transistor. I'm talking about pure basic research."[8] Vagelos wants Merck to find the correct pharmaceutical compound to conquer AIDS and mankind's other terrible scourges.

LEVERAGING ASSETS UNDERPINS STAYING POWER

To Peter Drucker, consultant, author, and management guru, the competitive leveraging of assets is an art rather than a science. His advice is as follows: Don't try to catch up, and don't add new products based on current technologies, markets, and financial resources.[9] Instead, leap ahead, and add new technologies, new customers, and new approaches to making money. Moreover, when leaping ahead, hijack the development efforts of rivals and devalue their assets and competitive advantages.[10] This strategic intent focuses the firm on a future winning strategy. If this strategy is carried out successfully, top management adds a tremendous value to the international firm.

What is the view of Merck's managers about the firm's assets? Do they think of them as financial assets, grouped together into an equity portfolio and available for sale based on the breakup value of the firm? Although many U.S. executives have succumbed to such financial strategies, Merck rejects these ideas because of their short-term nature and their unsuitability for buttressing the firm's competitive staying power.

Instead, Merck believes in real assets where present-day research feeds future sales and these together allow the company to leap ahead of its competitors. Real assets are its new drug compounds, its acquisitions, its "greenfield" plants (i.e., the construction of new plants), and, most recently, its strategic alliances to gain access to new markets and new technologies. Such long-term asset commitments give Merck the opportunity to contest U.S., Japanese, and European markets, to internalize the research and development of its Japanese subsidiaries, and to leverage sales into higher pretax results. These global competitive connections among assets, strategies, and results make Merck what it is today—a winner in the continuing battle for worldwide competitiveness.

The Breakthrough Japanese Acquisition

Almost a decade ago, Merck was the first foreign company to acquire a controlling interest of a Japanese corporation listed in the first section of the Tokyo Stock Exchange, the honor roll of Japan's most important companies."[11] Banyu Pharmaceutical Corporation, among Japan's top 12 pharmaceutical firms, gave Merck three important business successes: (1) increased sales in Japan; (2) an alliance with the Japan's MITI in setting market conforming trade rules as MITI consolidates 400 domestic drug producers down to about 60 firms, and (3) access to new research discoveries made in Japan.

Such benefits fly in the face of the claim made by some U.S. executives that their lack of competitiveness (and hence their inability to invest in Japan) is due to the lower cost of capital in Japan than in the United States. In both countries, the cost of capital is the pretax earnings that offer investors a high enough after-tax return to attract their funds. Capital costs are a bit lower in Japan because the Japanese government pursues a mix of fiscal and monetary (or market-conforming) policies that keeps interest rates low, whereas the United States, to the cost of U.S. firms, has done the opposite.[12] Moreover, Japanese equity capital is probably a little bit more expensive than the Japanese (and their foreign investors) are willing to acknowledge.[13] Nevertheless, these differences between the cost of capital in Japan and in the United States do not stop U.S. firms from taking over Japanese firms when such real assets are needed for market expansion.

Besides Banyu, Merck also took over Torii Yakuhin (Pharmaceutical) KK to buttress the parent firm's staying power in Japan and other world markets. Even though the current earnings of both Japanese firms were low, they had no difficulty luring Merck to become the primary equity investor. The real benefits from these acquisitions played a far greater role in Merck's thinking than any questions about low or high financial returns. Merck is willing to pay almost any price to get into markets where the potential future sales give the firm crucial competitive connections and long-term staying power worldwide.

Strategic Alliances with Du Pont and Johnson & Johnson

Recently, Merck began forging partnerships to gain access to new markets and new technologies.[14] With Du Pont, Merck is working to develop new heart disease medicines and in return to give the former comarketing rights for whatever drugs are discovered. Also, Merck has a 50-50 joint venture with Johnson & Johnson to develop and market over-the-counter drugs. Both deals offer additional ways for Merck to strengthen its assets overseas as dominance in global markets becomes the crucial effort for all pharmaceutical firms during the 1990s.

MERCK REINVENTS THE FIRM IN THE EUROPEAN ECONOMIC COMMUNITY

In 1978, Merck introduced a new drug to inhibit the buildup of fluid in the eye due to glaucoma.[15] (It's called timoptic in the U.S. and timoptol in Europe.) Because Merck needed to gain the endorsement of ophthalmologists, it set up the Chibret Division in France and gave it worldwide (except in North America) manufacturing and marketing responsibility for the drug. Chibret's strategy: to become known as the most knowledgeable source of information on eye diseases and treatment through free access to its computer-based data library. This division now contributes research breakthroughs and new products to, and in partnership with, the parent firm. Such success is a direct result of the worldwide responsibility given to the Chibret Division.

MERCK'S EIGHT INTERNATIONAL MARKETING TACTICS

- Uses research and development to create new core drugs
- Acquires foreign subsidiaries
- Goes into strategic alliances
- Positions assets (Chibret Division) in EEC
- Takes advantage of worldwide sales opportunities
- Selects higher-income European and Asian customers
- Creates global pharmaceutical network
- Stays ahead of its rival firms

By positioning timoptic (timoptol) in both the U.S. and Europe and later adding this new drug to its worldwide sales effort, Merck improved its market share. The firm is better off with Chibret as a division of Merck's worldwide business. Moreover, Merck's enhanced its pretax earnings. As a result, it quickly passed the cost of entry test. Its pretax results were then employed to expand research and development efforts in the U.S. and to purchase two subsidiaries in Japan.

STRATEGY ANALYSIS OF MERCK'S INTERNATIONAL BUSINESS PERFORMANCE

With $5 billion (in U.S. dollars) in annual drug sales, Merck has a 4.5 percent share of the world pharmaceutical market.[16] Other British, Swiss, German, and U.S. pharmaceutical firms have smaller market shares worldwide. Merck is responsible for 6 of the world's 50 top-selling drugs, twice as many as its nearest competitor. Clearly, Merck is winning worldwide, but it is not the Bell Laboratories of its industry.

Because of the fragmentation of the world pharmaceutical market, Merck must double its market share from 4.5 to about 10 percent before its pretax earnings and cash flow can stay far enough ahead of Glaxo, Ciba-Geigy, Hoechst, Baxter, SmithKline Beecham, Pfizer, Sandoz, Bayer, and Eli Lilly in research and marketing. Even as a $5 billion company, Merck's size and market position do not give it enough assets to dominate the pharmaceutical markets of the world, so Merck is still unable to restructure the industry in its favor.

INTERNATIONAL SALES POLICY

Merck and other drug and medical products companies position assets in the U.S., Europe, and Japan to grow sales, increase market share, and raise pretax earnings in their continuing battle to sustain international competitivenes. Exhibit 8–A shows the eighth international business decision. Exhibit 8–B shows the international marketing tactics for rolling out Decision 8. Exhibit

8–C lists the data elements for preparing a pro forma sales statement.

INTERNATIONAL MARKETING TACTICS AND DATA ELEMENTS FOR PREPARING THE PRO FORMA SALES STATEMENT

The following provides an explanation of how various pharmaceutical firms have used the three tactics listed in Exhibit 8–B for rolling out Decision 8. It also provides an explanation of most of the data elements listed in Exhibit 8–C for preparing the pro forma sales statement.

Tactic: Position Technical, Capital, Human Resources, and Other Assets

Leveraging research, marketing, and financial assets is crucial to making international firms contenders in markets outside their home countries. To create such staying power, ethical pharmaceutical companies must spend many millions of dollars upfront on research before they have products to market around the world. They must tie these strategies together with financial strategies so that sufficient pretax earnings are available to them as the industry moves through concentration, consolidation, and new rounds of foreign acquisitions. What follows is a second case study to show how rapid change is dealt with in the pharmaceuticals and medical products industry.

Pharmacia Becomes a Contender in the United States[17]

From Sweden, Pharmacia has brought its pharmaceutical drugs to treat autoimmune, inflammatory, and tumorous diseases; its high-performance liquid chromatography to separate complex biological compounds; its ophthalmic products for eye surgery; and its diagnostics equipment to detect diseases and allergies. The latter three have enhanced the firm's core drug business. From

EXHIBIT 8–A
International Business Decision 8: Success in Positioning Assets to Cope with Rapid Rate of Change in International Business

Technical
Financial
Marketing

Note: Executives must specify decisions to fit international business problems. How much should be invested in research and development? Can funds be raised locally? What is the cost of capital? Should exports or investments be the entry strategy?

EXHIBIT 8–B
International Marketing Tactics for Rolling Out Decision 8

Position technical, capital, human resources, and other assets
Prepare pro forma sales statement
Decide on market expansion strategy

EXHIBIT 8–C
Data Elements for Preparing a Pro Forma Sales Statement

Predict sales response function
Predict industry growth rate in each market
Predict the stability of sales in each market
Predict competitive lead time
Predict spillover effects
Predict costs of product adaptation
Predict costs of promotional adaptation
Predict costs of brand development
Predict costs of distribution
Predict costs of controls
Predict costs of constraints

this biochemical expertise, Pharmacia has developed its superior pumping and fluid metering system.

Within the United States, Pharmacia has pursued a niche marketing strategy. During the 1970s, it converted its export-based strategy to one of acquisitions and foreign direct investments. The U.S. is the initial overseas growth market for Pharmacia and, combined with Sweden, gives the firm the base to expand worldwide. Margins are good in the U.S. and in Europe so that now Pharmacia has investment funds to spend worldwide. Its success shows up in the increasing net revenue per share for Pharmacia's shareholders.

PHARMACIA'S FOUR INTERNATIONAL MARKETING TACTICS

- Positions biotechnology assets in North America, Europe, and Japan
- Uses alliances to transmit technological innovations and marketing data
- Diversifies through sales and investment opportunities
- Selects American customers with niche marketing

Since its stock first opened on the NASDAQ in 1981, Pharamcia's success has been recognized by U.S. equity investors. It is the sixth most actively traded stock among the 97 non-U.S. companies. In 1986, Pharmacia also began trading on the Tokyo Stock Exchange. Investors worldwide view Pharmacia as a shareholder value company whose efforts at product, geographic, and financial diversification are extraordinarily successful.

Therefore, by positioning biotechnology assets in the United States, Pharmacia improved its market share, made itself better off, plowed back its earnings into operations, increased the net revenue per share of its shareholders, and passed the cost-of-entry test. As a result, Pharmacia became a contender in the United States. Nevertheless, Pharmacia, just like Merck, has been unable to restructure the worldwide pharmaceutical industry in its favor.

Tactic: Prepare Pro Forma Sales Statement

Before reading further, go back to Chapters 6 and 7, to review the materials on the international marketing forecast and the four market expansion strategies. These are helpful in preparing the pro forma sales statement discussed below. This document assists executives in predicting expected overseas sales and in comparing these to actual international sales. If done correctly, it leads to better forecasts and choices about market expansion What follows is a third case study from the pharmaceutical and medical products industry that shows how to prepare the data elements that make up the pro forma sales statement.[18]

Baxter International Takes CAPD to Europe[19]

In 1982, Baxter International made a breakthrough with its continuous ambulatory peritonealdialysis (CAPD) product. Since then, CAPD has become the fastest growing form of artificial kidney replacement therapy, particularly for those patients who need this treatment for end-stage renal disease when transplants are not available. CAPD improves the quality of life for patients by giving them more mobility. Moreover, it is far less expensive than traditional hemodialysis therapy. Because of these factors, Baxter has achieved high levels of market penetration in the United States, Great Britain, and Sweden, and more modest levels of sales in West Germany, France, Italy, and Spain.

Today, Baxter derives 11 percent of its net sales and 15 percent of its profits from the EEC.[20] The firm needs to improve its performance there within the guidelines set for the industry by the European Commission, the Brussels headquarters of the EEC. For example, the coming common internal market for Europe in 1992 means lower average pharmaceutical prices; these reductions in cash flow are going to be held to an absolute minimum by raising prices as high as possible for medical products such as CAPD. Like Merck, Baxter is forming alliances with European-based community dialysis services to make other large U.S. and European firms appear as also-rans in the EEC for medical products.

Baxter chose dual (i.e., national and segment) concentration as its market expansion strategy within the 12-nation EEC and the 6-nation European Free Trade Association. The following are the data elements that went into the preparation of the pro forma sales statement and the decision about a market expansion strategy.

Data Element: Predict Sales Response Function
Generally, when preparing a pro forma sales statement, two sales response functions come to mind. One presumes slow growth and looks similar to an S-curve function when plotted on a graph. From this assumption about slow sales growth comes a market expansion strategy of concentrating in one or two national markets, several market segments, or both. Sometimes the product does not have obvious advantages in the eyes of local customers, or the firm does not have the capacity to manufacture the product everywhere at once. Until Merck and Pharmacia made their local acquisitions and tied themselves into local supplier and distribution outlets, neither could have become strong contenders in Japan or the United States.

The other sales response function presumes fast growth and looks similar to a concave curve when plotted on a graph. From rapid sales growth comes a market expansion strategy of diversifying in both national markets and market segments. In this case, the product has a unique set of advantages in technology, product design, or marketing image. Through advertising and other promotional techniques, executives become more effective in beating back their competition and overcoming customer resistance.

In the case of CAPD, Baxter knew that the population of Europe, the United States, and Japan is aging; about 220,000 patients throughout the world need dialysis, and this figure is growing by about 9 percent per year.[21] Moreover, the growth in the demand for CAPD is twice that of hemodialysis disposable products, or about 15 percent a year.

In the United States, 80 percent of home treatment is CAPD versus 55 percent in Sweden, 46 percent in Switzerland, 39 percent in Great Britain 27 percent in Denmark, 11.9 percent in Italy, 9.1 percent in West Germany, and 8.4 percent in France.[22] These data from Europe suggest that Baxter can expect rapid sales increases in most parts of Europe, that is, a concave sales response function. However, this conclusion must be tempered with follow-up information about the customer. In West Germany, for example, the medical profession prefers the technically sophisticated hospital equipment associated with hemodialysis rather than the home care quality of CAPD. Thus, sales growth will be less rapid than first anticipated in some of the most important, medically literate European countries. Hence, market concentration becomes the preferred market expansion strategy for Baxter.

Data Element: Predict Industry Growth Rate in Each Market

Baxter has first-mover advantage because it has dominated the CAPD market since 1982. Three other firms compete for market share: Fresenius (a strong number two); Abbott (U.S.-owned, and a weak number three); and Delmed (a very weak number four). All four of them are threatened by Gambro, the largest European manufacturer of hemodialysis equipment. Gambro could diversify into CAPD, a related product technology, at a relatively low cost. Although hemodialysis continues to be the dominant technology, the use of CAPD technology in Europe is growing at the expense of the other technologies. Hence, the potential for rapid sales growth in all segments of the European dialysis industry is sure to induce Gambro to jump in as one of Baxter's major competitors in the future. This prediction translates into a market expansion strategy of concentrating on key European markets, such as Germany, so that other continental European countries will follow the lead of this important market.

Data Element: Predict the Stability of Sales in Each Market

Because every indication suggests long-term growth in CAPD sales, irrespective of whether the national market is within the EEC or elsewhere in Europe, all possible alternative futures (1, 3, 5, and even 10 years) suggest long-term sales stability for Baxter and its competitors, This conclusion also underscores the importance of choosing a market expansion strategy of concentrating on key European markets.

Data Element: Predict Competitive Lead Time

Because Baxter developed the CAPD technology, it captured and maintained first-mover advantage over its rivals. Generally, between 5 to 10 years are needed in the pharmaceutical and medical products industry to do the required research and development, and to gain the necessary approvals from national governments to sell the product to hospitals and the general population, This long lead time works to the advantage of Baxter during the development period and against it during the marketing period. Once drug and medical technologies become generally available in the United States and Europe, they are easier for other firms to copy which whittles down the first mover's lead time. Until recently, long lead times encouraged Baxter to pursue a market expansion strategy of concentration on key national markets and market segments. Today, Baxter must diversify the sales of its CAPD technology worldwide so that no other competitor gains a significant market share in North America, Europe, or Japan.

Data Element: Predict Spillover Effects
Baxter's success in Great Britain goes back to 1961 when it first established its British operating subsidiary to provide intravenous therapy, dialysis, cardiology, and critical care support to the National Health Service (NHS). Its 20-year record gave Baxter an opening to convince the NHS to use its new CAPD technology. Moreover, Baxter priced the cost of CAPD treatment at $5,000 versus $25,000 (in U.S. dollars) for traditional hemodialysis. Once established with the NHS, Baxter entered into agreements with similar agencies in France, Spain, and Portugal. These spillover effects from the United States to Great Britain, and then from Great Britain to the rest of the EEC were not so extensive that they forced Baxter to shift away from its market expansion strategy of concentrating heavily on individual national markets.

Data Element: Predict Costs of Product Adaptation
Initial costs are usually high for new pharmaceutical and medical products. The high development and marketing costs of CAPD were no exception because of the need for government approval to sell the product to hospitals and to the general public. These initial high costs pushed Baxter toward a market expansion strategy of concentrating on key national markets. Once successful (i.e., with average costs of product adaptation dropping as sales increased rapidly), Baxter shifted its market expansion strategy from national concentration toward European-wide diversification.

Data Element: Predict Costs of Promotional Adaptation

Baxter used the following themes to introduce CAPD: cost-effectiveness, life-style improvement, and alternative site services. Because the ensuing promotional costs are not high, Baxter is free to pursue a market concentration strategy for a very long period of time.

Data Element: Predict Costs of Distribution

Baxter convinced the National Health Service to purchase and distribute CAPD for home use as an alternative to hospitalization. Because these costs are not high, Baxter is now free to concentrate on crucial national markets before trying to diversify throughout the EEC. This is a good choice because health care policy in Europe is in all essentials controlled by the national governments rather than by the European Commission.

Data Element: Predict Costs of Controls

Baxter must impose tight controls over quality (e.g., date and time of use) and sales price because of its close working relationships with government-owned hospitals and health services. These tight controls encourage a concentration market expansion strategy.

Data Element: Predict Costs of Constraints

In the United States, Great Britain, and Sweden, government approval of CAPD meant Baxter could sell the product freely to private and public health facilities. On the other hand, the preference of West German doctors for advanced medical equipment hindered the sale and use of CAPD. This constraint forced Baxter to pursue a concentration strategy in those markets more amenable to a new approach for treating kidney disease.

Using the Pro Forma Statement to Gain Staying Power

The foregoing sales data elements help Baxter make up its pro forma sales statement for CAPD. Each of them is estimated and expressed in terms of sales, prices, costs, and time necessary to accomplish the sales effort. From these calculations comes a computation of expected value and the variance of the net present value for each of the four market expansion strategies discussed previously (see Chapter 7). The following list summarizes these strategies:

1. When sales data favor concentration in both national markets and market segments, then executives should choose Market Expansion Strategy 1, dual concentration.
2. When sales data favor concentration in national markets and diversification in market segments, then executives should choose Market Expansion Strategy 2, market diversification.
3. When sales data favor diversification in national markets and concentration in market segments, then executives should choose Market Expansion Strategy 3, market concentration.
4. When sales data favor diversification in both national markets and market segments, then executives should choose Market Expansion Strategy 4, dual diversification.

International marketing executives must weigh the relative importance of each of these factors in preparing a pro forma sales statement and carrying out the appropriate market expansion strategy. The preparation of a pro forma sales statement concerning entry and expansion in national markets and market segments must include the option of aborting the start-up or abandoning the sales effort once it begins. Fortunately for Baxter, CAPD was a runaway success in most markets worldwide.

Tactic: Decide on Market Expansion Strategy

Most international marketing decisions are made incrementally. If mistakes occur in weighing the relative importance of one or more of the sales data, then executives should revise their calculations, redo their pro forma statement, and change their market expansion strategy. The pro forma statement is a way for marketing executives to put on paper their understanding of the competitive situation faced by their firms. From it flows the firm's acid test: the ability to finance its commitment to market expansion in the face of competition from other firms in its industry. Is the firm a contender? Does it have staying power? Can it gain long-term sustainable competitive advantage? What follows is a fourth example of how rapid change is dealt with in the pharmaceutical industry.

THE SMITHKLINE BEECHAM MEGAMERGER[23]

Although many U.S. pharmaceutical companies are strong in Europe, and although many European pharmaceutical firms are strong in the United States, the merger of the two groups only started in earnest during 1989. This was the beginning of consolidation in the pharmaceutical and medical products industry. The merger of U.S.-owned SmithKline Beckman and the British-owned Beecham Group offers a good example of how two also-rans were turned into a new North Atlantic company with the potential for great success.

Creating a New Management Culture

Robert P. Bauman, once an American coffee salesman, was the CEO of Beecham who acquired SmithKline. Instead of merging them immediately, he spent six months looking at the two companies. "We wanted to create a totally new company, different from both partners and with a new culture,"[24] Bauman has said. Then he instructed his managers to cut costs because it was "an ideal time to get at the internal bureaucracy."[25]

Bauman is now cutting out management layers and centralizing decision making regarding such issues as payroll systems and $2.8 billion (in U.S. dollars) a year in supply purchases[26] Still, Bauman took almost a full year to tell stock analysts what the restructuring or write-off charges would be from closing at least 12 major production factories that were not needed by the combined company—about $640 million.[27] Investors "are getting fed up. They can't understand why it has taken SmithKline Beecham [almost a year] to come up with their rationalization number,"[28] Paul Woodhouse, a drug industry analyst at Smith New Court Securities PLC in London, has said.

Bauman also told his sales force to boost market share of existing SmithKline Beecham over-the-counter drugs, for example,

Contac, Tums, Geritol, and Sucrets. He believes this will provide his firm with the necessary cash flow to invest in new pharmaceutical research.

Bauman's goal is to get two new drug compounds approved each year by the Food and Drug Administration. "That's incredible," Ernest Mario, chief executive of Glaxo Holdings, has said; "We've had 6 in the last 10 years, and we're a very productive company."[29] In fact, no major drugs loom to replace Tagamet, SmithKline's biggest money-maker.[30] The firm soon will have an enormous new product gap, a gap that "has been papered over by the [immediate] benefits of the combination,"[31] according to Samuel Isaly. "A lot of [SmithKline's current research products] are probably useful as stocking fillers, but that's about as far as you can go,"[32] Woodhouse has said. Bauman has responded that SmithKline Beecham's over-the-counter and animal drugs provide extra sales and earnings stability, and the cash for research into new pharmaceutical[33] compounds.

STRATEGY ANALYSIS OF BEECHAM'S INTERNATIONAL BUSINESS PERFORMANCE

Research is expensive; new drug development costs a hefty 15.5 percent to 20 percent of product value.[34] It is not clear that SmithKline Beecham can afford these exorbitant costs, compete head-to-head with Merck, build market share to a minimum 10 percent, and be a major player in the newly consolidated industry.[35] Beecham's return on equity and assets peaked in 1984 and went down after that until 1988. However, its pharmaceutical business (especially Augmentin, a leading antibiotic whose sales are growing twice as fast as the market) did better than the whole company. This is Bauman's important building block for the future.

STRATEGY INSIGHT

International competitiveness comes from creating a new management culture that enhances international business performance in Japan, the United States, and the EEC.

The following is what the merger means to Beecham: First, Beecham made the acquisition when both the dollar and the stock price of SmithKline were low, so Beecham positioned itself in the United States at a relatively low cost. That was the smart part of the deal. Second, Beecham obtained additional research and development capacity in the United States; however, in reality, it bought SmithKline's poor track record in coming up with new compounds to cure major human ailments. That was the major downside risk of the deal. Third, Beecham gained direct and immediate access to the U.S. market, which was not the case prior to the SmithKline acquisition. Still, Beecham must acquire or go into joint ventures with other research-based U.S. pharmaceutical companies for it to gain a commanding presence in the United States. That's the great unknown of the deal. Finally, through SmithKline's joint venture with Fujisawa, Beecham gained a toehold in the Japanese market, which amounts to 30 percent of the total pharmaceutical market worldwide. Unless Beecham can do better and gain substantial market share in Japan, it will not be a major player in the world market by the end of the decade. That is the major risk facing Beecham in the future.

Beecham's current market expansion strategy is to concentrate on the U.S. market. The spillover effects from Great Britain and previous SmithKline business in the U.S. make concentrating on the U.S. market a good managerial decision. However, Bauman is pushing for faster sales growth with existing pharmaceutical and over-the-counter drugs and for shorter lead times with new compounds. Both goals are thought to be unrealistic by the CEOs of other drug companies.

JAPANESE DRUGMAKERS

For U.S. and European pharmaceutical companies, the 1990s will be far different from the 1980s. This is because Japanese drugmakers are about to jump into the world's markets with the active support of both their U.S. and British joint-venture partners and of MITI. The following is another example of how market-conforming trade and investment practices by Japan are helping Japanese firms gain, maintain, and sustain competitive advantage. For example, Sankyo, Japan's number two drugmaker has licensed Bristol Myers Squibb to sell provachol, a drug free of side effects, to compete against Merck's mevacor, both designed to lower cholesterol.[36] Takeda, Fujisawa, Yamanouchi, and Chugai all are making acquisitions, going into joint ventures, and licensing products to build up market share in the U.S. and Europe. They have the money but not yet the research and development assets to become very big players in an industry going through consolidation. This will change by the end of the decade.

STRATEGY ANALYSIS OF INTERNATIONAL SALES POLICY

An eighth future has already happened in international business: Increases in sales, market share, and returns on sales are crucial to managing successfully the rapid rates of change occurring in the world's markets. Good pro forma sales data offer marketing executives the option of choosing the most appropriate market expansion policy for national markets, segments, and niches overseas. The pharmaceutical and medical products industries are pushing up sales around the world to throw off cash for more expensive research and development. They must do this to sustain their competitive advantage.

CONCLUSIONS FROM THE CASES

The success of Merck, Pharmacia, and Baxter in positioning their assets in Europe, the United States, and Japan must be tempered with the threat from new competitors, such as SmithKline Beecham and the Japanese drugmakers. The first three are better off today and continue to pay back their costs of entry and ongoing research and development. Merck has a research plan to boost sales and market share so that in the future it will (1) be twice as large as its nearest competitor, SmithKline Beecham; (2) dominate the pharmaceutical industry worldwide; and (3) perhaps restructure the industry in its favor. That is a tall order for any international firm.

EXECUTIVE SUMMARY

Merck, Pharmacia, Baxter, and Beecham offer good cases in which to observe how assets are positioned around the world. Merck positioned its assets in Europe and Japan to take advantage of new market opportunities among high-income customers Merck has carefully selected customers for its new pharmaceuticals and thereby created new market segments. On the other hand, Pharmacia took market niches already in existence in the U.S. and developed medical products for its U.S. customers. Both firms used their core skills to create strategic alliances, to acquire new subsidiaries, and to build an international network. All four drug and medical products firms are better off today than they were 10 years ago. Because the worldwide pharmaceutical industry continues to be fragmented and lacks highly concentrated firms, neither Merck, Pharmacia, Baxter, nor Beecham has the accumulated assets to restructure the industry in its favor. That is the international business problem for the 1990s.

CHAPTER 9

NATIONAL DIFFERENCES TRANSLATED INTO COMPETITIVE ADVANTAGE

Dramatic change often comes only as a response to imminent collapse.[1]
Tom Peters, *the guru of excellence in management.*

The primary reason hurried efforts fail, the reason it takes so long to establish a global presence in Japan (or in any other market), the reason that checkbook driven shortcuts do not work is people—and the *values* they do or do not carry with them. . . . This sort of learning takes time, lots of time.[2]
Kenichi Ohmae, *head of McKinsey & Company's office in Tokyo.*

American manufacturers with Western European ventures substantially increased their market penetration. . . . In Japan a good many companies bought out their joint-venture partners. . . . These benefits required a transnational base, strategy and marketing effort.[3]
Peter Drucker, *Clarke Professor of Social Science at the Claremont Graduate School.*

COMPETITIVENESS: THE IMPORTANCE OF GETTING THERE FIRST

Restructure the industry (Boeing and Airbus), reinvent the firm (Merck, Pharmacia, and Beecham), rebuild market share (Black & Decker and Quaker Oats)—and shareholder value will grow as long as the firm continues investing above its cost of capital. The duration of this period of growth in shareholder value is dependent on how many of the firm's proprietary technologies, patented products, product life cycles, and established brands have lasting value for customers. Over a decade or more, this growth in shareholder value translates into sustainable competitive advantage for the firm in the United States, Europe, and Japan.[4]

STRATEGY INSIGHT

International competitiveness comes from knowing how to build up sales and market share to become the dominant firm in all world markets.

However, all these financial successes depend on one crucial marketing success: sales. Get into markets first. Gain significant market share first. Be the sales leader first.

When rolling out a product worldwide, executives must prepare an international marketing plan concerning market expansion; product, geographic, and financial diversification; forecasts of domestic, export, and global sales; and decisions about targeting upmarket versus traditional market segments. This plan must reflect local preferences for tailored goods and services as well as the growing convergence of consumer preferences worldwide. For some products, it means fast sales growth, and for others it means much slower sales growth. The right choice fosters international competitiveness. What follows are two examples of how U.S. firms attempted to sustain competitive advantage in Europe and then a series of suggestions of how U.S. firms can sustain competitive advantage in Japan.

BLACK & DECKER OPTS FOR FAST SALES GROWTH[5]

When the marketing executives at Black & Decker predicted a concave sales function for their products, they expected to grow sales first in high-income or upmarket segments. Once successful with their product launch, they expanded sales very rapidly into middle-income market segments. Once Black & Decker's power tools became products of universal need, then sales were also expanded into lower income market segments.

Getting There First Through Diversification

Although the physical characteristics of Black & Decker's products are similar throughout the world, the price, quality, distribution, and image of individual products are sometimes different in Japan, the United States, and Europe. These differences reflect local preferences, cultural differences, and other norms of behavior on the part of customers. Notwithstanding small national differences, Black & Decker has turned them into competitive advantage through a strategy of related product and geographic diversification. The products are thought to be similar among trendsetters and those customers who want to be like trendsetters. Everybody wants Black & Decker's power tools. This is called the convergence of consumer preferences worldwide.

Such a fast sales growth policy can be reflected in a dual diversification expansion strategy for country and market segments (e.g., Unilever with Pond's, Vaseline, and Cutex in the United States, Japan, Europe, and elsewhere in the world). Or this fast sales growth can be reflected in a market diversification strategy coupled with a concentration strategy for specific market segments (e.g., Caterpillar with its earthmoving equipment in the United States, with its excavators in Japan, and with its other materials handling equipment elsewhere in the world). Black & Decker has practiced the former rather than the latter. It has gotten into markets first and translated this fast sales growth policy (through dual diversification) into competitive advantage.

Black & Decker's International Marketing Plan

With strong geographic diversification in more than 100 countries and with strong product market concentration in two segments—power tools and household products—today, Black & Decker is a world leader.[6] This was not always the case.

Data Element: Predict Spillover Effects

In the early 1980s, with the onset of the Reagan recession, sales of power tools slowed dramatically. Then the dollar rose against the yen, an unanticipated external event, and management was unprepared for the quick grab by Japan's Makita Electric Works Ltd. of market share in the United States.[7]. Moreover, Black & Decker's management was even having a hard time competing against U.S.-owned Emerson Electric.

Data Element: Predict Costs of Brand Development

By the mid-1980s, Black & Decker was fighting back. It brought out a new product line of cordless tools. Also, the company acquired prestigious power-tool accessories, such as Piranha saw blades and Bullet drill bits, as well as General Electric's small appliances division. Within two years and without losing market share or trade support, the GE brand name was gone from 150 products and replaced by Black & Decker's logo. The firm also took over ELU Machines of Switzerland to challenge Makita's dominance in fine woodworking tools.[8] However, this piecemeal brand and acquisition strategy was not enough.

Data Element: Target Upmarket Segments

To accomplish its turnaround in the mid-1980s, Black & Decker created a global strategy for its two product market segments. It leveraged its strong brand name in power tools into leadership of household small appliances. Moreover, it turned its brand name into a proprietary name for the specific product market segment (e.g., in England, all do-it-yourself tools are called Black & Decker). Finally, it licensed its brand name to a toy manufacturer, Creative Design, to produce a line of battery-operated toy appliances that look like Black & Decker products and carry the Black & Decker logo.[9] As a consequence, in France, someone who is plugged into the social scene is *très Black et Decker*.[10]

Data Element: Predict Competitive Lead Times

Today, Black & Decker's 10 world-scale manufacturing plants (60 percent in the United States and 40 percent in Europe) produce global products that have broad functional and design appeal.[11] These tools and appliances have standardized components (i.e.,

20 motors instead of 100, as previously) to give the company economies in purchasing, sourcing, and manufacturing.

However, the company's factories can be modified easily to meet
the special requirements of different national market segments.[12]
For example, in Europe, consumers demand substantially higher
power in their tools than customers do in the United States.[13] Moreover, the company now guarantees either four-hour or overnight repair for industrial users of Black & Decker tools. And it guarantees
its products for twice as long as its competitors do. These strong operating results are producing the cash flow necessary to finance
Black & Decker's growth throughout the 1990s.

*Data Element: Know Customers and How to Reach
Them*
National differences refer to different safety and industry standards that hinder product standardization (e.g., the various volt-
ages, such as 110V, 220V, and 240V, and the various cycles, 50 Hz
and 60 Hz). They also pertain to different local preferences for
product designs and colors; for example, European designs are accepted in the United States, but the reverse is not true. Moreover,
Europeans prefer high power from their tools, whereas Americans want convenience, compactness, and light weight in their
tools; as a result, European power tools have more powerful motors and U.S. tools are designed to be cordless.

STRATEGY ANALYSIS OF BLACK &
DECKER'S INTERNATIONAL BUSINESS
PERFORMANCE

Throughout the 1980s, Black & Decker began shifting its administrative culture from being a multidomestic firm with independent manufacturing and marketing operations in 50 countries to
one of standardizing the selection of raw materials, the preparation of blueprints, and the design of components for the purpose of
rationalizing manufacturing in the U.S. and Europe. Black &
Decker moved to a higher level of coordination among its research and development centers and its 10 focused factories. In
the 1990s, Black & Decker's managerial efforts are designed to

strengthen its international business network—especially in Japan, India, Brazil, and eastern Europe.

Is Black & Decker better off? In terms of improved returns on sales, the firm is doing much better today than it did 10 years ago. All of its sales and marketing strategies are working to build the international company.

Has Black & Decker employed its assets wisely? Did it increase the income from its assets in the U.S. and Europe? Because its acquisitions only occurred in the mid- to late-1980s, it is too early to tell whether or not the firm has passed the cost-of-entry test.

Although Black & Decker is dominant in several market segments, it is not the dominant firm in the industry, nor has it reached the level of sustainable competitive advantage. To accomplish these objectives, Black & Decker must develop global products with a broad functional appeal, invest in core technologies, and establish stronger distribution links. Some of these products, technologies, and links could come from internal growth and others might come from acquisitions.

All in all, Black & Decker is on the fast track for rapid sales growth, product and geographic diversification, and worldwide market expansion. Its management thinks globally, but acts locally. The firm gets there first. These are all ingredients for sustaining long-term competitive advantage.

QUAKER OATS OPTS FOR SLOW SALES GROWTH IN PET FOODS IN EUROPE

When the executives of Quaker Oats predicted an S-curve sales function for their pet food products in Europe, they expected to grow sales slowly in traditional market segments and in a few countries. Even when successful, these executives may or may not launch their products outside traditional segments because of the problems discussed above and in Chapter 8.

Getting There Second Through Concentration

Although the physical characteristics of Quaker Oat's products, especially pet food, are similar throughout the world, the price, quality, distribution, and image characteristics of its products are vastly different in Japan, the United States, and Europe. These reflect cultural differences regarding whether or not pets should be kept inside houses, which animals should be pets, and how pets should be fed. Notwithstanding these great national differences, Quaker Oats has turned them into competitive advantage through a strategy of national and segment concentration: Roll out pet food first in the United States, and then sell it with a different set of cultural attributes in Europe and elsewhere in the world. This follows the fragmentation of the mass market for pet foods on both sides of the Atlantic Ocean.

Such a slow sales growth policy is reflected in a dual concentration expansion strategy for country and market segments (e.g., Molson in Canada and the United States). Or, this slow sales growth is reflected in a country concentration strategy coupled with a diversification strategy for specific market segments (e.g., Kodak and Fuji in the United States and in Japan). Quaker Oats has practiced the former rather than the latter and has translated this slow sales growth policy (through dual concentration) into limited competitive advantage.

QUAKER OATS'S EUROPEAN MARKETING PLAN[14]

With a 13 percent market share, Quaker Oats is the number two seller of pet food in the EEC. It is far behind Mars—the market leader and dominant firm in France, Italy, and Great Britain—which has a 53 percent market share throughout Europe. The rest of the market is highly fragmented among many U.S. and European firms. Given the strong competition in the pet food industry, increased sales are hard to come by except through coupons, rebates, and sweepstakes. These promotional techniques are used by all firms, not just Quaker Oats. Therefore, the firm has sought sales growth through acquisitions and by pushing a whole new market segment, dry pet food.

Currently, moist pet food is the most popular market segment in Europe because Europeans do not think dry pet food is good enough for their pampered pets. However, because it costs more to produce moist pet food and because of the rising prices of tin-plate, Quaker Oats is pushing dry pet food as an alternative in both France and Great Britain. This is a high-risk strategy, given that the market still prefers moist and semimoist pet food. As a way to raise margins, increase sales, and improve cash flow, Mars, Quaker Oats, and the other firms are also encouraging the use of gourmet pet foods, healthy pet foods, pet snacks, and pet toys.

STRATEGY INSIGHT

International competitiveness comes from knowing how to build up sales and market share in becoming the number two firm in one crucial world market.

When neither Mars nor Quaker Oats takes aggressive action against one another or the other pet food manufacturers, Quaker Oats's sales are stable. However, Mars has the strength to use aggressive marketing tactics against other firms as it did against the Quaker-Henkel partnership in Germany in 1985.[15]Quaker is the dominant firm only in the Netherlands, Belgium, and Luxembourg and cannot depend on taking sales from Mars in the larger European countries.

STRATEGY ANALYSIS OF QUAKER OATS'S INTERNATIONAL BUSINESS PERFORMANCE

Quaker Oats prefers to acquire other pet food manufacturers, such as the Gaines brand (Anderson Clayton) and Ralston Purina's European operations. Quaker Oats is also avoiding placing new manufacturing investment in France and Great Britain because it does not want to compete head-on with Mars. Rather, Quaker Oats is consolidating its operations in the other countries of the EEC.

Is Quaker Oats better off in Europe? Yes. It has solidified its number two position within the EEC. Also, Quaker Oats has paid off its acquisitions and is now throwing off cash for future investment in Europe and elsewhere in the world. However, Quaker Oats is not the dominant firm now, nor will it be so during the 1990s. Quaker Oats will grow sales much more slowly in the next few years because of its number two position and because of the competitive position of the industry relative to other household purchases. Here, too, Quaker Oats is thinking globally, but acting locally. Whether Quaker Oats is able to transfer America's preference for dry pet food to Europe is yet to be decided. Quaker Oats has not been able to sustain its competitive advantage against the strong number one firm in the industry, Mars.

INTERNATIONAL TAILORED MARKETING POLICY

Black & Decker understands well how cultural differences affect products sold to customers, putting more power in the tools sold to Europeans, and selling cordless tools in the United States. In this way, Black & Decker sustains its competitive advantage. Exhibit 9–A shows the ninth international business decision. Exhibit 9–B shows the international marketing tactics for rolling out Decision 9. Exhibit 9–C lists the data elements for preparing an international marketing plan.

INTERNATIONAL MARKETING TACTICS AND DATA ELEMENTS FOR PREPARING INTERNATIONAL MARKETING PLAN

The following provides an explanation of how various firms have used the three tactics listed in Exhibit 9–B. It also includes an explanation of most of the data elements listed in Exhibit 9–C (and also 8–C), which are useful in preparing the international marketing plan.

EXHIBIT 9-A
International Business Decision 9: Success in Understanding National
Differences to Cope with Rapid Rate of Change in International Business

Cultural
Marketing
Business

Note: Executives must specify decisions to fit international business problems. Is it
important to develop products that fit local cultural practices? Or should they conform
to regional standards? What local business practices must be included in corporate
strategic decisions?

EXHIBIT 9-B
International Marketing Tactics for Rolling Out Decision 9

Manage competitive connections among countries
Turn pro forma statement into international marketing plan
Integrate international marketing plan into corporate strategy

EXHIBIT 9-C
Data Elements for Preparing an International Marketing Plan

Target upmarket segments
Know customers and how to reach them
Prepare coherent marketing strategy
Create high-priced products for upmarket segments
Sales tips
Carry out market launch by targeting customers
Match marketing investment with expansion of working capital
Take advantage of currency swings, cuts in prices, and increases in market share
Use local distribution system effectively
Modify products to conform to local culture
Forge long-term links with suppliers, distributors, and customers

Tactic: Manage Competitive Connections among Countries

Black & Decker, Quaker Oats, and other firms discussed in this
book have developed competitive connections among markets in
developed and third-world countries. They do this by catering to

the cultural differences, norms of local behavior, and national preferences apparent in every country. At the same time, they do not forget economic trends worldwide; emerging standards in North America and Europe; and converging consumption habits in the Asian, Caribbean, and Pacific Basin countries.

To find "chunks" of local cultural preferences within national markets, international executives must tailor their marketing strategies to local market segments within countries. They begin this by carrying out life-style research to find market niches. Then executives study their existing products worldwide to see whether some of them fit the needs of local customers. Sometimes, they customize products to fit the specific needs of their new overseas customers.

Once international marketing executives have products to match markets, segments, and niches, they must decide the following: Should the sales growth policy be fast or slow? Should sales be made through exports or by investing overseas? Should they internalize or hire out distribution, promotion, and other marketing management activities? When they have made these decisions, they are in the process of turning their pro forma sales statement into an international marketing plan.

Tactic: Turn Pro Forma Sales Statement into International Marketing Plan

Elements of the international marketing plan include knowing who the existing and potential customers are, concentrating marketing investments on high potential growth markets, reacting offensively to foreign penetration of home markets, creating high-priced products for upmarket segments, differentiating products by superior quality and profitability, targeting and positioning products for the market launch, matching products to local market segments, establishing strong sales management organization, and focusing on long-term market position and growth in market share.

The international marketing plan is a technique for measuring sales performance overseas at the level of individual markets or product lines. The international marketing plan shows the success (or failure) of product managers in targeting market segments, positioning products in national markets, increasing market share and cost competitiveness, dominating markets, and growing aggressively in all possible world markets. The marketing plan must have one-, three-, and five-year milestones to check whether or not international product managers are accomplishing their goals.

The following are some crucial marketing data that marketing executives should have in formulating their international marketing plans for one crucial market—Japan.

Data Element: Know Customers and How to Reach Them

International marketing executives carry out life-style research about their existing and potential customers. For example, the Japanese are internationalizing their palate.[16] Japanese children prefer curry rice, hamburgers, and spaghetti as their favorite dishes. Japanese families like to eat at McDonald's, Kentucky Fried Chicken, Denny's, Häagan-Dazs, and Mister Donut. Because of the increased intake of beef and dairy products since 1950, the Japanese have increased their height by 4 inches (10.2 cm) and their weight by 15 pounds (6.8kg). However, Western food must be adapted to Japanese tastes. For example, *kasutera* (Castella, Spanish pound cake), *tonkatsu* (pork cutlet), and *tempura* went through a transformation that took into account the Japanese cultural norms and taste preferences.

Now, the doughnut is going through the same transformation. Most Japanese have not developed the taste for sweets that Westerners have, so one finds curry doughnuts, *yakisoba* (fried noodle) doughnuts, sausage doughnuts, *an* (red bean) doughnuts, and other adaptations of the doughnut concept.

Because the Japanese dislike strong tastes and smells, odors must be masked, and hot or spicy dishes must be made milder. Usually, soy sauce masks odors, and original curry or Mexican food is made less spicy to please Japanese palates.

Another difference between Japan and the United States is how pizza is consumed. American-style pepperoni pizza and Japanese-style *ika* (squid) pizza suit the palate of each nation and are merely national market differences for the worldwide product, pizza.

Even rice balls are going through substantial product transformation. In Japan, rice balls have been traditionally sold with a tidbit of pickled plum or some kind of fish inside them. They are now found with bacon and mayonnaise, beef, or tuna fish in the center. Moreover, these new-style rice balls are sold at convenience stores, such as the 7–11, which few Japanese know originally comes from the United States; they believe it is a Japanese retail institution.

Also in Japan, food must be served precut into bite-size pieces because the Japanese use chopsticks and consider carving food at the dinner table a barbarous custom. The Japanese also eat smaller portions than Americans and Europeans do. Hence, prepackaged food must come in smaller containers. Frozen foods are used for snacks rather than as part of the main meal; they are used the same day they are purchased, which is quite different than how they are used in the United States.

In some cases, national differences take a unique twist in finding potential customers for existing products. In the case of the soy bean product tofu, Japan exported it to the United States, where it became popular due to the shift to health food. Because of the American craving for sweets, a healthy dessert, tofu ice cream, was created. This dessert is now finding its way into the Japanese market unchanged from the United States.

Data Element: Prepare Coherent Marketing Strategy

International marketing executives must prepare a coherent marketing strategy based on product positioning and market segmentation. For example, in 1986, the Japanese consumed the biggest share of the 66,000 tons of frozen french fries exported by the United States.[17] These were sold in two market segments in Japan. The first was to the U.S. and Japanese *fast-food chains* such as McDonald's, Kentucky Fried Chicken, and Lotteria. In the United States, 85 percent of the fast-food orders include fries or hash browns, whereas in Japan only 40 percent of these orders include fries, so there is great growth potential for orders of french fries in Japan. The second market segment was the *at-home* market. Almost 40 percent of Japanese women work, and 65 percent of the 24 million in the work force are married and another 10 percent are widowed or divorced. U.S. manufacturers of french fries have been slow to reach this second market segment because Japanese supermarkets have limited freezer space.

For the fast-food chain market segment, U.S. firms must increase their expenditures on promotion to convince more Japanese to order fries with their hamburgers and chicken. For the at-home market, these firms must increase their expenditures on retail distribution, perhaps buying the freezers and placing them in the supermarkets as Kraft did for its cheese when it was introducing this product in the United States.

Ore-Ida Foods, a unit of H. J. Heinz Co., captured a 26 percent market share against its Japanese competitors in the frozen potatoes market. It did this in spite of not selling to McDonald's in Japan. When Ore-Ida first came to Japan, it found demand for frozen potatoes about 3 percent of what it was in the United States. Also, Japanese home freezers were small, and few Japanese had ovens in which french fries could be reheated. Moreover, few Japanese thought of eating french fries or hash browns for breakfast.

Then McDonald's began promoting its breakfast menu, including hash brown potatoes similar to those produced by Ore-Ida. Now, nearly 10 percent of the Japanese consider eating potatoes for breakfast and Ore-Ida has become number one in the Japanese market.

Ore-Ida found that its Japanese trading company partner, Mitsubishi Corporation, could only reach about 40 percent of the retail outlets Ore-Ida wanted. Ore-Ida asked supermarkets to persuade wholesalers to handle its products. Now, 60 percent of Ore-Ida's potatoes pass through only one distributor rather than two or more, which is common in Japan. About 11,000 stores, which do about 84 percent of the business, stock Ore-Ida frozen potatoes in Japan.

Also, Ore-Ida adopted the Japanese promotional technique of selling cute cartoon characters as the image for its Japanese products.[18] The cartoon-like potato character is a big Idaho potato with a goofy face, arms and legs, farmer's blue overalls, and a farmer's hat. Now, 64 percent of Tokyo housewives and 92 percent of children recognize the Ore-Ida frozen potato through its cartoon-like character. This is very high product recognition.

Ore-Ida has a coherent marketing strategy for Japan. This firm is concentrating on the at-home market segment. Ore-Ida is pushing the marketing idea that potatoes are a good breakfast meal; finding ways to get its product into supermarkets throughout the country; and making sure that Mr. Ore-Ida is as familiar a cartoon character as Peepokun, the floppy-eared mouse mascot of the Tokyo police, or Hello Kitty, the smiling cat cartoon character worn by college women on their coats.

Data Element: Create High-Priced Products for Upmarket Segments

In many cases, international marketing executives must concentrate their marketing investments on high potential customer groups rather than spreading their investments across the entire market. For example, Daiei, Japan's largest retailer with annual sales of $6 billion (in U.S. dollars), decided to market lingerie from Marks and Spencer, one of Great Britain's best-known retailers, through the home-party system, like Tupperware in the United States.[19] Daiei has 3,600 "life-stylists," mainly housewives who host parties and sell underwear on commission. In Japan, direct selling to the home is fairly common. These housewives learn how to wear Western merchandise in the privacy of their homes rather than changing their cultural habits in public.

Exporting to Japan is crucial because it is the second biggest market in the world, and export marketers must have an aggressive market share policy for Japan. Since 1978, Marks and Spencer has been selling its goods in Japan through Daiei. The following are some of the problems Marks and Spencer has overcome to gain sales among upmarket customer groups in Japan.

At first, Marks and Spencer biscuits had uneven thickness, and this made the product unmarketable in Japan. Once the thickness was made uniform for all biscuits, the product sold well year-round in Japan. Also, Marks and Spencer towels were too big and heavy for the Japanese. Once they were made smaller and lighter—that is, equivalent to Japanese bath towels—the product sold well in department stores. Finally, Marks and Spencer polyester shirts were too warm in summer and created too much static electricity in winter. Moreover, their price and design were not competitive with locally made products, and their sizes and shapes were better suited to Europeans rather than to the Japanese, who are smaller people. Marks and Spencer allowed Japanese firms to manufacture its brand name products, such as Woolmark sweaters, under a licensing agreement.

For many years, Daiei set up Marks and Spencer corners in its stores where customers could find all of the British supplier's goods. Today, Marks and Spencer goods are scattered throughout Daiei's department stores, and some of these goods are sold through direct selling in the home.

Data Element: Sales Tips[20]

Here are some sales tips that have been used for selling to Japanese customers. First, go to the Isetan department stores to hunt for things the Japanese like best. These are gimmicks with a clever design that sell at a high price—for example, a credit card that contains a tiny ballpoint pen and propelling pencil.

Second, roam Isetan to see whether or not imported products are staying ahead of local imitators. For example, Japan's Aylesbury House clothes are nearly identical to Scotch House clothes, a British import. And Japan's Ashford sells a memo and date book system that is almost identical to Great Britain's Filofax brand name. This has resulted in Filofax's being dropped from Isetan stores.

Third, accept Isetan's use of unacceptable English in its promotional material. "Let's active Britain" is a slogan that sounds ridiculous to English-speaking people but works for the Japanese.

Fourth, aim sales to Isetan for the two Japanese gift-giving seasons, one in the winter (*O-Seibu*) and one in the summer (*O-Chungen*). There are two Christmas seasons rather than one in Japan. The Japanese like to give seaweed soap, salad oil, foods from Marks and Spencer, Scotch whiskey, and—as the Japanese internationalize their palate and tastes—high-price, high-prestige goods from overseas.

Data Element: Carry Out Market Launch by Targeting Customers

International marketing executives must link their new products with an innovative marketing strategy in pricing and distribution. They assign an international product manager to coordinate the marketing side of the organization with research and development. This product market link is called the market launch.

Zantac, an anti-ulcer wonder drug, was launched by Glaxo of Great Britain by marrying a brilliant scientific discovery with innovative marketing, such as unconventional sales partnerships in the United States and Japan, and an upmarket pricing policy.[21] This is an example of "scrum and scramble" teamwork. Research on the ranitidine molecule (the generic name for Zantac), toxicity tests in animals, clinical trials on humans, construction of mass production facilities, and setting up the distribution system were all done in parallel, not just in one country but in all major markets. The result is that Zantac is the first pharmaceutical to sell $1 billion (in U.S. dollars) a year.

As early as the mid-1980s, Glaxo assigned an international product manager to prepare the launch of a new antimigraine compound in the early 1990s. Who are the competitors? What does the term *migraine* mean to doctors in different countries? What are their preferred methods of medication? How can migraine sufferers be convinced to go to doctors for medication when they don't think the treatment is worth the effort? These are some of the questions that must be answered in the market launch.

Japan is especially important to Glaxo because it is the second biggest drug market in the world.[22] Japan spends 5 percent of its gross domestic product on health care, and this is expected to increase to 12 percent by 2025. Sales of prescription and over-the-counter drugs are worth $30 billion (in U.S. dollars) annually. The Japanese already swallow more pills than do people of other nations because Japanese doctors receive a percentage of the sales of the drugs they prescribe. In Japan, drug salesmen (or detail men) are known as *propas*, a Japanese contraction of the English word for propagandist. Unusually, Japanese drug firms have been slow to develop drugs that can hold their own on the domestic and international market.

In preparation for this new business, Glaxo got itself listed on the Tokyo Stock Exchange. Between 1987 and 1993, it plans to double its share of the Japanese pharmaceuticals market to 2.5 percent. Zantac, Ventolin (its antiasthma drug), and its still unnamed antimigraine compound should do well in the Japanese market. The Japanese government rewards companies that offer drugs with significant new benefits by allowing them to be priced far higher than generic copycat products. Thus, Glaxo's competitive strategy of only launching drugs with significantly new therapeutic benefits and that can command upmarket prices will be well-rewarded in Japan.

In 1987, there were 59 foreign companies with investments in Japanese pharmaceutical and health care firms, 43 of them involving equity stakes and 16 technical licensing agreements. Ten foreign firms are going it alone in Japan, including Merck, the world's largest drug firm; Dow; G. D. Searle, a subsidiary of Monsanto; Hoffmann-La Roche; and Hoechst. These firms are Glaxo's competition in the Japanese market. They, too, will be launching their new products with the same parallel scrum and scramble teamwork followed by Glaxo.

Data Element: Match Marketing Investment with Expansion of Working Capital

International marketing executives must link their market launch with timely collection and payments. From the beginning, they should set out clearly (1) the terms of payment—that is, cash, open account, letters of credit, or factoring receivables (or forfeiting); (2) the process for correctly completing the documents so that much-needed funds are not trapped in the banking system; (3) the maintenance of export credit insurance; and (4) the timely expansion of working capital.

For example, when Smith and Telford, a British manufacturer of cashmere and lambswool knitwear, first built up its sales in Japan, the company began using one ton of cashmere a week, worth $150,000 (in U.S. dollars).[23] As a result, the company easily ran up overdrafts of $1.2 million. To match its Japanese marketing investment with its need for additional capital, Smith and Telford ran its bank credit up to the limit. Then it obtained an increase in share capital of $300,000 from the Scottish Development Agency.

A successful export marketing campaign requires a carefully thought-out plan for maintenance of cash flow and the expansion of working capital. Sometimes additional capital can be obtained from the Japanese importer, particularly when these importers are trading companies, large retailers, and international firms. All of them have close working ties with large, medium, and small banks in Japan that are willing to finance imports.

Data Element: Take Advantage of Currency Swings, Cuts in Prices, and Increases in Market Share

When the currency of a host country rises in terms of the currency of the home country, marketing executives must realize they have a golden opportunity to cut prices of imported goods below those of domestic producers and, therefore, to increase on a permanent basis the market share of the imported goods in the host country market. Between 1985 and May 1987, the Japanese yen rose 89 percent in terms of the U.S. dollar. This one-time significant change in the foreign exchange value of the yen permitted the Campbell Soup Company to cut its soup prices and make Campbell Soup a part of Japanese consciousness.[24] This step to increase market share gave Campbell Soup a stronger base in Japan from which to launch other products in the future.

Campbell initiated its market launch in 1983, when it began urging Japanese retail store managers to give shelf space in their cramped stores for its seven varieties of soup, including corn potage, a soup made exclusively for Japan. Campbell made numerous changes in its products for the Japanese market, such as putting shiny lids on cans to appeal to quality-conscious Japanese housewives and making expiration codes readable in Japanese. Campbell's managing director in Japan, an American with a Ph.D. in Japanese history and who is fluent in Japanese, also drank with the store managers and listened to their comments about Campbell soups. When the yen rose, Campbell dropped its store price of soup by 16 percent. This permitted Japanese store managers to increase their volume and make a lot more money on their sales of Campbell soups. Now, two of the largest grocery chains in Japan sell Campbell soups.

At the same time, Teradyne Inc., a Boston-based maker of electronic test equipment, deeply cut prices in Japan so it could stick with its long-term goal of becoming more like a Japanese company. This strategy gave the company an increase of 3 percentage points of market share from its Japanese competitors. Now it is cultivating long-term relationships with Japanese firms. With the help of Mitsubishi Electric Corporation, Teradyne designed a system to check computer-chip memories. For Sony, Teradyne designed a machine that tests a solid-state image sensor in Sony's tiny 8mm videocamera. This image sensor can be used in photocopying and facsimile machines, industrial robots, and even toys.

Data Element: Use Local Distribution System Effectively

When marketing executives seek entry into the Japanese market, they do not tackle the retail distribution system head-on. This would be folly because there are over 1.7 million retailers to serve Japan's population of 120 million, and because many of these retailers are small, mom-and-pop stores that have a long-term, trusting relationship with their suppliers. Instead, marketing executives must hire or go into a joint venture with one of the 8,000 domestic trading companies.

In 1960, two Japanese companies controlled 80 percent of the razor market. Schick challenged Japanese dominance of the razor market by hiring as its exclusive agent a cutlery distributor, Hattori Seiko. Then Schick carried out an advertising campaign showing that stainless steel blades were safer and more durable than Japanese carbon steel, double-edged blades. Schick also mailed 5 million stainless steel blades to Japanese men to convince them to switch to this imported product. Today, Schick controls 71 percent of the market.

The California Almond Growers Exchange was unsuccessful in getting a trading company or a wholesale distributor to push its products in Japan. Because these distributors may handle as many as 2,000 different items of merchandise, new products have a difficult time getting accepted among the chocolates, liquors, and other related items they usually carry. The almond growers exchange finally broke into the Japanese market by getting Coca-Cola in Japan to distribute nuts as part of a promotional campaign. With 15,000 salespeople, 500 sales offices, and 1.1 million sales locations, the Coca-Cola network helped the almond growers to corner 70 percent of the market in Japan.

Data Element: Modify Products to Conform to Local Culture

International marketing executives must alter their products to conform to local culture and conditions. For example, S. C. Johnson & Son's furniture polish, Lemon Pledge, smelled like a latrine disinfectant widely used in Japan during World War II. Because of this, Japanese people over 40 resisted buying the product. When the lemon odor was reduced in the Japanese product, the sales of Lemon Pledge rose sharply.

Another example: Mattel replaced Barbie's blonde, curly hair with straight, black hair, and the doll's eyes with oriental eyes. This was the new Barbie doll for Japan.

Another example: Procter & Gamble developed a new liquid detergent based on the cooler water temperature in Japanese washing machines. This was a substitute for the company's powder detergent, which dissolved too slowly in the cooler water. P&G's liquid detergent, which was developed for the Japanese market, is now sold in the United States as well.

More examples: SmithKline Beecham lowered the amount of antihistamines per capsule in its cold medicine, Contac, because the average body weight of the Japanese is less than that of Americans and Europeans. Melitta, a manufacturer of coffee filters, introduced a 25-gram vacuum pack because the Japanese use less coffee than Americans do. McDonald's changed the name of its Quarter Pounder to Double Burger because the Japanese use the metric system which does not include the concept of a quarter of a pound of meat.

Data Element: Forge Long-Term Links with Suppliers, Distributors, and Customers

International marketing executives must build long-term relationships with their overseas customers. These ties include exchanging information with sales agents and partners, understanding how local business is carried out, building rapport with employees and customers, meeting testing and certification requirements of local governments, and providing local markets with quality goods.

Over 50,000 U.S. products have been launched in Japan. They are being sold in 85 percent of Japan's 126 industrial sectors. Many of them hold the number one market position in their field. Examples of these firms and products include: Coca-Cola, Warner Lambert's Schick razors, McDonald's, Digital Equipment, Polaroid, Gleason Corporation's bevel gear-cutting machines, Ben Hogan golf equipment, Baskin Robbins, SmithKline Beecham, Lipton, Del Monte tomato juice, Kimberly-Clark tissues, and Corning Glass Works.[25]

Tactic: Integrate International Marketing Plan into Corporate Strategy

International marketing executives must nurture the success of their overseas businesses. The following are several diversification strategies that are appropriate.

First, diversification through adding similar products for sale provides economies of scale and scope. Marketing executives should not forego such diversification opportunities because local culture and conditions are different. Instead, they should diversify by creating high-priced products for upmarket segments.

Second, diversification by adding dissimilar products for sale through the same distribution system also provides economies of scale and scope. International executives should not forego such diversification opportunities because local conditions require changes in packaging, branding, and labeling. Instead, these executives should diversify by tailoring products to meet the special requirements of distributors, wholesalers, and retailers.

Third, diversification into overseas markets must add value to international business firms. Such growth in shareholder value must offset the costs of market expansion overseas or be above the cost of capital in local overseas markets. The duration of this successful period of growth in shareholder value is dependent on how many of the firm's products have lasting value for customers. Over a decade or more, this growth in shareholder value translates into sustainable competitive advantage for the firm in the United States, Europe, and Japan.

STRATEGY ANALYSIS OF INTERNATIONAL TAILORED MARKETING POLICY

A ninth future has already happened in international business: Knowledge of Japanese national differences is essential to sales and marketing success in Japan and similarly so in Europe and the United States. Good data help executives tailor their marketing plans to meet the supply-demand conditions of each national market. From these plans come an international marketing strategy about product and geographic (international) diversification. If done correctly, marketing strategy dovetails nicely into the firm's overall corporate strategy. The following are three ways to link marketing to corporate strategy.[26]

Shift Export Marketing Focus to Asia

Restructuring is one way in which marketing executives carry out their international business. For example, when the sovereign debt crisis hit the Latin American countries, U.S. firms switched their export business away from Mexico, Brazil, and Venezuela to the newly industrialized countries in Asia. The firms established a critical mass of marketing, transportation, and freight-forwarding core skills in the new region and applied them to these growth markets to create value for themselves. International marketing executives must be able to spot market segments and niches that need new or additional products, and then must proceed to apply core skills to these growth markets.

Shift International Marketing Focus to Asia

International executives manage a discrete set of business activities (or value activities). They are linked together in a set as a value chain of international marketing activities. These include the design of the product, sales and marketing efforts, logistics, the sales management organization, and other activities in terms of what is demanded by Koreans, Taiwanese, Thais, Malaysians, and so on. International marketing executives must be able to transfer these skills of positioning products, market segmentation, and promotional techniques from the home country market to the host country markets. Such a transfer of skills by marketing executives becomes a source of sustainable competitive advantage.

Shift Global Marketing Focus to Asia

International executives are very successful when they share activities in value chains among the parent and subsidiaries. For example, Mattel uses the same distribution system (from Hong Kong and China to Japan and the United States) for its Barbie dolls and other toys. Such sharing lowers costs. These shared activities must be the significant value items in creating sustainable competitive advantage. Over time, this sharing of activities changes completely the ways in which competitive advantage is gained and maintained.

These three links between marketing and corporate strategies are not mutually exclusive. The two most powerful strategies for international marketing are transferring skills and sharing activities. The work of international marketing executives is to put in place a corporate strategy that identifies the competitive connections among national markets and market segments, matches core skills with growth markets, puts together a sales management organization linking the international network together, shares activities, transfers skills, and creates value for the shareholders of the international firm.

EXECUTIVE SUMMARY

Black & Decker and Quaker Oats are good cases in which to see how different sales policies affect success overseas. Black & Decker understood local preferences well in both Europe and the U.S. for power and cordless tools, whereas Quaker Oats was trying to change European preferences for moist versus dry dog food. Both firms are better off today than they were 10 years ago, yet Black & Decker is poised to expand its dual diversification strategy to other areas of the world, whereas Quaker Oats remains with a lower level of sales and its dual concentration strategy. Today, a fast sales growth international marketing strategy tends to work out better than a slow sales growth marketing strategy.

STRATEGY ANALYSIS OF ORGANIZATIONAL LEARNING AND INTERNATIONAL BUSINESS: INTERNATIONAL BUSINESS FORECAST

In Part III, the focus is on what executives need to know about the future and how they can sustain their firm's competitive advantage over long periods of time. Clearly, three things help firms sustain competitive advantage: (1) getting the answers right, (2) staying power, and (3) getting into markets first.

An international business forecast requires firms to project their sales, cash flows, and other important data for periods of time in the future—one year, three years, and five years. The period of time can be extended indefinitely as long as firms invest funds above the cost of capital and thus create shareholder value. In this way, the market is telling executives whether or not their firm's proprietary technologies, patented products, brand names, and other intellectual property are competitive among customers for long periods of time.

PART IV

GLOBALIZATION AND INTERNATIONAL BUSINESS

How to Gain, Maintain, and Sustain Competitive Advantage

Globalizing the Firm

CHAPTER 10

GLOBALIZING THE FIRM, ITS PRODUCTS, AND ITS MARKETS

One day Electrolux will have to consider spreading its headquarters people around the globe, just like the Catholic Church—the only real multinational in the world.[1]
Anders Scharp, *president of Electrolux.*

Well, we really do do all three corporate parenting roles . . . financial control, coaching and fully fledged orchestrating.[2]
Anders Scharp.

We're all learning new roles.[3]
Don Blasius, *Electrolux's top manager in the United States.*

I see a world developing where there will be a handful of players worldwide. We'll be one. Electrolux will be one. There will be one or two Far Eastern players. We're going to have a far stronger foothold in Asia.[4]
David R. Whitwam, *chairman of Whirlpool.*

COMPETITIVENESS: THE IMPORTANCE OF CORPORATE PARENTING

"Anders Scharp acts as an orchestrator towards white goods, for instance, as a coach towards Granges (the aluminum subsidiary), and as a controller towards agricultural machinery. . . . This [corporate parenting] is one of the real skills of Electrolux top management,"[5] says one industry insider.

For example, Electrolux management insists that local firms, particularly those in noncore businesses (such as Granges), participate in coaching programs to improve quality, just-in-time inventory, and accounts receivable.[6] Management has also demanded that its core subsidiaries (such as Zanussi and other appliance firms) go through a thorough redesign of their plant layouts and product designs on the basis of guidance from the parent firm.

Scharp's goal is for all subsidiaries to provide the parent Electrolux with a 15 percent return on shareholders' equity and operating income.[7] The strains from this emphasis on corporate parenting and improved financial performance are an inevitable by-product of a transnational firm going through a major change in the way it does business in Europe, the United States, and Japan. It is up to Scharp to keep the corporate staff from overturning the independence of product line managers and national subsidiaries while insisting that the financial, marketing, and international objectives be met by the world firm. Such is the elusive balance and ambiguous nature of Electrolux.[8]

ELECTROLUX: A TRANSNATIONAL FIRM

Electrolux creates value for its shareholders by aiming its products at Europe, the United States, and Japan. In all three markets, consumers prefer an international life-style. They expect their large kitchen appliances—especially their microwave ovens, washing machines, and freezers—to provide them with the good life. Thus, the firm has taken advantage of the convergence of consumer preferences among the developed countries to manufacture similar products salable on all three continents.

However, Electrolux's executives are aware that strong local preferences exist among national consumers for certain whiteline appliances. For example, with refrigerators, the depth of the shelves on the door must take various sizes of milk, juice, and soda cartons because consumer drinks do not come in standard packages even in the developed countries.

Moreover, Electrolux lets its local subsidiaries carry out distribution because local preferences for this marketing strategy are a great deal stronger than the need for global integration. Wherever it can, the firm is devolving more international responsibility onto its product line subsidiaries.

Although Electrolux is a Swedish firm, its common business language around the world is English. Even the managers at Zanussi, the Italian subsidiary, are learning English at the rate of 500 managers per year. But many Italian and U.S. executives complain that the most crucial decisions are made in Swedish over coffee by Stockholm-based executives.

Because the parent firm is actively pushing for greater benefits for its shareholders, the global business network has had great success in shrinking its product design down to months from years, transferring technology among subsidiaries, and being sure none of its local companies works in isolation of the whole firm. This is Electrolux, a global network unique in the large kitchen appliance industry.

An Impossible Organization . . . That Works[9]

Electrolux's corporate strategy is to make acquisitions to fill gaps in products and markets rather than to diversify for the sake of diversification. By making 100 acquisitions during the 1980s, it has become the largest producer of chain saws, garden appliances, vacuum cleaners, and large kitchen (or white-line) appliances.[10] The firm is the second largest producer of seat belts for automobiles, professional catering equipment, and refrigerator compressors. It is also active in aluminum smelting (Granges), commercial cleaning and laundry services, farm machinery and road surfacing equipment (Blaw Knox), industrial shelving, sewing machines, and artificial flowers. What most companies call divisions, Electrolux labels "product lines" because it wants to focus its executive time and managerial efforts on product markets.

In 1989, Electrolux launched its Quattro 500, a fridge-freezer with several different temperature zones. This new large kitchen appliance was designed by a high-tech team of executives from Europe and the United States under the leadership of Electrolux's Mr. Cold, Heikki Takanen, a Finn based in Stockholm who is responsible for refrigerators and freezers. He has called this executive team "organisational high-tech . . . a model for the future" and has said, "We want not only to create common projects that span several units, but a process that allows responsibilities to be transferred between them as the projects develop."[11] For example, the design work was done in Italy, the product was engineered in Finland, and the marketing input came from Great Britain. Now, manufacturing for the Quattro 500 is done in Finland.

The parent firm has only three international product and manufacturing managers—one for refrigerators, freezers, and other cold products; another for stoves, microwaves, and hot products; and a third for washing machines, dishwashers, and other wet products. This is an organizational structure that tolerates ambiguity, informality, and a willingness to communicate. All three product managers report to Leif Johansson, who heads the white goods product line. According to Johansson, "If you ask me who makes the decisions, it's not at all clear. . . . It's a quite impossible organisation, but the only one that will work."[12]

For Italians and Americans who entered the Electrolux organization through the Zanussi and White Consolidated acquisitions and who are used to a hierarchical relationship, Electrolux's matrix organization pattern is more difficult to get used to. The balance of power is not with powerful country managers, decentralized business units, or international product divisions. Instead, the parent firm wants built-in conflicts resolved through informal discussion rather than by orders from the headquarters in Sweden.

However, each product division has international responsibilities for several sets of products. Electrolux insists that these not be duplicated elsewhere in the global business network. When Zanussi was taken over, it was given manufacturing responsibilities that had once been the province of the French and Scandinavian subsidiaries. Because 70 percent of Zanussi's revenues comes from exports, this subsidiary has direct control over the negotiation of sales volume and transfer prices between itself and other subsidiaries as well as with the parent.[13] Electrolux requires product divisions and sales companies to operate at arm's length as if they have a customer-supplier relationship.

Blending a Swedish Corporate Culture with Foreign Acquisitions[14]

During the 1980s, Electrolux took over the following white-line businesses: in Italy, Zanussi; in Great Britain, Thorn-EMI's Tricity and Bendix interests; in Spain, Corbero and Domar; and in West Germany, Zanker. By doing so, Electrolux preempted its rivals in the headlong rush to build up scale economies within Europe. Through its timely acquisition of White Consolidated (i.e., long before its European rivals saw the benefits of competitive connections with the United States), Electrolux also preempted its rivals in building up scale economies across the North Atlantic.

Today, two strategic alliances between U.S. and European firms (Whirlpool-Philips and GE-Hotpoint, as well as Maytag, with its acquisition of Hoover), are trying to follow in the footsteps of Scharp and Electrolux. These other firms were not first into cross-border and transcontinental deals, and they may not have the staying power to catch up and beat Electrolux. None of them practice corporate parenting with the great success found at Electrolux.

Electrolux believes in decentralization, but it has sought to span national frontiers with product development, manufacturing, and inventory management. All of these require additional managerial time in the configuration of responsibilities and the coordination of product market results. Electrolux wants to become a flexible global business firm that is better integrated within Europe, and with the United States and Japan. The end result is that the firm might wind up with more centralization at the top—an outcome dreaded by product managers and unwelcomed by Scharp.

STRATEGY ANALYSIS OF ELECTROLUX'S INTERNATIONAL BUSINESS PERFORMANCE

Is Electrolux better off? In terms of improved market share and a 15 percent increase in returns on sales, the firm's product lines—particularly in large kitchen appliances and compressors—and the firm's foreign subsidiaries with international responsibilities—such as Zanussi, White Consolidated, Tricity, and Zanker—are doing better. Thus, the parent firm itself is better off.

Has Electrolux employed its assets wisely? Its acquisitions have paid back the cost of entering the Italian, U.S., British, and German markets. Now these subsidiaries earn enough to cover their cost of doing business, and they are throwing off sufficient additional cash to provide Electrolux with funds to invest elsewhere in the world, most recently in Spain.

Is Electrolux the dominant firm? The firm has set a new standard for its competitors in developing standardized parts, components, and finished goods for its kitchen appliances in Europe, the United States, and Japan. Electrolux is the industry's leader.

Since the mid-1980s, Electrolux has won most of the battles over international competitiveness. For half a decade, the firm has had sustainable competitive advantage in white-line appliances over Philips in continental Europe. However, the Italian, British, and U.S. subsidiaries still remain nondominant firms in competition against Ariston, Hotpoint, and Whirlpool. Electrolux seeks to change this with its new product development tied to more global marketing in the large kitchen appliance business.

Today, Electrolux is a good example of a transnational firm, a global business, and a worldwide manufacturing and marketing network. It has successfully implemented the international business decisions discussed in this book and, by doing so, has improved its performance worldwide.

GLOBAL MARKETING POLICY

Electrolux and several other firms discussed in previous chapters create international business networks that circle the globe. Exhibit 10–A shows the 10th international business decision, which is made once all the other business decisions have been made and successfully completed. Exhibit 10–B shows the international marketing tactics for rolling out Decision 10. Exhibit 10–C lists the data elements for developing an international business strategy.

EXHIBIT 10–A
International Business Decision 10: Success in Globalizing the Firm

Note: Executives must specify decisions to fit international business problems. Substantially different organizational problems exist for international firms whether they are starting up or seeking to stay ahead of their competitors in the quest for a strong global business network.

EXHIBIT 10–B
International Marketing Tactics for Rolling Out Decision 10

Coordinate global and local marketing strategies
Foster organizational learning
Balance interdependence among subsidiaries
Create profit sanctuaries

EXHIBIT 10–C
Data Elements for Preparing an International Business Strategy

Global and Local Marketing Strategies
Barriers to contesting markets
Preemptive marketing strategies
Improvements in company operations
Competitive connections
World operations
Global business network
Long-term viability

Organizational Learning
Incremental commitments
Cultural (psychic) distance
Marketing institutions

Interdependence among Subsidiaries
Sole-source subsidiaries
Export platforms
Internalization

Profit Sanctuaries
Standardization
Adaptation
Marketing management

INTERNATIONAL MARKETING TACTICS AND DATA ELEMENTS FOR PREPARING AN INTERNATIONAL BUSINESS STRATEGY

The following provides an explanation of how Electrolux and other companies have used the four tactics listed in Exhibit 10–B for rolling out Decision 10. It also includes an explanation of the data elements listed in Exhibit 10–C for preparing an international business strategy.

Tactic: Coordinate Global and Local Marketing Strategies

When international executives think globally, and act locally, they tailor products, channels of distribution, and promotional themes to fit specific local and regional markets. They also try to standardize as much of the marketing mix as possible. These are the twin elements of global marketing management. Their coordination is a primary source of competitive advantage.

Data Element: Barriers to Contesting Markets

Until Electrolux came into Italy, the largest firm selling white-line appliances was Ariston. Zanussi and Indesit each were half as large, followed by a smaller Candy and by IRE, the Philips subsidiary.[15] Ariston was the dominant firm, the price giver, and the market leader in exporting Italian-made appliances throughout Europe. Together with Zanussi and Indesit the three firms formed one strategic group within the large kitchen appliance industry of Italy. Their size, their breadth of models, and their exporting capability separated them from other Italian manufacturers.

These price and nonprice barriers remained until Electrolux took over Zanussi. Then the latter was linked to a global enterprise, to its international business network, and to markets on three continents. Through these crucial competitive connections, Zanussi became a different firm.

Zanussi obtained new capital, was coached on improving manufacturing and plant layout, and orchestrated into providing sophisticated marketing strategies to customers in Italy, France, and Great Britain. Moreover, Zanussi was given major international responsibilities by its new parent firm, especially in the design of new kitchen appliances. Although Zanussi still has not become as large as Ariston, the former is much better connected internationally to raise new barriers against Ariston throughout Europe.

Ariston fought back by bringing in Japanese and European advisors on technology, management, marketing, and finance. With computer-aided design, Ariston halved its idea-to-production time to two years, automated production, and installed an integrated information system. This is an example of the use of scrum-and-scramble teamwork to change the cost and efficiency barriers facing Ariston in its fight to stay competitive against the new Zanussi.

To finance these competitive changes, Ariston switched from financing expansion through cash flow and debt growth to using a bigger capital base and access to international money markets via listings on European stock exchanges. Between 1983 and 1987, Ariston lowered its cost of finance from 6 percent of turnover to less than 3 percent of sales. Ariston is investing these funds to double its share of the European appliance market to about 10 percent. The company's objective is to be one third the size of Electrolux in every European country except for its home market, Italy.

Data Element: Preemptive Marketing Strategies

To sustain an international marketing strategy, Ariston must export 40 percent of the white goods it produces in Italy to other European countries. The national output of Italian white-line goods manufacturers is 13 million appliances, second only to the 18.5 million units produced in the United States and double the production in West Germany. Italy has 38 percent of European production within its borders, but its home market consumes only 16 percent of European demand; therefore, Italy has 8 million (and Ariston has 3.2 million) appliances to export annually.

The two European markets with production deficits are Great Britain and France. Appliance manufacturers from West Germany, Spain, and Italy also are actively contesting for market share in both Great Britain and France; Zanussi has international responsibility from Electrolux for these other European markets. Therefore, Ariston will have a hard time keeping up with the new Zanussi.

Data Element: Improvements in Company Operations

Nevertheless, Ariston is building on traditional Italian strengths in innovation and product design, and is extending to the maximum its flexible manufacturing systems. Ariston produces 1,400 different models and versions of appliances. Fifteen percent of its annual sales comes from new products such as multipurpose, multifuel cookers and the Four Seasons fridge-freezer (an appliance with compartments that have their own microclimates and one that has been copied recently by Zanussi).

Ariston produces 740 appliances per worker per year; this is double Zanussi's and IRE's production. Moreover, the company has halved its failure costs—that is, mechanical faults, cabinet flaws, and the manpower and testing equipment costs associated with prevention and process control. This is a better track record than that found at Zanussi.

The new Zanussi aroused Ariston to purchase smaller Italian appliance businesses. This move toward more concentration was coupled with Ariston's either modernizing its newly acquired plants or closing them down. When industries go through consolidation, the competitively more effective firms (such as Ariston in Italy and Electrolux in Great Britain) can enter and exit the weaker firm's markets at will, with very limited incremental investment given their total resources. The strong firms in fact drive the weaker ones out.

Ariston is building up the scale of its business in Italy and making itself the most efficient producer in Italy. Its streamlining of company operations coupled with its drive to cut costs helps Ariston avoid being trapped by Electrolux as a mere market niche competitor and the target of an unfriendly takeover by Philips-Whirlpool or some other international firm.

Data Element: Competitive Connections

Before Electrolux contested for market share in Italy, it had captured Scandinavia and had built up a strong position in France and Switzerland. With the Zanussi acquisition in 1984, Electrolux gained market share also in West Germany, Austria, Spain, and Italy and eventually doubled its share of the European market for white-line goods and equipment used in the catering industry.

In 1987, Electrolux went into Great Britain and took over Thorn EMI's loss-making appliance division as well as its profitable food-services equipment division. Through this acquisition Electrolux gained control over the brand names of Tricity, Moffat, Parkinson Cowan, and Bendix. It can now manufacture gas and electric cookers and microwave ovens in Great Britain. From this acquisition Electrolux gained a 25 percent market share of the British large kitchen appliances market, enabling it to compete effectively against Ariston's strategy of creating a strong brand image in Great Britain and Europe.

In 1986, Electrolux took over White Consolidated Industries, the third largest household-appliance maker in the United States after General Electric and Whirlpool. Electrolux now owns the well-known brand names of Frigidaire and Kelvinator, and can compete effectively against Ariston's strategy of creating a strong brand image. For example, Frigidaire has the responsibility for competing against Ariston's Four Seasons fridge-freezer in the new market segment of multiclimate refrigerators.

Data Element: World Operations

All of these acquisitions made Electrolux the world's biggest household appliance maker. They put this international firm in the forefront of restructuring an industry weighed down by overcapacity, price wars, and poor profitability. Nevertheless, some marketing and financial problems do exist with Electrolux's strategy of low-cost investments for developing world-scale operations.

For example, cookers, refrigerators, and washing machines differ significantly from country to country because their cultural grounding (e.g., whether meat should be served well-done or rare;

which fruits, vegetables, eggs, and dairy products must be kept cold to be considered fresh and safe to eat; and how hot water must get for clothes to wash clean) varies considerably from country to country.

Moreover, between 1977 and 1986, Electrolux's equity-to-assets ratio fell from 32 to 24 percent, a number that is unacceptable among U.S. chief financial officers. This decrease came about because the company carried out its expansion by acquiring loss-making or poorly performing companies and gained market share through restructuring and rationalization. In the case of Zanussi, Electrolux bought only a minority share in 1984 to avoid the balance-sheet pressures of consolidation; however, in 1986, Electrolux increased its share of Zanussi to 90 percent. Such higher gearing is the price Electrolux was willing to pay for building world-scale capacity and market leadership in Europe.

Finally, with each acquisition, whether in Europe or North America, Electrolux has closed plants and cut the work force, consolidated warehousing and transportation, reduced inventories, and cut corporate overhead. These actions have amounted to significant savings for Zanussi, White Consolidated, and Thorn EMI's appliance division.

Data Element: Global Business Network

Notwithstanding these important managerial problems facing Electrolux, this firm has made great gains in coordinating the local marketing operations of Zanussi, White, and Thorn EMI into the parent firm's global marketing strategy. The following is what Electrolux is doing to create, maintain, and expand its international business network.

First, Electrolux views microwave ovens as the first global product of the white-line industry because they have similar designs and similar uses throughout the world. Second, it is concentrating on producing common components for all of its household appliances, such as compressors and controls for refrigerators, and motors and pumps for washing machines. Finally, Electrolux chose its Zanussi division in Italy to be the company's export platform for the design, manufacture, and supply of motors and compressors for both Europe and North America. In this way, Electrolux will achieve economies of scale, commonality of parts, more uniformity in product design, targeting of export products to market segments, and an export platform able to serve Electrolux's international business network worldwide.

Data Element: Long-Term Viability

Clearly, the three international giants of the household appliance industry (Electrolux of Sweden, Whirlpool of the United States, and Philips of the Netherlands) are pursuing a growth-by-takeover strategy. In the United States, the industry has shrunk from including over 100 manufacturers in the early 1980s to including 4 today: Whirlpool, General Electric, Maytag, and White Consolidated (now owned by Electrolux). In Europe, there were still 300 manufacturers in the late 1980s, and Europe was further behind in the effort to restructure and rationalize the kitchen appliance industry. The following explains how the large-scale international firms are competing against one another and against the smaller national firms.

Starting in 1987, Whirlpool's products were introduced into Europe by Philips as a way for the latter to complete against its rival, Electrolux. This joint marketing agreement accelerated the restructuring and rationalization of European industry because it tied Whirlpool's prime range of products and unbeatable marketing skills to the competitive power of Philips.

Today, Electrolux controls 25 percent of the European market. Philips has 13 percent. Bosch-Siemens of West Germany, 12.5 percent; AEG, another West German company, 8 percent; Thomson Brandt and Indesit, 6 percent each; and Hotpoint (a subsidiary of Great Britain's GEC) and 300 smaller firms (including Ariston) scramble for the remaining 29.5 percent.

The big international firms (Electrolux and Philips, together with Whirlpool) with production, distribution, and marketing capability in North America and Europe form a separate strategic group in the United States, Great Britain, France, West Germany, the Low Countries, and Italy. They gain their competitive strength by increasing their competitive connections among these national groups, for example, Electrolux's policies of concentrating components production and achieving global scale by making Italy (and more recently Spain) the export platform for the international firm.

As with the situation in Italy after Electrolux's acquisition of Zanussi, most of the smaller firms in the household appliance industry do not compete in the same strategic group as the international firms. These smaller firms tend to be restricted to niche markets within each country. Ariston is seeking to avoid this market niche trap by attempting to create its own barriers, to implement preemptive international marketing strategies, and to contest for market share within the strategic groups of Italy, West Germany, and Great Britain. By the late 1980s, Ariston still lacked the ability to coordinate global and local marketing strategies among the European countries, and it had no products positioned in the important North American market.

Hotpoint, the GEC subsidiary, is also seeking to avoid becoming a mere niche player in Great Britain's household appliance industry. In 1987, Hotpoint was still Great Britain's only substantive indigenous, full-range appliance company. It has been one of the consistently profitable appliance makers in Europe. Hotpoint has 33 percent of Great Britain's washing machine market, 30 percent of the tumble drier market, and 20 percent of the dishwasher market. Hotpoint refuses to cut prices; instead, it has a good distribution and service network, and uses advertising and promotion to pull its quality products through the channel to the consumer. Marketing within Great Britain comes first at Hotpoint. The company does not export to continental Europe because it believes the costs of duplicating its distribution and service network would be too high. Rather, it seeks to be the producer of common components for other appliance manufacturers and to make its plants in Wales and England export platforms for one or more worldwide international firms. If it cannot succeed in joint production and marketing agreements overseas, then it will be forced to retreat into its British fortress and lose the global marketing benefits that come from the competitive connections among countries worldwide.

For both Ariston and Hotpoint, the time for action may be over already. Toshiba, Hitachi, Sharp, and other Japanese firms are quickly entering the competition for market share in the white-line market of both Europe and North America. All appliance manufacturers will have to compete more aggressively to maintain their long-term viability in a more concentrated world market.

Tactic: Foster Organizational Learning[16]

When international marketing executives think globally and act locally, they try to learn about the distribution and other business practices of the local country and to determine how these might mesh with those encountered elsewhere, especially in the major markets of the world. This type of organizational learning is another primary source of competitive advantage.

Data Element: Incremental Commitments

Ariston is at the beginning of its quest to export extensively throughout Europe, whereas Zanussi, with the backing of Electrolux, is further along in making commitments to markets outside of Italy and even outside of the EEC. Furthermore, under Electrolux's coaching, Zanussi has been given the international responsibility to bring along the Spanish subsidiary so that the latter also contributes 15 percent of operating income to the parent firm.

Data Element: Cultural (Psychic) Distance

The speed of diffusion of knowledge about exporting, international marketing, and global marketing depends on the cultural (psychic) distance between domestic and foreign marketing executives. In the Zanussi case, cultural distance starts with preference of its Italian executives for a hierarchical administrative structure versus the informal matrix organization favored by Electrolux. It continues with the Italian executives' minimal ability in the English language, which prevents the free flow of information between Italy, Sweden, Finland, Germany, and Great Britain.

According to Jim Ringler, Electrolux's second most senior executive in the United States, Electrolux "is not a multinational, but an international company run by Swedes. . . . No American has the ambition to get into Electrolux group management, nor to speak Swedish." This refers to the fact that, although the company's official language is English, many of the most important discussions take place informally in Swedish, either over coffee back in Stockholm, or during the commute between meetings around the world.[17]

Anders Scharp, Electrolux's president, agrees: "The group is too Swedish today. . . . I've said many times that its future depends very much on the internationalisation of management. We've been trying to allocate group responsibilities internationally—but I'm worried that we're not acting as quickly as we ought to."[18] Leif Johansson, the head of the firm's largest division, the white-goods product line, agrees that good non-Swedish managers lower down in the organization "need to have a way to grow and develop international roles—otherwise we'll lose them."[19]

However, executives at Zanussi and Electrolux share several common managerial traits, especially the need to position products and segment markets properly. Both sets of international marketing executives are in agreement about the desirability of tailoring market segments for standardized and differentiated products. Moreover, both groups want to shrink the cultural distance between themselves and the product market ideas they wish to make paramount in the global firm.

Data Element: Marketing Institutions

As Zanussi and Ariston executives make incremental commitments to overseas markets and shrink the psychic distance between themselves and foreign customers, they will add the following marketing institutions to their international networks. Initial forays into new overseas markets might mean hiring freight forwarders, transportation companies, and export agents to take care of a limited volume of foreign sales. Neither Zanussi nor Ariston had experts immediately available on the Spanish and British markets; their export specialists for the French market had to add these new markets to their portfolio. As long as the total of export sales to these new markets remains less than 5 percent of total sales, neither company will make any significant changes in its marketing organization. In this case, the export intensity is low.

As foreign sales increase to Spain and Great Britain, the marketing executives of the two companies must hire import agents and other foreign distributors to expand export sales. At this point, the firms will set up a separate export sales department or division and give one or more managers responsibility for in-

creasing export sales. Export intensity will then double to between 5 and 10 percent.

With a sufficient volume of export sales, the marketing executives of Zanussi and Ariston will decide to rent, lease, or buy
warehouse facilities for breaking bulk, storing, sorting, and
wholesaling goods to foreign distributors or retailers. They will
manage the physical distribution aspect of marketing on a local
basis but leave sales management and promotion policy to others
in the network. These firms must convert their export divisions
into international marketing divisions whose managerial time is
taken up by gaining experience in maintaining a limited physical
presence in overseas markets. Export intensity will then double
again, to between 10 and 20 percent.

At this point in the expansion overseas, the international
marketing executives of Zanussi and Ariston must set up sales
branches and sales subsidiaries for checking daily, weekly, and
monthly sales volumes and inventory levels at all distributors
and retailers. They must sell products under their own brand
names and begin to employ special marketing techniques, such as
positioning products and segmenting markets, to expand their
sales overseas. These international firms must redesign their international marketing division into one focused on geographic
markets, products, or functional activities, which may all change
depending on each firm's successes or failures. These international firms must compete as a multidomestic firm, and export intensity will then double again, to between 20 and 40 percent.

To obtain a feel for overseas markets, the marketing executives of Zanussi and Ariston need to establish the physical presence of one or more manufacturing subsidiaries in host countries.[20] They must add such services as repairing, packaging,
mixing, finishing, processing, assembling, and full-line manufacturing. Through their competitive connections, these international marketing executives must gather the best information
about product markets. Finally, these international firms must
compete as global firms. Export intensity will jump to more than
40 percent and be sustained as part of the global firm's worldwide
competitive advantage.

All of these efforts will form the international business network of Ariston within Europe. On the other hand, the develop-

ment of a global network by Zanussi is truncated by its position as a wholly owned subsidiary of Electrolux. Instead, Zanussi has been assigned the task of manufacturing components for the worldwide company.

The result: Zanussi of Italy is the export platform for Electrolux, whereas Ariston must compete with Electrolux and Philips for overseas markets, foreign marketing institutions, and sites for direct investment abroad. Because of the formation of international business networks, organizational learning is taking place at both firms. However, the new Zanussi (as a part of a truly global enterprise) has the advantage over the old Ariston in the quest for export sales, market share, returns on investment, and long-term competitiveness.

Tactic: Balance Interdependence among Subsidiaries

When international marketing executives "think global, act local," they put together alliances among their subsidiaries and with outside partners so that their international business network acts in conformity with local government laws on foreign ownership, repatriation of profits and licensing fees, and the development of national research and development centers. This process of balancing interdependence among subsidiaries, affiliates, partners, and others is another primary source of competitive advantage.

Data Element: Sole-Source Subsidiaries[21]
Sole-source national subsidiaries such as Zanussi provide the following benefits to the international firm and its global network.

1. Economies of scale:
   - World-scale technology, product design, and distribution.
   - Commonality of parts and components.
   - Lower ocean and air freight costs.
2. Economies of scope:
   - Joint or multiproduct output across product lines.

- Commonality of distribution and promotion services.
- Lower managerial costs.
3. Economies of variety:
   - Products matched to segments and niches among countries.
   - Expansion of demand for world, national, and local goods.
   - Lower network costs.

Data Element: Export Platforms

Electrolux's success in turning Zanussi into an export platform was dependent on creating scale and scope economies; using either Zanussi's or Electrolux's dominant position in the exporting country to gain competitive advantage (on the import side) in other countries; and internalizing knowledge about markets, segments, and niches within the global firm. Both sets of international executives transfer technological skills and share marketing activities on the basis of a strong sense of corporate identity, values, and corporate culture. Within half a decade, Zanussi has become an integral part of the Electrolux corporate family.

Data Element: Internalization

Now, both groups of executives are screening opportunities, redesigning products, and reconfiguring distribution channels to meet the needs of importers. As exporters, Zanussi and Electrolux executives are clearly dependent on the importers for signals about demand for products in foreign markets. Over time, this dependency has become a burden, and exporting executives are looking for alternative ways to manage sales overseas.

With knowledge learned from exporting, these executives are looking for ways to gain first-mover advantage through a combination of exporting, licensing, offshore sourcing, and foreign direct investment. All four of these international business activities may be carried out separately. When the managerial costs of coordinating these efforts rise significantly, executives will be forced to look for alternative ways to manage their marketing activities overseas.

Today, Electrolux executives are implementing marketing

strategies based on a similarity of markets, a keen understanding of sales response activities, and a perception that local preferences dominate supply and demand decisions. Over time, the managerial costs of not fostering organizational learning within the international network will rise, forcing marketing executives to seek out a new, more global approach toward marketing both at home and abroad.

As global marketing enters the thoughts of Zanussi executives as well, they are learning that the primary sources of competitive advantage are coordination, organizational learning, and network interdependence. To make these sources of international competitiveness sustainable worldwide, Zanussi executives have agreed for their subsidiary to become the sole-source supplier of products for the parent firm. Together with Electrolux executives, they are implementing a series of preemptive marketing strategies against Ariston and Philips, and for the promotion of a global business now known as Electrolux.

Tactic: Create Profit Sanctuaries

International marketing executives who "think global, act local" use several marketing management techniques to create profit sanctuaries for their firms overseas. This is another source of competitive advantage.

Data Element: Standardization[22]
Electrolux executives are trying to obtain the benefits of economies of scale, scope, and variety by standardizing business functions among countries through global products, prices, promotion, and distribution. Through standardization, their subsidiaries are gaining a more coherent international image, more rapid diffusion of products and ideas worldwide, and greater control and coordination from the corporate headquarters.

This work is based on the assumption that consumer preferences are converging worldwide. For some products this is true: Electrolux washing machines, driers, and microwave ovens; Matsushita and Sony VCRs; and other homogeneous goods. Moreover, Procter & Gamble has taken its popular U.S. product, Head & Shoulders dandruff shampoo, and turned it into a European favorite. This product is manufactured in a single European plant and comes in a "Euro-bottle" that is labeled in eight languages. Through standardization within Europe and between the EEC and the United States, P&G has been successful in establishing profitable market segments in many developed countries.

Yet Electrolux and others are bound to the local cultural practices of countries. For example, some Europeans (and most Americans) prefer top loaders in their washing machines because additional clothes can be added in the middle of the washing cycle. Other Europeans prefer front loaders because they require less soap. Both Zanussi and Electrolux produce both types.

Moreover, customers in the home country may react to television advertising and other types of media differently from consumers in host countries. For example, in the United States, new consumer preferences sweep across the country on nationwide television and through coast-to-coast advertising networks. Neither White Consolidated nor Electrolux has mastered local U.S. cultural practices. The same ideas in Europe sometimes stop at the national borders because language, culture, and television transmissions stop at national borders.

Data Element: Adaptation
Nevertheless, total adaptation in terms of all elements of the marketing mix, marketing planning, and marketing control processes is rare. For example, Electrolux adapts the doors in its refrigerators to the various sizes of milk, juice, and cola cartons in use around the world; the remainder of the product design is standardized. However, advertising themes and copy, distribution, sales promotion, and customer service are fully adapted to local conditions and subject to the control of national subsidiaries.

Too much adaptation leads to inconsistent brand identities, limited product focus, and slow launches of new products. These inherent difficulties put at a disadvantage firms that use adoption as their prime thrust behind their marketing strategy. Thus, their executives are driven to reconsider the benefits of standardization.

The following explains how product and image adaptation were carried out successfully by Beecham. Between 1983 and

1987, the Beecham Group took the oblivion-bound Brylcreem (which was stuck in time with a dated image, a shrinking market, and sinking sales) and repositioned it in the market.[23] In the 1920s, this men's hairdressing cream was instantly successful, and it went with Allied soldiers to war in Europe during the late 30s and 40s. In the 60s, it lost out to flower power and flowing locks. Briefly, in the 70s, with the ad "Just a little dab'll do ya," Brylcreem came back. However, its users were aging, dying, and taking Brylcreem with them to the grave.

The mid-80s ushered in a Brylcreem revolution. Beecham sought to capture two diverse market groups—the aging, lapsed users and the new market of trendy young males. Because style was back in fashion and the market for male toiletries was growing fast, Beecham wanted a major share of this market. It had to hook its customers once again by reminding its lapsed users what they were missing and to excite its new young users with a new fashion image.

Using footage from the 60s with contemporary slow-motion, freeze-frame techniques, Beecham made commercials that gained cult status in Great Britain. Nostalgia appealed to both target market groups. Using rock music of the 80s, the ad firmly put the product in the modern period. These ads established Brylcreem's contemporary image.

Then Beecham launched two new Brylcreem products, the mousse and the gel. With success in Great Britain assured, Beecham used the same product positioning and promotional strategies in the United States to change the image of Brylcreem.

In the case of Brylcreem, successful adaptation came about by adapting the marketing mix element of advertising copy and then by adapting the product to suit new consumer tastes in both home and host country markets. None of these adaptations could have taken place, however, if Beecham's management had been unwilling to change its marketing management practices. The standard Brylcreem product, which had always been packaged in a black and red tube, would have been a dying product in growing markets both in Great Britain and the United States.

Data Element: Marketing Management
To accomplish the appropriate level of standardization and adaptation, and thereby create profit sanctuaries, international exec-

utives must define the market share, profit, and cash flow sought from overseas product markets.[24] Electrolux has done this with its demand for 15 percent of operating revenues from its subsidiaries.

Can entry be stimulated by an offensive strategy that wins over the customers of competitors? Can a business be established that targets products to those customers with sufficient income to buy these goods over a long period of time? Can high price and quality barriers be raised against competitors so the firm keeps the value-added portion of the market? Can the firm keep its customers happy with good after-market services?

If the firm's executives answer yes to these questions, then the firm is on the way to creating sustainable competitive advantage. The new Zanussi is on the way, but with a little bit of help from Electrolux.

STRATEGY ANALYSIS OF GLOBAL MARKETING POLICY

A 10th future already has happened in international business: Electrolux is developing an administrative culture suitable to becoming a global firm. Its organizational design for product development is both flexible nationally and integrated globally. For example, three Italian managers have been given senior international coordination roles within Electrolux for washing machine development, European white-goods marketing, and the components product line.[25] This new breed of international executives is able to take the measure of its rivals and outdo them in matching products with customer needs.

However, the responsibility for leveraging assets is with the senior group management, and virtually all of the senior managers reside in Stockholm. As a consequence, many of the most important research, technical, and marketing decisions are made informally in Swedish rather than in the firm's official language, English, and not by executives who reside in Turin, Italy, or in the United States.

In this respect, Electrolux is no different from New York-based U.S. firms or Tokyo-based Japanese firms. To overcome home market bias, international managers travel frequently.

The next step for European, U.S., and Japanese international firms is to decentralize crucial functions away from the corporate headquarters. Only by spreading headquarters personnel around the world will Electrolux, Procter & Gamble, and Fuji become truly global firms and sustain their worldwide competitive advantage.

EXECUTIVE SUMMARY

Electrolux made a smart move in taking over Zanussi, and the latter made a smart move in joining the former's corporate family. During the 1980s, the large kitchen appliance industry moved toward becoming a global business based on more universal consumer preferences worldwide. Electrolux saw this change coming and acted on it through acquisitions, new product development, and changes in organizational design and by forcing its subsidiaries to become mini-international firms in their own right. In the 1990s, Electrolux is far ahead of its rivals in global integration and with a global marketing policy that is tailored to needs of local, regional, and international markets.

CONCLUSIONS

[Global corporations are the] most powerful human organization yet devised for colonizing the future. . . . [They are] exporters of dreams.[1]
Richard Barnet and Ronald Mueller, *well-known critics of multinationals.*

Multinationals are the 'dominant institution' in a new era of global trade and investment.[2]
P. O. Gabriel, *a business consultant.*

Why do some companies based in some nations innovate more than others? Why do some nations provide an environment that enables companies to improve and innovate faster than foreign rivals?[3]
Michael Porter, *professor, Harvard Business School.*

GROPING FOR A THEORY OF INTERNATIONAL BUSINESS

International business forces its attention on all nations because global firms from three regions (Europe, the United States, and Japan) dominate trade and investment. Even so, some governments (including successive U.S. administrations) are trying to swim against the transnational tide. They act irrationally by trying to impose market-defying trade and investment practices on foreign goods, services, and firms. Global firms are learning to withstand these disruptions and get around them by doing a better job in managing their competitive links among countries, subsidiaries, suppliers, and distributors against all comers, foreign and domestic.

The 10 international business strategies provide the common, unifying framework for firms to strengthen their competitive advantage relative to the best competitors worldwide. They are the decisive characteristics of global firms that allow them to create, maintain, and sustain competitive advantage. These are the determinants for success worldwide—in research, technology, managerial skills, and marketing. They underpin increases in productivity, market share, return on investments, and shareholder value.

The 10 international business strategies provide a new theory about why some companies based in some nations innovate faster than their domestic and foreign rivals. Some firms win and others lose; this suggests that the theory is able to discriminate between successes and failures in the quest for competitive advantage. Moreover, the results can be compared across firms, industries, and countries; this indicates that the theory is able to provide a road map for other firms (from other nations) to march toward the universal goal of competitive advantage.

This new theory of international business is both dynamic and evolving. It awaits further refinement by others who will test it out with their own case studies in situations outside North America, Western Europe, and Japan.

THE 10 INTERNATIONAL BUSINESS STRATEGIES

The 10 international business strategies discussed in this book provide the basis for a new theory of international business. The cases in this book show how the 10 strategies are applied to firms in vastly different industries and from widely different home countries. They provide the reality check to the new theory and show whether these firms were able to gain, maintain, and sustain their competitive advantage. These 10 strategies can be grouped together as follows:

Countries and International Business

1. *Success in choosing market opportunities.* Are executives able to deal with the wide variety of cultural, economic, and political differences that exist in the world?

2. *Success in fitting core skills.* Do executives have a strong enough home base from which to deliver their proprietary goods to other countries? Do they need to establish a second home base to improve the chances for success?

3. *Success in overcoming barriers.* Are executives willing to make special arrangements with local firms to get into difficult markets?

Marketing Management and International Business

4. *Success in sourcing.* Can executives find the least costly, most productive resources for their firms and do this task better than their competitors?

5. *Success in selecting customers.* Can executives find customers with the highest quality of demand for the products of their firms and do this task better than their competitors?

6. *Success in creating value.* Can executives create valuable proprietary goods and do this task better than their competitors?

Organizational Learning and International Business

7. *Success in using information.* Are executives able to integrate the rapid changes in technology, management, and resources into their worldwide business firm?

8. *Success in positioning assets.* Are executives able to employ their assets more effectively than their worldwide competitors?

9. *Success in understanding national differences.* Can executives tailor their strategies to conform to the wide variety of differences around the world?

Globalization and International Business

10. *Success in globalizing the firm, its products, and its markets.* Can executives craft global strategies for global markets?

CONTINUING BATTLE FOR INTERNATIONAL COMPETITIVENESS

Competitiveness is making sales, earning profits, and increasing shareholder value from the trend toward globalization, the convergence of consumer demand worldwide, and the fragmentation of mass consumer markets in the United States, Europe, and Japan. The following are the things firms must do to gain, maintain, and sustain competitive advantage:

- Use intuition, hunches, and good guesses.
- Create an international management culture.
- Beat rival firms in the United States, Europe, and Japan.
- Become an insider in all overseas markets.
- Implant a set of commonly held beliefs.
- Build a dominant position at home and abroad.
- Get the answers right about the future.
- Stay in overseas markets for the long haul.
- Be first in all important markets.
- Take on the role of corporate parent.

Competitiveness is a continuing battle waged on all fronts by international executives who seek to globalize their firm, its products, and its markets. First, firms must be better off. Then they must pay back the cost of entering markets. Third, they must begin to dominate some of their home or host country markets. Finally, firms must restructure the industry in their favor and become the source of new technology for their competitors. This is what sustainable competitive advantage is all about.

THE FUTURE OF INTERNATIONAL BUSINESS

Because global firms are the dominant economic institution in the international economy of the 1990s, their future has several important cautions for the dominant political institution in the world, the nation-state. These are the warning notices.

Executives are better able today than at anytime in the past to manage country risk. They avoid governments, peoples, and nations where trade-defying practices make up the preponderance of government policy toward business firms. Japan, the United States, and Europe are exceptions because of their large internal markets. Canada and other small, developed and less-developed countries must conform to what executives expect from governments or face the loss of revenues from future foreign direct investments. Because executives live within an international management culture that transcends national political differences and looks for new ways to link up with others across industries, nations, and continents, global firms will continue to be more powerful than most nation-states, irrespective of resources, macroeconomic policies, or Nobel peace prize winners.

Also, executives are more competent today than at anytime in the past at managing product sourcing, customer selection, and value creation. They have internalized within their firms the export platforms created by countries, the high-quality consumers trained by educational ministries, and the proprietary information first created by now privatized (but formerly government-owned) laboratories and enterprises. With the decline of socialism in central, eastern, and Soviet Europe, these three processes of internalization will quicken until only the most backward regions of the world are left outside the world's market economy.

Finally, executives seem to be better able than most government officials in planning for the rapid rate of changes in the world economy. Although both national governments and big global firms share the problem of entrenched bureaucracies, the latter seem to understand better the need for organizational learning, if only because financial markets demand increases in sales, profits, and shareholder value. Very few national governments can match the success of a Unilever or an Electrolux in globalizing the firm, its products, and markets so that consumers worldwide benefit from the material success of such global firms.

Although nation-states will be the dominant political institution well into the next century, their role in the world economy and their relationship to transnational firms is evolving from what it used to be to what it might become. The willingness of governments to form common markets, customs unions, and free trade agreements is a hopeful sign that even nation-states see the benefits of freely competitive, open markets. If executives of global firms argue for free markets first regionally and then worldwide, they will become as active a set of players in world politics as they are in the world economy. This is the most important task facing international executives as they plan for the future of their firms in the world economy.

APPENDIX

MODELING INTERNATIONAL BUSINESS PERFORMANCE

Expert systems mimic the way people think. . . . Most of the biggest benefits of expert systems are turning out to be their unique abilities to spread knowledge through an organisation, to teach, and to improve quality. . . . Unlike the jobs computers have done in the past, . . . there are no right or wrong answers in most expert systems applications. . . . There is only better or worse.[1]
Edward Feigenbaum, *author.*

There's no question but that [resampling statistics, i.e., the bootstrap and the jackknife are] very, very important. [Because the method replaces standard, and simplifying assumptions about data with extensive computer calculations, it can be a powerful tool.] It gives us another way to get empirical information in circumstances that almost defy mathematical analysis. It's a nice way of letting the data speak almost for themselves.[2]
Frederick Mosteller, *a statistician at Harvard University.*

[Resampling is] the most important new idea in statistics in the last 20 years, and probably the last 50. Eventually, it will take over the field, I think.[3]
Jerome H. Friedman, *a statistician at Stanford University.*

THE EXPERT SYSTEMS MODEL

The material in this appendix is for readers who have an interest in the chaos theory of mathematics, resampling statistical techniques, intuitive decision making, and expert systems modeling. All of these underpin the theory of international business developed in the book. They are a part of the teaching notes used at the Kellogg Graduate School of Management for students who are studying the international business performance of global firms. A Lotus 123 tutorial exercise organizes the financial and market data, runs the regressions, and calculates the t-test results for students. It is an interactive tutorial exercise that falls within the class of models known as expert systems (or decision support) models.

This appendix explains an intuitive process for modeling the managerial performance of international business executives. It combines the basic theories of international business and decision support systems. It uses the skills of the model user to determine whether good business decisions are being made by management. Although there are many possible decisions that can be made by international executives, 10 are highlighted by the model; in the judgment of the model builder, these 10 decisions seem to capture a great deal of the relevant areas of managerial decision making in exporting to and investing in overseas markets. Together, these 10 international business decisions are the independent variables in a set of regression equations that show the success (or lack of success) of firms in international markets. This relationship between international business decisions and international business performance is the heart of the expert systems model.

TESTS OF INTERNATIONAL BUSINESS PERFORMANCE

Throughout this book, the research shows that the variation among international firms (e.g., between exporters and global firms; among U.S., European, and Japanese firms; or both) comes from specific differences in a firm's set of international business decisions. By observing the implementation of these 10 decisions, researchers separate successful from unsuccessful international firms. Successful international firms pass one or more of the four tests for international business performance. The following is a review of what they mean and how they were applied throughout this book.

Is the firm increasing market share or returns on sales or both? See the discussion of Molson before 1986 and L'Oréal during the initial fast sales growth period for Free Hold styling mousse for successful examples of being better off. See the discussion of both companies in the later 1980s for unsuccessful examples of international business performance. The better-off test requires a good understanding of country risk and some skill in marketing management.

Does the firm go into a host country at a cost lower than expected returns? Because both Molson and L'Oréal set up only captive distributors (or the internalization of U.S. distribution), their costs of entry were low and were easy to maintain even when a slump in sales occurred. Labatt, Procter & Gamble, and others made foreign direct investments in the United States and Japan; their costs of entry were higher, and it took them a long time (more than a decade in the case of some firms) before the costs of entry were successfully paid back. Sometimes, firms such as Airbus get their costs of entry subsidized by national governments. This gives an inconclusive result to the cost-of-entry test. Again, this test requires a good understanding of country risk and some skill in marketing management.

Can the firm make its overseas markets structurally attractive by dominating local industry? Caterpillar followed a second-best strategy with its equity joint venture in Japan; that is, it sought to make Komatsu less dominant in its home market and thus eliminate a profit sanctuary for Komatsu. MacMillan Bloedel sought to reinvent the paper industry by combining two national markets, the Canadian and the U.S., into one regional North American market. Both Kodak and Fuji sought dominance in each other's home markets. Both Boeing and Black & Decker reinvented their industries in their favor and passed the attractiveness test. Quaker Oats was unable to restructure the European pet food industry and, hence, failed the attractiveness test. This test requires a good understanding of country risk, excellent marketing management skills, and some insight into organizational learning.

Finally, is the firm able to get others to use its technology as the world standard? Boeing, Unilever (in Europe), and Electrolux successfully passed the sustainable competitiveness test. Airbus, Merck, and Black & Decker are trying very hard to join this short list of successful firms, but it takes a long time, perhaps decades of increases in sales, market share, returns on investments, and shareholder value. The sustainable competitive test is the most difficult test to pass because it requires firms to deal successfully with rapid rates of change worldwide.

PREDICTIVE VALUE OF THE 10 INTERNATIONAL BUSINESS DECISIONS

From the qualitative evidence presented in Chapters 1 through 10, the following assumptions can be made about the quantitative relationships among the 10 international business decisions, and between them and the four tests of international business performance. First, the 10 decisions are intuitively correct. Second, they are highly correlated among themselves. And third, their linear combination predicts international business performance.

In statistical theory, the four tests are called criterion (or dependent) variables and the 10 decisions are called predictor (or independent) variables. The goal of this appendix is to show readers a statistically meaningful way to make statements about international business and to explain why successful business decisions account for the variation in performance among international firms.[4]

JACKKNIFE METHOD OF STATISTICAL ESTIMATION[5]

The methodology described above using criterion variables (i.e., the tests of international business performance as the dependent variables) and predictor variables (i.e., the 10 international business decisions as the independent variables) requires measuring the influence of a variety of factors and then assessing their influence jointly rather than individually. This methodology needs the use of a multivariate approach in the quantitative measurement of international business performance.

Because of the nature of line-of-business financial and market data, the following three statistical problems confront research about international business performance:

1. The samples are likely to be small.
2. The stability of the estimates is likely to questioned.
3. The validity of the analysis is likely to be challenged.

In attempts to overcome the problems of small samples, the stability of the estimates, and the validity of the analysis, some researchers use the jackknife method of statistical estimation. As with any statistical procedure, there are pros and cons about its use because of data availability, collinearity (or near dependence) among variables, and the purposes of the research.

Pros and Cons of Using the Jackknife

The jackknife method of estimating the discriminant function in international business is carried out by a *t*-test procedure and by making estimates of canonical coefficients. Jackknife procedures in canonical analysis yield estimates of standard errors for weights, loadings, and cross-loadings. They also provide statistical evidence for interpreting linear relationships between predictor and criterion variables.

Unfortunately, the jackknife is dependent on the proper scaling of data. In terms of international business data, where the variables may be measured on different scales, researchers have to decide whether weights should be given to the variables, the standardized data, and the correlation matrix. Researchers also have to decide whether to do this the same across the board for the whole sample or do it differently for each of the subsets of the sample. The problem in drawing conclusions about international business performance is that this restandardizing of subset samples does not lead to simple linear relationships between predictor and criterion variables.

Moreover, the jackknife is unable to reduce the difficulties of statistical interpretation that can be traced to collinearity (or near dependence) between two or more predictor variables. The problem in drawing conclusions about international business is that intuitively we know collinearity exists among international business predictor variables. Also, this near dependence crosses the discrete boundaries set up in Parts I through III for country risk, marketing management and organizational learning, and the distinctive differences among the 10 international business decisions themselves. Overall, the pros outweigh the cons in using the jackknife method of estimating the discriminant function for international business performance, hence its use as a technique of resampling statistics in the expert systems model.

Intuitive Modeling and the Jackknife

The jackknife helps researchers fit a regression model to a set of data when they are not certain of the model's form. This fitting is based on a hunch, a guess, or intuition. The real model remains a mystery to researchers. They try to explain the properties they think the model has through the research design (i.e., deciding which and how many of the 10 decisions should be used) and the data collected as information about international business problems. (See Exhibits 1–C through 10–C in Chapters 1 through 10 for data needed to assess a set of decisions.)

Notwithstanding these judgments, researchers assume that the true distribution is supported on these observed data points. Still, they do not know for sure which predictor variables to include, whether or not to make a logarithmic transformation on the response variable, or which interactions to include in the model.

With the jackknife (or the bootstrap, other resampling plans, or other methods of cross-validation), anything goes to get started in understanding the information that the data are conveying. First, use hunches. Second, carry out preliminary testing. Look for patterns. Try a large number of different models. Seek to eliminate "outliers," or data that don't seem to fit.

What is important is consistency in assumptions about what the model should look like after the data are compiled and after the regression analysis is carried out. Then the intuitive model approximates the real model for international business. This is the benefit of using the jackknife statistical procedure in the expert systems model.

Jackknife Method of Estimating the
Discriminant Function[6]

The jackknife is carried out as follows. First, one must analyze the entire sample of successful and unsuccessful international firms. To be included in the sample, international firms must be exporters, equity or nonequity joint venture partners, or foreign direct investors. Because of this range in possible international involvement by firms, stratification is possible for the sample. Technically, the mean of the k values for this sample of successful and unsuccessful firms is the jackknifed estimate of the discriminant function. One must use the standard deviation of these k values to test the significance of this estimate by employing a t-test procedure.

Second, one must divide the sample into subsets of successful and unsuccessful firms by industry, product markets, experience with exporting and foreign investment, ability to gather country risk and other market information, sophistication of marketing management both at home and abroad, organizational learning toward global business, and the other international business characteristics discussed in Chapters 1 through 10.[7]

Third, one must repeat the analysis, omit each subset in turn, fit the model to the remaining points, and see how well the model predicts the excluded subset. Technically, the average of the predicted errors, with each subset being left out once, is the cross-validated measure of the prediction error.

The jackknife can cause the problem of excess error in the analysis of the discriminant function. The jackknife variance estimate tends to be conservative in the sense that its expectation is greater than the true variance. Technically, the excess error is the difference between the true and the apparent rates of classification errors.

Also, the jackknife can be seriously misleading in setting confidence intervals. Technically, smoothing helps overcome this problem. However, smoothing puts a parametric element into an estimation procedure that is designed for nonparametric statistics and multivariate analysis.

Finally, the jackknife simply does not go all the way in presenting as normal a model as possible for the complicated international business situations faced in measuring export or investment performance as a proxy for global business policy.

PREVIOUS RESEARCH STUDIES

Before the creation of the expert systems model of international business performance, a search was made for previous research studies that used resampling statistics to measure business performance. Two jackknife studies were found to be useful in developing the expert systems model.

British Clothing Exporters

In a study of British clothing exporters, the following three variables exerted a significant influence in discriminating between successful and unsuccessful exporters:[8]

- Attitude and commitment of management toward exporting (International Business Decision 1).
- Willingness of management to adapt products to foreign markets (International Business Decision 6).
- Years of export experience (International Business Decision 2).

Technically, to test the validity of the discriminant function in this case, the researchers need to compute the jackknifed estimates of the canonical coefficients. Such canonical functions are particularly sensitive to changes in sample composition; when the omission of one or more observations changes the order in which the canonical functions are extracted, a comparison among functions (or variables) is made more difficult.

Nevertheless, from the study of British clothing exporters, the following are the most significant predictors at the 10 percent level:

- Years of export experience (International Business Decision 2).
- Similarity of distribution policies in home and host country markets (International Business Decision 3).

For the British study, the jackknifed estimate of the discriminant function is reliable because it provides a correct and independent classification for 66 percent of the companies in the sample.

Israeli Exporters

In a study of Israeli exporters, the canonical correlation coefficient between the predictor variable set and the criterion set was highly significant statistically.[9] In fact, when a Stewart and Love Redundancy Index was calculated, it showed that 46 percent of the variance in the criterion set was accounted for by the single canonical variate developed from the predictor set.

The predictor variable set includes the following variables:

1. *Market share*: the increase in the firm's exports (by product category) sold in the target markets of the importing country (International Business Decision 1).
2. *Market size*: the increased demand in overseas markets for imported products (International Business Decision 6).
3. *Absolute skill intensity*: the experience of employees to manufacture and market products for overseas markets (International Business Decision 2).
4. *Relative production experience*: the long-term record of manufacturing overseas (International Business Decision 4).
5. *Market growth rate*: the increase in economic activity in the importing country (International Business Decision 3).
6. *Product differentiation index*: the ability to produce higher value-added products with increasing inputs of more sophisticated technology for specific market segments (International Business Decision 6).
7. *Relative skill intensity*: the experience of employees in manufacturing and marketing products for overseas markets in competition with other firms in the strategic group and industry (International Business Decision 2).

The criterion set includes the following variables: (1) Exports per employee (better-off test), and (2) Exports per dollar of capital invested (cost-of-entry test).

The following conclusions were drawn in the Israeli study. Market share (International Business Decision 1) is by far the largest relative contributor of the predictors to both exports per employee (better-off test) and exports per dollar of capital invested (cost-of-entry test) of the criterion set. Market size and absolute skill intensity (International Business Decision 2) also provide significant positive contributions. The other four predictors offer little additions to the variance explained, and relative production experience and relative skill intensity had a negative sign with both variables of the criterion set. These correlations between marketing predictor factors and success criterion factors are measures of "net" linear association.

In these two studies, the use of the jackknife helped researchers test the stability of their results against changes in the composition of the sample without requiring that new data be collected. However, the jackknifed canonical correlations did not do as well in predicting the level of business performance among these same companies.

ONGOING RESEARCH IN INTERNATIONAL BUSINESS

To predict the level of international business performance among firms, researchers must disaggregate the specific product market activities of the firm following the 10 international business decisions outlined in Chapters 1 through 10. These 10 variables are presented in Exhibit A–1. The list of successful and unsuccessful firms comes from both case analyses in this book and other case analyses done at the Kellogg Graduate School of Management. These firms and others are the sample for the jackknife. The discriminant analysis is performed on the entire sample; then the sample is split into the subsets listed in Exhibit A–1, and the analysis is repeated, omitting each subset in turn. This jackknife technique tests the stability of the results against changes in sample composition without requiring the collection of more new data.

EXHIBIT A-1
International Business Decisions

Variable	Conditions for Firms to Score 1	Firm	
		Success	No Success
Country risk:			
X_1	Choosing market opportunities	Molson* L'Oréal* Corona Heineken	Molson† L'Oréal† Labatt Other beers
X_2	Fitting core skills	L'Oréal Epson Canon Honda	P&G Renault British Telecom
X_3	Overcoming barriers	Caterpillar Brother	Komatsu GEC
Marketing management:			
X_4	Sourcing	MacMillan Bloedel Stone Container Stelco Dofasco Sanyo Ricoh Helene Curtis	Olivetti Micron
X_5	Selecting customers	Kodak Fuji Mattel	Cadbury Rover Magna
X_6	Creating value	Unliver Merck Abbott	Konica
Organizational learning:			
X_7	Using information	Boeing Airbus Henkel Colgate	BSN

EXHIBIT A–1
(concluded)

Variable	Conditions for Firms to Score 1	Firm	
		Success	No Success
X_8	Positioning assets	Merck Pharmacia Baxter Northern Telecom Bayer	Beecham Upjohn
X_9	Understanding national differences	Black & Decker Ore-Ida Campbells Schick Matsushita Sony	Quaker Oats
Globalization: X_{10}	Globalizing the firm, its products, and its markets	Electrolux 3M NEC Sumitomo McDonald's Benetton Coca-Cola Nestlé ASEA	Hotpoint Ariston Dunlop

* Pre-1986.
† Late 1980s.

Splitting the Sample into Subsets[10]

To simplify the research, researchers split the sample in Exhibit A–1 into 20 subsets. Each subset contains one successful and one unsuccessful firm. Then researchers performed 20 discriminant analyses; each excluded a different pair of successful and unsuccessful companies. Technically, the mean of the subsets is the jackknife estimate of the discriminant function. The standard deviation of the subsets is used to test the significance of the estimate; this is done by a *t*-test procedure. This statistical procedure determines which of the 10 international business variables exert a significant influence in discriminating between successful and unsuccessful firms.

Testing for Validity

In testing the validity of the discriminant function, researchers are able to provide an unbiased validation of the analysis with 40 individual validations, or they can exclude one subset and obtain a further 19 discriminant functions. Through a canonical correlation analysis, researchers can attempt to provide a multidimensional measure of international business performance.[11] To accomplish this, researchers must prepare performance measures such as the four tests of international business performance. A canonical correlation analysis using the jackknife technique is then carried out between the predictor variables (i.e., the 10 decisions) and the criterion variables (i.e. the four performance tests). The highest loadings (or performance measures) should be explained by the 10 decision variables. If the canonical function is particularly sensitive to changes in the sample composition, these comparisons among international business variables are difficult to make. This is one of the disappointments in using the jackknife technique for measuring international business performance.

APPLICABILITY OF JACKKNIFE IN INTERNATIONAL BUSINESS

The following is what the jackknife can and cannot do in helping researchers understand and predict a firm's transition from exporting to global business. The jackknife model:

1. Helps construct an intuitive model based upon the available information.
2. Gives a good fit to the available quantitative data.

3. Discriminates between successful and unsuccessful international firms.
4. Gives a meaningful assessment of significance even with a small sample.
5. Does not give rules for successful exporting and foreign direct investment.
6. Does not predict the level of international business performance.
7. Does not give researchers a robust explanation of exporting and global business management.

Dummy Variables

Because so many country, commercial, and competitive factors influence decisions to export and grow markets overseas, it is impossible to test the role of each without going beyond the degrees of freedom of all but the largest sample. However, 10 important influences were isolated because they have a significant impact on the management of international business. In Chapters 1 through 10, their multivariate content was carefully specified. This gives researchers two important tools of analysis:

1. The ability to discuss all aspects of the attitudes held by executives toward exports, joint ventures, and global business.
2. The means to summarize all the detailed information available about a firm's policies toward international business.

To measure international business performance, these decisions become the dummy variables in the regression equation.

Technically, there is no clear-cut means for selecting a set of dummy variables except by making hunches, doing preliminary testing, looking for patterns, trying large numbers of models, and eliminating outliers. Once the variables are selected, there are problems with the structure of the matrix and the use of the explanatory variable data to search for an appropriate model.

Example: International Business Decision 1

For example, X_1 (which quantifies what is known about international marketing research) is a measure of a researcher's ability in choosing market opportunities. X_1 takes the value of 1 when executives are choosing product market segments; determining the level of country risk; identifying sales opportunities; and mastering changes in terms of trade based on increases in sales, market share, or returns on sales. X_1 takes the value of 0 when one or more of these crucial international marketing tactics are not carried out by executives. Similar relationships can be shown for decisions 2 through 10.

Proper Use of Dummy Variables in International Business

Three important technical results occur when dummy variables are properly used. First, researchers avoid the problem of having to determine the scaling intervals of an executive's ability to choose market opportunities for high rates of return. Technically, researchers do not have to make judgments about the professional background, competence, and experience of international executives.

Second, researchers can summarize detailed information about a firm's policies toward international business without worrying about specific gaps in the data base. Technically, researchers are not left with an inability to make an analysis because one or more data sets reflect improperly recorded data, observational errors, extreme observations or outliers, residuals or harmful departures from normality, collinearity that degrades regression estimates, or condition indices that cause high variance and decomposition.

Third, the use of several or all of the dummy variables in discussing the shift from exporting to global business gives researchers the ability to measure all aspects of the attitude toward international business held by the firm's executives. Technically, researchers do not have to worry about the exact boundaries among country risk, marketing management, organizational learning, and globalization.

INFLUENTIAL OBSERVATIONS AND SOURCES OF NEAR DEPENDENCE[12]

In using multivariate statistical analysis to measure international business performance, researchers assume the stability of their model. That is, they believe that the 10 dummy variables (i.e., the 10 international business decisions represented as X_1 through X_{10}) explain the long-term change from exporting to global business for all firms in Europe, North America, Japan, and elsewhere in the world. Also, they believe the model is stable among its 10 dummy variables and among all of the subsets of data that explain specific international business decisions.

To answer these important research questions, they need to know whether the data they collect support the assumption of model stability or are in conflict with the model. Technically, researchers ask the following questions: How much of the results are dependent on specific data points? Do they have an unknown error because of how the data were collected? Do they have anomalous data points? Is collinearity or near dependence causing troubles with the regression results? Do regressions based on different subsets produce different results? Do small subsets have a disproportionate influence on the results?

Criteria for Influential Observations

As researchers grow in their understanding of the relationship between competitive analysis and international business, they answer these data questions based on their judgment (what they know about the past) and their intuition (what they expect in the future). To provide successful answers time and again, they need to have a set of criteria for choosing influential observations and for determining when particular measures of leverage or influence are large enough to merit attention.

These criteria must be based on statistical theory. Technically, researchers must do three things: (1) choose cutoffs that are reasonable for the problem under study, (2) examine how these deletions change the estimated regression coefficients, and (3) determine whether or not the conclusions from the hypothesis testing will be affected.

Unfortunately, these three statistical procedures can be misused. Some researchers remove high-influence data points so that a desired result comes about in a particular estimated coefficient, its *t*-value, or other regression outputs. These types of cutoffs must not be carried out.

How to Employ Cutoffs

If researchers remove high-influence data points and employ cutoffs, they must practice the following rule: Delete a high-influence data point only when it is in error and when the error cannot be corrected. Technically, if researchers employ cutoffs, the latter must be based on one of the following three sources of information:

1. *External scaling.* In this case, researchers use statistical theory to scale *t*-values by an appropriate estimated standard error. Under the Gaussian assumption, the estimated standard error is stochastically independent of the *t*-values (or other regression diagnostics). This is a stringent criterion for setting absolute cutoffs. It means these cutoffs are not dependent on the sample size. For large data sets, a less stringent criterion for setting size-adjusted cutoffs can be used.

2. *Internal scaling.* For this case, researchers use the "weight of evidence" of the regression diagnostic measure to define extreme values and delete high-influence data points. Because researchers do not have a more exact distribution theory, the use of a jackknife estimate, hat-matrix diagonal, and interquartile range gives a more robust estimate spread than the standard deviation. These are particularly useful when the high-influence observations and their distribution are heavily tailed.

3. *Gaps.* Otherwise, researchers usually find that the large majority of their data sets bunch in the middle and that the tails usually contain only a small number of observations. These latter data points are generally detached from the data sets in the middle. These detached data points should show different regression values from those in the middle.

These three sources of information help researchers practice the rule of deleting high-influence data points when the data points are in error and when these errors cannot be corrected. If researchers can work within the boundaries of this rule, then the good information they obtain from high-influence data points, which usually far outweighs the dangers from their misuse, can be used successfully in setting cutoffs.

The application of multivariate analysis to exporting and foreign direct investment is fraught with the problems of outliers, extreme values, multiple tests, and multiple comparisons. Researchers must not remain ignorant of the potential dangers from high-influence data and observations. Instead, researchers must be cautious in their use of these data in hypothesis testing and in determining whether the results are significant or not significant.

Significance Tests in International Marketing Research[13]

At this point in the discussion, researchers should stop for a moment and warn themselves about overvaluing the role of inferential statistics in research on international business. Technically, the following is a list of what they *cannot* infer when they find a null hypothesis statistically significant:

1. The results occurred because of chance.
2. The results will reoccur in the future.
3. The alternative hypothesis is true.
4. More confidence will be obtained by increasing sample size.

The goal is to render implausible one or more alternative explanations for the research hypothesis. In the literature, the use of nearest neighbor exporter and global marketer are used to explain annual increases in exports and the growth in overseas sales. These say little about rates of return on investments in people, resources, and organizations, and even less about the relationship between competitive analysis and international business.

Directional Hypotheses

The goal is to come up with directional hypotheses about a firm's international business performance. For example, in testing the first decision or research hypothesis, researchers want to show the approximate agreement of observations concerning product market segments, level of country risk, sales opportunities, and changes in terms of trade to the success of executives in choosing market opportunities around the world.

When executives do nothing they get no results; when they do something they get some results. When they do a great job in choosing market opportunities they have the chance of becoming very successful in exporting, and, over the long run, they have the opportunity to become successful in global marketing as well.

These are the expectations about success in international business. They are stated in terms of a direction for executives to follow, hence the name *directional hypothesis*. Directional hypotheses are preferred to null hypotheses because of the tentativeness of international business theory; the lack of suitable comparable data; and the difficulty of replicating studies from among countries, market segments, and market niches worldwide.

Role of International Business Data

Researchers must carry out the following steps in their quest for suitable international business data for their jackknife multivariate analysis:

1. Examine all data based on their suitability for the directional hypotheses, the questions asked, the models proposed, and the regressions to be calculated.
2. Handle the data properly and use appropriate cutoffs when necessary.
3. Reject data when they are in error.
4. Determine whether the regression results depend on the specific data sample employed.
5. Reduce the sensitivity of the estimating model to some parts of the data.
6. Find data that can be replicated in additional statistical tests.

Types of Data

In econometric forecasting, marketing research, and other quantitative business analysis, researchers use the following types of natural data: (1) "levels" data, such as manufacturing output, territorial sales, and market share information; (2) "trended" data, such as gross national product, income, consumption, savings, and expenditures on a market basket of goods; and (3) "rate of change" data, such as inventories, sales levels, and investments. In Chapters 1 through 10, both natural and empirical data are used. Their combination within an intuitive model causes several regression problems.

For example, a wide range of data types may cause many different types of collinearity—simple relationships between two variates, complex relationships among many variates, near dependencies among data sets, and high influence data points with difficult scaling problems. These dependencies are generated from unscaled natural data, then transformed into unscaled and scaled dummy variables, and finally transformed into a predictor variable set of scaled columns of equal length (more about this to follow). The following explains what to do about the problem.

Need for Column Scaling
These different types of data are in effect equivalent models of international business. Unfortunately, when researchers specify outputs in terms of productivity, sales volume, percent of market, gross national product deflator, personal income, marginal propensity to consume or save, minimum order quantity, returns on investment, or other data results, they are affecting the numerical properties of these data models, their matrixes, the decomposition of data, and the condition indexes.

Researchers must make adjustments, or else the near dependencies among structurally equivalent economic, marketing, and business data will result in greatly differing condition indexes. They must make adjustments in such a way that the comparisons of condition indexes are meaningful. That is why they scale each column of their data matrices to have an equal length. Then they subject their data models to an analysis of regressions, variance, decomposition, near dependencies, and other diagnostics.

Constructing Condition Indexes
Without going into all the regression diagnostics that are necessary to turn international business decisions from dummy vari-

ables into a predictor variable set, researchers must agree with these *technical steps*—that is, with parameterization, transforming the data to conform to this parameter, and allowing the intercept term to remain explicit so that X_1 has a column of ones.

Researchers must avoid centering the data because this could mask the role of the constant in the underlying near dependencies and produce misleading regression results. The following are the *technical steps*:

1. Scale the data matrices to have equal column length.
2. Obtain the singular-value decomposition, and from this calculate the condition indexes.
3. Determine the number and relative strengths of the near dependencies by the condition indexes.
4. Select a threshold for the condition indexes that shows tightness.
5. Examine the condition indexes for the presence of competing and dominating dependencies.
6. Determine the involvement (and the resulting degradation to the regression estimates) of the variates in the near dependencies.
7. Form the auxiliary regressions to display the relations among the indicated variates.
8. Determine those variates that remain unaffected by the presence of the collinear relations.

Transforming Raw Data into Useful Statistical Observations

By scaling columns and constructing condition indexes, researchers are able to make several decisions about the statistical properties of international business data. These are as follows: (1) how many near dependencies exist, what they are, and what their impact will be on the data set; (2) which variates have coefficient estimates adversely affected by the presence of these dependencies; (3) whether there is a need to obtain better conditioned data or to sharpen prior information through a Bayesian estimation; and (4) finally whether the prediction intervals on the estimated model are inflated by the presence of ill-conditioned data.

Readers should note that this is a brief technical discussion of influential observations and the sources of near dependence (or collinearity) among data sets. The literature should be reviewed for further refinements and more technical details.

PREDICTOR VARIABLE SET AND CRITERION SET

The final step in an analysis of international business performance is to investigate the multivariate relationships between the 10 decisions and the four tests. Canonical correlation analysis can be employed to determine the relative contributions of the 10 decision variables (i.e., the predictor variable set) to the explanation of the variance in the performance tests (i.e. the criterion set).

Multiple Regression Problems[14]

Multiple regression models are one of the favorite tools of researchers to show the relative contributions of predictor variables in accounting for variance in criterion variables. Unfortunately, several difficult regression problems crop up when researchers use this statistical procedure in analyzing dependence structures between predictor and criterion variables.

First, when two predictor variables in a multiple regression analysis are themselves intercorrelated, no unambiguous measure of predictor importance is available to the researcher. Second, each of the three measures of relative contribution of predictor variables to accounted-for variance in criterion variables has regression problems. The three measures are the squared simple correlations (or validities) of the criterion with each predictor in turn, the squared beta weights, and the "independent" contribution measure. Some researchers either ignore the multiple regression aspects of the problem or rank the importance of the predictors differently.

Overcoming the Ranking Problem

Researchers should make the following assumptions:

1. The 10 decisions, or predictor variables (i.e. X_1 through X_{10}), are themselves highly correlated.

2. The four tests or criterion variables (i.e., Y_1 through Y_4) are correlated with each decision predictor variable, but are slightly more highly correlated with X_1, as an example, than with X_1 through X_{10}.

3. Given these conditions, the criterion variables can be predicted perfectly from an appropriate linear combination of X_1 through X_{10}; geometrically, X_1 through X_{10} can be shown as 10 vectors.

4. Therefore, we parcel out almost all of the variance almost evenly, but with slightly more going to X_1 than to X_1 through X_{10}.

This model for ranking predictor variables as they account for variance in the criterion variables is intuitively correct. It fits the hunches researchers have about exporting and the importance of choosing market opportunities for high rates of return.

As executives shift the focus of their firms from exporting to global marketing, researchers must change the assumption about which predictor variable is slightly more highly correlated with the criterion variables. Again, this change in the model is intuitively correct. It fits the hunches researchers have about organizational learning within firms and the importance of creating, maintaining, and sustaining competitive advantage.

INTERNATIONAL BUSINESS PERFORMANCE

All 10 international business predictor variables (as a set) are contributors to the better-off, cost-of-entry, attractiveness, and sustainable competitiveness tests. As the focus of firms changes from exporting to global marketing, researchers change the assumptions about which predictor variable is slightly more highly correlated with the four criterion variables. These correlations between the predictor set and the criterion set are measures of the "net" linear association between the two. This association tells us that the 10 international business decisions (when applied in the multivariate format described in Chapters 1 through 10) explain successful international business performance among firms. This intuitive qualitative model of organizational learning within international firms is quantifiable. Therefore, researchers can replicate the analysis and, over time, make predictions about the level of performance needed within international firms.

THEORY OF INTERNATIONAL BUSINESS

In summary, these qualitative and quantitative analyses provide a theory about competitiveness and international business. This theory fits within the analytical framework of international business strategy. Further research must be done to determine whether or not this theory applies in all international business cases, and to determine the nature of and the extent to which the exceptions to this theory about international business hinder its usefulness in understanding competitive behavior among international business firms.

THE USE OF JACKKNIFE COMPUTER PROGRAM WITH LOTUS 1-2-3

Exhibit A–2 provides a step-by-step approach to using the jackknife computer program with Lotus 1-2-3®. The following are a few main points to keep in mind:

1. You must choose which test you want the computer to run. There are four tests: better-off, cost-of-entry, attractiveness, and sustainable competitiveness.

2. You must decide which of the 10 Xs to include in the equation. One or more of the decision variables must be included. You *must* have at *least* two more observations (data points) than the number of decision variables or the regression will malfunction.

3. You must scale the data. This means you must use the same type of data for all entries. For example, all entries must be in actual numbers or percentages or index numbers. Sometimes one year's data show an aberration or an anomaly. Then you should smooth the data using data from the previous year, the problem year, and the next year to come up with data appropriate for the regression model.

4. You must make two intuitive judgments concerning the

company under study. You are asked to order the Xs by their relative importance to one another; some may share the same rank. These ranks are entered as coefficient weights to the Xs; a ranking of 1 is understood and is not shown in the equation. A ranking of 2 means that X_3 is twice as important as X_1 or X_2.

Moreover, you are asked to judge the relative failure or success of the firm's management in accomplishing the Xs; some may be judged to be of equal failure or equal success. These judgments are entered as exponent weights to the Xs. A ranking of .8 means that management was highly successful in carrying out the Xs; and a ranking of .4 means management was not successful in carrying out the Xs.

Both the coefficient weights and the exponent weights are based on your intuitive judgment concerning the qualitative and quantitative data you have observed for the company. These may be altered on the basis of a change in judgment or upon the receipt of new information by returning to the appropriate jackknife worksheet. They should not be altered simply because the R^2 or the t-test results are too low. This is misuse of the intuitive modeling process.

5. When you are finished specifying and weighing the Xs, enter the proxy data. It should be noted that some of the Xs can be left out of the final equation. This is because the jackknife regression model requires two more data points for each of the Xs than the number of Xs specified in the equation. If you miss this important data entry requirement, the regression model will crash and you will have to correct your error.

6. You now are ready to name and enter your proxy data. Remember, as shown in the third point above, you must scale your data properly or the regression model will crash.

7. Once you have completed entering all of your proxy data, you can view them and check for errors. Then you are ready for the Lotus 1-2-3 program to carry out your multiple regression analysis.

8. The regression will give an R^2 to show whether or not there is correlation between Y and the Xs, and t-test results to show whether or not there is causation between Y and the Xs. You should interpret your findings. If your R^2 is too low or if your t-test results are insignificant, you may recluster the X variables by

EXHIBIT A–2
How to Use the Lamont Model Builder (or Jackknife) Computer Program with Lotus 1-2-3

Steps	Screen	Instruction
1		Boot up computer.
2		Enter date.
3		Enter time.
4		Change to 123 subdirectory.
5	C>	Type 123, then press ENTER.
6	Lotus Main Menu	Lotus worksheet.
7		Put IBMODEL.WK1 diskette in drive B.
8		Press back slash.
9	Worksheet	Press FILE.
10		Press RETRIEVE.
11	IBMODEL.WK1	Press ENTER.
12		Take Jackknife diskette out of drive B.
13		Put in DOS-formatted blank diskette.
14	Consent form	Press CONSENT.
15	Main Menu	Select Better Off.
16	Menu	Press Y, then ENTER.
17	Data Entry Table	Use Arrow keys to Enter % Annual Return on Sales. (Note: Make sure the data values are entered in subsequent rows beginning with Data Value 1. Note that this approach to entering proxy data applies whenever data proxy data is being entered in the Data Entry Table.)
18		Enter proxy data:
		0.3
		1.3
		1.5
		1.3
		1.3
19		Press ENTER when finished.
20	Main Menu	Select Look.
21	Menu	Choose coefficients.
22	Coefficient Discussion	Read discussion; Press Y or N then ENTER.
23	Data Entry Table	If Y, enter coefficients (see below), then press ENTER.
24	Main Menu	Select Look.
25	Main Menu	Choose exponents.

EXHIBIT A–2
(continued)

Steps	Screen	Instruction
26	Exponent Discussion	Read discussion; Press Y or N then ENTER.
27	Data Entry Table	If Y, enter exponents (see below), then press ENTER.
		Intuitive judgment.
		Importance: weighing of Xs—any value for coefficients: order the Xs by relative importance.
		Success: Weighing of Xs—from 0 to 1 to show relative failure to success.
28		Enter weights:

		Coefficients	Exponents
	Rule 1	1	0.7
	Rule 2	1.3	0.6
	Rule 8	1.5	0.5

Steps	Screen	Instruction
29		Press ENTER after completion of entries.
30	Main Menu	Select CHOOSE then press ENTER.
31	Menu	Select 1–5 Decision Rules.
32	Menu	Select Rule 1.
33	Discussion of Rule 1	Press Y since Rule 1 is appropriate.
34	Data Entry Table	Enter % Annual Change.
35		Enter proxy data:
		.0862
		.1429
		.0972
		.1139
		.0682
36		Press ENTER after completion of entries.
37	Main Menu	Select CHOOSE then press ENTER.
38	Menu	Select 1–5 Decision Rules.
39	Menu	Select Rule 2.
40	Discussion of Rule 2	Press Y since Rule 2 is appropriate.
41	Data Entry Table	Enter % Annual Change in Inventory to Sales Ratio.
42		Enter proxy data:
		0.87
		1.25
		2.08
		3.40
		1.59

EXHIBIT A–2
(concluded)

Steps	Screen	Instruction
43		Press ENTER after completion of entries.
44	Main Menu	Select CHOOSE then press ENTER.
45	Menu	Select 6–10 Decision Rules.
46	Menu	Select Rule 8.
47	Discussion of Rule 8	Press Y since Rule 8 is appropriate.
48	Data Entry Table	Enter % Annual Change in Capital Investment.
49		Enter proxy data:
		2.2
		8.0
		6.9
		0.6
		6.9
50		Press ENTER.
51	Main Menu	Press REGRESS.
52	Menu	Choose Run.
53		If you get regression error, hit ESC key until LOTUS 123 READY mode is shown. At this time hit FR then "LAMONT" for file name followed by ENTER to reboot model. Always be sure to save your files under unique file names and **never** under the original "LAMONT" or "BACKUP" file names. In this way you will always have two (2) copies of the original model, one called LAMONT.wk1 and one called BACKUP.wk1. Once you reboot you may once again begin your modeling operations.
54	Main Menu	Press REGRESS.
55	Menu	Press VIEW and look at regression results. (Note that if regression failed to run, you have either no regression data, which is the result of booting original models, i.e., LAMONT.wk1 or BACKUP.wk1, or you have the results of a previously run model. Interpret your results.
56	Regression Output	Press Y or N as appropriate.
57	Main Menu	Select Print.
58	Menu	Select from among the various Print options.
59	Main Menu	Select Utility.
60	UTILITY Discussion	Follow directions on your particular statistical utility to configure your hardware and run the F test as well as other statistical tests.

eliminating one or more of them from the equation, or by running several regressions with different clusters of X variables.

If you like what you have done, then save the results and exit to another statistical utility program to perform the F-test as well as other statistical and graphical displays.

Model users in most cases have available only that information available to the general public. This limited information affects the jackknife method in two important aspects. First, the jackknife model requires at least two data points more than the number of decision variables to be used in the model. Therefore, a jackknife model utilizing 10 decision variables would require a minimum of 12 data points, that is, 12 years of data. Second, proxy data must be used in lieu of nonpublic corporate data to simulate the decision variables.

ENDNOTES

Introduction

1. Peter F. Drucker, "The Transnational Economy," *Wall Street Journal* (August 25, 1987), p. 30.
2. Kenichi Ohmae, "Planting for a Global Harvest," *Harvard Business Review,* 67:3 (July-August 1989): 136–45.
3. Drucker, "The Transnational Economy."
4. John Dunning, "The Eclectic Paradigm of International Production: A Restatement and Some Possible Extensions," *Journal of International Business Studies* 19:1 (Spring 1988): 1–31.
5. Ibid., p. 7.
6. Ibid., p. 6.
7. Ibid., p. 7.
8. Christopher Lorenz, "Diversification: The Trouble with Takeovers," *Financial Times* (December 8, 1986), p. 11. Lorenz quotes a study by Michael Porter (which was then unpublished) about the average disinvestment rate of those firms that grew through acquisitions. The study later appeared as Michael E. Porter, "From Competitive Advantage to Corporate Strategy," *Harvard Business Review* 65:3 (May-June 1987): 43–59. Porter's three tests of international diversification (better-off, cost-of-entry, and attractiveness) are adapted in this book for use in studying export marketing and foreign direct investment strategies. The sustainable competitiveness test was suggested by Patricia Panaia, a student at the Kellogg Graduate School of Management, and adapted by the author of this book for use in studying international business.
9. O. B. Hardison, Jr., *Disappearing Through the Skylight: Culture and Technology in the 20th Century* (New York: Viking Press, 1989).
10. "Peter Drucker's 1990s: The Futures That Have Already Happened," *Economist* (October 21, 1989), pp. 19–20, 24.

Chapter 1

1. Seagram quoted in Suzanne McGee, "Molson's Cohen Has Little Taste for Beer," *Wall Street Journal* (February 22, 1989), p. B12.
2. Widdrington quoted in Edith Terry, "Canada's Labatt Has Just One Way to Grow: South," *Business Week* (November 9, 1987), p. 70.
3. Romm quoted in Vigor Fung, "Molson, Elders Canadian Brewers to Join, Seeking to Lift U.S. Sales, *Wall Street Journal* (January 19, 1989), p. B6.
4. The research for the Molson case was funded by a grant from the Business Fund for Canadian Studies in the United States to the Kellogg Graduate School of Management of Northwestern University. The preliminary analysis comes from a research paper prepared by Debbie Fuhr, Julie Jasica, and Lyle Wright, graduate students at Kellogg. Their general information on the beer and beverage industry came from current issues of *Beverage World, Beverage Industry, Beer Marketing Management,* and *Advertising Age.* Their specific information on Molson's place in the beer industry comes from interviews at the Beer Institute, Brewers Association of America, the National Beer Wholesalers, Brewers Association of Canada, Martlet Importing, Molson Breweries of Canada, and Molson Companies Limited. Peter Lawyer, also a graduate student at Kellogg and the first coordinator of the project to prepare Canadian business cases, refined the hypotheses, data sets, and statistical estimating equations. The data and analysis cited in Chapter 1 comes from Douglas Lamont, "Intuitive Modelling and the Use of the Jackknife Method of Estimating International Business Performance: The Case of Molson Breweries of Canada." Paper presented at the School of Management, National University of Singapore, August 1988.
5. R. E. Caves and M. E. Porter, "From Entry Barriers to Mobility Barriers: Conjectural Decisions and Contrived Deterrence to New Competition," *Quarterly Journal of Economics* 90 (May 1977): 241–61. These two authors discuss the prisoner's dilemma facing many number two firms in a strategic group of an industry.
6. Marj Charlier, "Beer Imports' Brisk Growth Is Bottled Up By Soft Dollar, Stiffer U.S. Competition," *Wall Street Journal* (January 11, 1989), p. B1.
7. Ibid.
8. The source used for this section was Richard E. Caves, *Multinational Enterprise and Economic Analysis* (Cambridge: Cambridge University Press, 1982), pp. 36–40, 43–44.
9. Terry, "Canada's Labatt."

10. Kavafian quoted in Terry, "Canada's Labatt."
11. The source used for this section was Douglas Lamont, *Forcing Our Hand: America's Trade Wars in the 1980s* (Lexington, Mass.: Lexington Books, 1986).
12. The source used for this section was Daniel I. Okimoto, *Between MITI and The Market: Japanese Industrial Policy and High Technology* (Palo Alto, Calif.: Stanford University Press, 1989).
13. "Managing Your Oyster," *Economist*, (October 28, 1989), pp. 78–79.
14. Mary Williams Walsh, "A Mexican Beer Export Scores in the U.S.," *Wall Street Journal* (December 17, 1986), p. 24.
15. Lamont, *Forcing Our Hand*, pp. 55–104.
16. Peter N. T. Widdrington, Speech given at the Kellogg Graduate School of Management of Northwestern University, April 1988.

Chapter 2

1. Owen-Jones quoted in Paul Betts, "Marketing More than Simple Hope in a Jar," *Financial Times* (November 29, 1988), p. 25.
2. Ibid.
3. Charles R. Morris, "The Coming Global Boom," *The Atlantic Monthly* (October 1989), p. 52.
4. Ibid., p. 56.
5. A. C. Nielsen Scantrade, "Unit Volume," (December 30, 1989). The unit share data and their interpretation were provided by Robert Shipley, a graduate student at the Kellogg Graduate School of Management of Northwestern University.
6. Betts, "Hope in a Jar."
7. The preliminary analysis on L'Oréal comes from a research paper prepared by Gretchen Spoo, a graduate student at the Kellogg Graduate School of Management of Northwestern University.
8. Betts, "Hope in a Jar."
9. Ibid.
10. The preliminary analysis on Pampers comes from a research paper prepared by Jacqueline E. Celestin, Joselina A. Concio, and Maria Carolina V. Dominguez, graduate students at the Kellogg Graduate School of Management of Northwestern University.
11. Bruce Dumaine, "P&G Rewrites the Marketing Rules," *Fortune* (November 6, 1989), pp. 40, 42.
12. "P&G Far East," *Marketing Week* (October 23, 1987), p. 63.
13. H. E. Swift, interview with Kellogg students. Advertising Department, The Procter & Gamble Co., Cincinnati, Ohio, February 1988.

14. Barbara Buell, "How P&G Was Brought to a Crawl in Japan's Diaper Market," *Business Week* (October 13, 1986), p. 71.
15. H. E. Swift, interview with Kellogg students.
16. Artzt quoted in Alecia Swasy, "Japan Brings Its Packaged Goods to U.S.," *Wall Street Journal* (January 17, 1989), p. B1.
17. Dumaine, "P&G Rewrites," pp. 40, 42.
18. Ibid., p. 48.
19. Ibid., p. 38.
20. Bernard Avishai and William Taylor, "Customers Drive a Technology-Driven Company: An Interview with George Fisher," *Harvard Business Review* 67:6 (November–December 1989): 107–14. See also "The Rival Japan Respects, Motorola's Secrets: Strong R&D, Built-In Quality, and Zealous Service, *Business Week*, (November 13, 1989), pp. 108–21.
21. Bruce Dumaine, "How Managers Can Succeed Through Speed," *Fortune* (February 13, 1989), pp. 54–59.
22. Yasukawa quoted in Christopher Lorenz, "Tactical Advantage: 'Scrum and Scramble'—the Japanese Style," *Financial Times* (June 19, 1987), p. 19.
23. Ibid.
24. Ibid.
25. Dumaine, "Succeed Through Speed," p. 54.
26. Ibid.
27. Ibid., p. 58.
28. Ibid.
29. Ibid., p. 54.
30. Gary Reiner, "Cutting Your Competitor to the Quick," *Wall Street Journal* (November 21, 1988), p. A14. See also Lorenz, "Tactical Advantage," p. 19.
31. Peter Marsh, "The Ideas Engine Which Drives Japan," *Financial Times* (May 29, 1987), p. 14. See also Peter Marsh, "Why Research Is in the Driving Seat," *Financial Times* (June 2, 1987), p. 12.
32. Christopher Lorenz, "The Product Race: Seizing the Initiative in a Struggle for Survival," *Financial Times* (June 17, 1987), p. 12.
33. The following sources were used for this section: S. Tamer Cavusgil and John R. Nevin, "Internal Determinants of Export Marketing Behavior: An Empirical Investigation," *Journal of Marketing Research* 18 (February 1981): 114–19. Warren J. Bilkey, "An Attempted Integration of the Literature on the Export Behavior of Firms," *Journal of International Business Studies* 9 (1978): 33–46. Kenneth Simmonds and Helen Smith, "The First Export Order: A Marketing Innovation," *British Journal of Marketing* 2 (1968):

93–100. Finn Wiedersheim-Paul, Hans C. Olson, and Lawrence A. Welch, "Pre-Export Activity: The First Step in Internationalization," *Journal of International Business Studies* 9 (1978): 47–58.

Chapter 3

1. Schaefer quoted in Eric N. Berg, "Thinking Long Term Is Costly to Caterpillar," *New York Times* (November 24, 1989), p. 25.
2. Stark quoted in Ronald Henkoff, "This Cat Is Acting Like a Tiger, *Fortune* (December 19, 1988), p. 76.
3. Ibid.
4. The four management tactics are excerpted from Thomas Hout, Michael Porter, and Eileen Rudden, "How Global Companies Win Out," *Harvard Business Review* 60:3 (September–October 1982): 96–108.
5. Henkoff, "This Cat," p. 72.
6. Ibid., p. 74.
7. Ibid.
8. Kawai quoted in Ian Rodgers, "Komatsu Calls for a Ceasefire," *Financial Times* (December 4, 1985), p. 10.
9. Nowaga quoted, ibid.
10. Katada quoted in Nick Garnett, "Komatsu: Hoping for a Smooth Global Ride," *Financial Times* (November 15, 1989), p. 14.
11. The following sources were used for this section: William J. Baumol, John C. Panzar, and Robert D. Willig, *Contestable Markets and the Theory of Industry Structure* (New York: Harcourt Brace Jovanovich, 1982). William Baumol, "Contestable Markets: An Uprising in the Theory of Industry Structure," *American Economic Review* 72:1 (March 1982): 1–15. Michael Spence, "Contestable Markets and the Theory of Industry Structure: A Review Article," *Journal of Economic Literature* 21 (September 1983): 981–90. William A. Brock, "Contestable Markets and the Theory of Industry Structure: A Review Article," *Journal of Political Economy* 91:6 (1983): 1055–66. William G. Shepherd, "Contestability vs. Competition," *American Economic Review* 74 (March 1984): 572–87. Martin L. Weitzman, "Contestable Markets: An Uprising in the Theory of Industry Structure: Comment," *American Economic Review* 73:3 (June 1983): 486–87. Marius Schwartz and Robert J. Reynolds, "Contestable Markets: An Uprising in the Theory of Industry Structure: Comment," *American Economic Review* 73:3 (June 1983): 488–90. William J. Baumol, John C. Panzar, and Robert D. Willig, "Contestable Markets: An Uprising in the Theory of Indus-

try Structure: Reply," *American Economic Review* 73:3 (June 1983): 491–93.

12. The following sources were used for this section: Richard E. Caves, Multinational Enterprises and Economic Analysis (Cambridge: Cambridge University Press, 1982), Chapters 4 and 7. R. E. Caves and M. E. Porter, "From Entry Barriers to Mobility Barriers: Conjectural Decisions and Contrived Deterrence to New Competition," *Quarterly Journal of Economics* 91 (1977): 241–62. Sharon Oster, "Intraindustry Structure and the Ease of Strategic Change," *Review of Economics and Statistics* 64:3 (1982): 376–83. Karel O. Cool and Dan Schendel, "Strategic Group Formation and Performance: The Case of the U.S. Pharmaceutical Industry, 1963–1982," *Management Science* 33:9 (September 1987): 1102–23. James Leontiades, "Market Share and Corporate Strategy in International Industries," *Journal of Business Strategy* 5:1 (Summer 1984): 30–37.

13. Paul Krugman and Richard Baldwin, "Persistent Trade Effects of Large Exchange Rate Shocks," *NBER Working Paper No. 2017.* Cited by Mushtag Shah, "Economic Report," UBS–Phillips & Drew Global Research Group, *Continental European Economics* 6 (May 17, 1988), p. 3.

14. Ibid.

15. The preliminary analysis for Caterpillar comes from two research papers, one prepared by Norm Gilsdorf and the other by Susan M. Barry, both graduate students at the Kellogg Graduate School of Management of Northwestern University.

16. Barry Stavro, "Digging Out," *Forbes* (November 3, 1986), pp. 127–28.

17. Henkoff, "This Cat."

18. The following sources were used for this section: Hout et al., "How Global Companies," pp. 100–102. Lisa Gross, "Bargained Birthright?" *Forbes* (June 6, 1983), pp. 46, 50.

19. "Peter Drucker's 1990s: The Futures That Have Already Happened," *Economist* (October 21, 1989), pp. 19–20.

20. The following sources were used for this section: Edward M. Graham, "Transatlantic Investment by Multinational Firms: A Rivalistic Phenomenon?" *Journal of Post-Keynesian Economics* 1:1 (Fall 1978): 82–99. Ongoing studies on concentration from the Multinational Enterprise Project at Harvard University. Burton H. Klein, *Dynamic Economics* (Cambridge, Mass.: Harvard University Press, 1977). Kiyoshi Kojima, *Direct Foreign Investment: A Japanese Model of Multinational Business Operations* (London: Croom Helm, 1978). Kiyoshi Kojima, "Macroeconomic Versus International

Business Approach to Direct Foreign Investment," *Hitotsubashi Journal of Economics* 23:1 (June 1982): 1–19. Peter J. Buckley, "Macroeconomic Versus International Business Approach to Direct Foreign Investment: A Comment on Professor Kojima's Interpretation," *Hitotsubashi Journal of Economics* 24:1 (January 1983): 95–100.

21. "Japan (SIC Code 35100) Statistics for 1987," *World-Regional-Casts* (Summer 1987), pp. B–222 and B–273.

22. Rodgers, "Komatsu Calls." See also Jack Willoughby, "Decision Time in Peoria," *Forbes* (January 27, 1986), p. 36.

23. Caterpillar, Inc., *1987 Annual Report*, p. 32.

24. Thomas J. Peters and Robert H. Waterman, Jr., *In Search of Excellence* (New York: Harper & Row, 1982), pp. 45, 171–72, 178–79, 283.

25. The following sources were used for this section: Warren J. Bilkey, "Toward a Theory of the Export Marketing Mix," paper presented to the Academy of International Business, New York, New York, October 17–19, 1985. Bilkey, "Variables Associated with Export Profitability," *Journal of International Business Studies* (Fall 1982): 39–55. Bilkey, "Export Marketing Practices and Export Profitability," in J. N. Sheth, ed., *Research in Marketing*, vol. 7 (Greenwich, Conn.: JAI Press, 1984). Bilkey, "Needed: Managerial Guidelines Regarding Export Marketing Practices," in V. H. Kirpalani, ed. *International Marketing: Managerial Issues, Research and Opportunities* (Chicago: American Marketing Association, 1984), pp. 12–24. Bilkey, "Development of Export Marketing Guidelines," *International Marketing Review* 2:1 (Spring 1985): 31–40. P. R. Cateora, *International Marketing* (Homewood, Ill.: Richard D. Irwin, 1983), p. 7.

26. Greener quoted in Peter Montagnon, "Breaching a Cultural Barrier," *Financial Times* (June 25, 1987), p. 12.

27. Greener quoted, ibid.

28. The following sources were used for this section: Daniel C. Bello and Nicholas C. Williamson, "Contractual Arrangements and Marketing Practices in the Indirect Export Channels," *Journal of International Business Studies*, 16:2 (Summer 1985): 65–82. R. S. Achrol, T. Reve, and L. W. Stern, "The Environment of Marketing Channel Dyads: A Framework for Comparative Analysis," *Journal of Marketing* (Fall 1985): 55–67. J. J. Brasch, "Export Management Companies," *Journal of International Business Studies* (Spring/Summer 1978): 59–71. P. J. Rosson and I. D. Ford, "Manufacturer-Overseas Distributor Relations and Export Performance," *Journal of International Business Studies* (Fall 1982): 57–72.

29. "The World's In-House Traders," *Economist* (March 1, 1986), p. 61.

30. Ibid.

31. The following sources were used for this section: Alan M. Rugman, *Inside the Multinationals: The Economics of Internal Markets* (New York: Columbia University Press, 1981). Ronald H. Coase, "The Nature of the Firm," *Economica* (1937): 386–405, reprinted in *Readings in Price Theory,* eds. G. Stigler and K. Boulding (Homewood, Ill.: Richard D. Irwin, 1952). Stephen H. Hymer, *The International Operations of National Firms: A Study of Direct Foreign Investment* (Cambridge, Mass.: MIT Press, 1976). Christopher Lorenz, "Multinationals Grope Towards an Inner Metamorphosis," *Financial Times* (November 20, 1987), 19. C. L. Prahalad and Yves Doz, *The Multinational Mission* (London: Macmillan, 1987).

32. "Peter Drucker's 1990s: The Futures That Have Already Happened," *Economist* (October 21, 1989), p. 24.

Chapter 4

1. "Peter Drucker's 1990s: The Futures That Have Already Happened," *Economist* (October 21, 1989), p. 19.

2. Pace quoted in Jonathan P. Hicks, "Forest Products on a Rebound," *New York Times* (April 27, 1987), p. D6.

3. Quoted in Linda Sandler, "Heard on the Street," *Wall Street Journal* (October 15, 1987), p. D–71.

4. Kenichi Ohmae, "Planting for a Global Harvest," *Harvard Business Review,* 67:4 (July–August 1989): 137–38.

5. Ibid, p. 138.

6. Ibid.

7. Douglas Lamont, *Forcing Our Hand: America's Trade Wars in the 1980s* (Lexington, Mass.: Lexington Books, 1986), pp. 55–104.

8. "Peter Drucker's 1990s," p. 24.

9. Hicks, "Forest Products," pp. D1 and D6.

10. Ibid.

11. Ohmae, "Global Harvest," p. 138.

12. Ibid.

13. Ibid.

14. The research for the MacMillan Bloedel case was supported by a grant from the Business Fund for Canadian Studies in the U.S. to the Kellogg Graduate School of Management of Northwestern University. The preliminary research comes from a research paper prepared by John Kuehne and John Paolini. Substantive primary research and additional secondary research was completed by Amy LaBan, the researcher assigned to work up the case material. Peter Lawyer, the first coordinator of the project to prepare Canadian business cases, refined the hypotheses, data sets, and statistical estimating equations. All are graduate students at Kellogg. The data analysis cited in this chapter comes from Douglas Lamont, "Intuitive Modelling and The Use of The Jackknife Method of Estimating International Business Performance: The Case of MacMillan-Bloedel Limited." Paper delivered at Martinadale Center for the Study of Private Enterprise, Lehigh University, Bethlehem, Penn., November 16, 1988.

15. The following sources were used for this section: Douglas Lamont, *Foreign State Enterprises: A Threat to American Business* (New York: Basic Books, Inc., 1979). Lamont, *Forcing Our Hand*, pp. 55–104. Yves Doz, *Strategic Management in Multinational Companies* (Oxford, England: Pergamon Press, 1986), pp. 35–44.

16. The following sources were used for this section: Christopher Lorenz, "Multinationals Grope Towards an Inner Metamorphosis," *Financial Times* (November 20, 1987), p. 19. C. L. Prahalad and Yves Doz, *The Multinational Mission* (London: Macmillan, 1987). Christopher Lorenz, "An Outdated View of Globalisation," *Financial Times* (December 12, 1988), p. 13. Christopher A. Bartlett and Sumantra Ghoshal, "Organizing for Worldwide Effectiveness: The Transnational Solution," *California Management Review* 31:1 (Fall 1988): 54–74.

17. The following sources were used for this section: Alan M. Rugman, *Inside the Multinationals: The Economics of Internal Markets* (New York: Columbia University Press, 1981). Alan M. Rugman, "Internalization and Non-Equity Forms of International Involvement," in *New Theories of the Multinational Enterprise,* ed. Alan M. Rugman (New York: St. Martin's Press, 1982), pp. 10–11. Mark C. Casson, "Transaction Costs and the Theory of the Multinational Enterprise," in *New Theories of the Multinational Enterprise,* ed. Alan H. Rugman (New York: St. Martin's Press, 1982), pp. 24–43. Ronald H. Coase, "The Nature of the Firm," *Economica,* (1937): 386–405, reprinted in *Readings in Price Theory,* eds. G. Stigler and K. Boulding (Homewood, Ill.: Richard D. Irwin, 1952). Stephen H. Hymer, *The International Operations of National Firms: A Study of Direct Foreign Investment* (Cambridge, Mass.: MIT Press, 1976).

18. James P. Miller, "Lumber Firms Rebound on Dollar's Fall," *Wall Street Journal* (March 11, 1987), p. 14.

19. Bruce Kogut, "Designing Global Strategies: Comparative and

Competitive Value-Added Chains," *Sloan Management Review* 26:4 (Summer 1985): 15–28.

20. "Two Newsprint Producers in Canada Increase Prices," *Wall Street Journal* (September 29, 1987), p. 46.
21. Hicks, "Forest Products," p. D6.
22. Miller, "Lumber Firms Rebound."
23. The source used for this section was Warren J. Keegan, "Multinational Product Planning: Strategic Alternatives," *Journal of Marketing* 33:1 (January 1969): 58–62.
24. The following sources were used for this section: Ian Rodger, "Caterpillar Faces Long Haul to Head Off Komatsu," *Financial Times* (June 30, 1987), p. 24. Brian Robins, "Gearing Up for Change," *Financial Times* (May 13, 1987), p. 9, reprinted as an advertisement.
25. Douglas R. Sease, "Japanese Firms Export U.S.-Made Goods," *Wall Street Journal* (March 3, 1987), p. 6.
26. Douglas R. Sease, "Trade Tangle: Taiwan's Export Boom to U.S. Owes Much to American Firms," *Wall Street Journal* (May 27, 1987), pp. 1, 21.
27. Christopher Lorenz, "Volvo's Drive for Shorter Cycles," *Financial Times* (June 26, 1987), p. 6.
28. "Sony's Challenge," *Business Week* (June 1, 1987), pp. 64–69.
29. Richard I. Kirkland, Jr., "The Bright Future of Service Exports," *Fortune* (June 8, 1987), pp. 32–38.
30. David Housego, "French Companies Criticised for Failure to Adapt," *Financial Times* (January 30, 1986), p. 3.
31. David Dowdell, "Toy Production: World's Leading Exporter," *Financial Times* (June 18, 1987), p. xii.

Chapter 5

1. Roderick Oram, "Eastman Kodak Buys a Billion-Dollar Dance Ticket," *Financial Times* (January 25, 1988), p. 10.
2. Ibid.
3. Ibid.
4. Ibid.
5. Mansfield interviewed by author at the U.S. Embassy in Tokyo, December 1984.
6. Murray Sayle, "The Yellow Peril and the Red-Haired Devils," *Harper's* (November 1982): 23–35.
7. Murray Sayle, "Bureaucracy and the Barriers That Do Not Exist," *Far Eastern Review* (April 16, 1982): 64–65.
8. Michael Borrus, with James Millstein and John Zysman, "Re-

sponses to the Japanese Challenge in High Technology: Innovation, Maturity, and U.S.-Japanese Competition in Microelectronics," (Berkeley: Institute of International Studies, University of California at Berkeley, 1983), pp. 112–13.

9. Clyde Prestowitz, *Trading Places: How We Allowed Japan to Take the Lead* (New York: Basic Books, Inc. 1988).

10. "America and Japan: The Unhappy Alliance," *Economist* (February 17, 1990), p. 21.

11. "Peter Drucker's 1990s: The Futures That Have Already Happened," *Economist* (October 21, 1989), p. 19.

12. Daniel I. Okimoto, *Between MITI and The Market: Japanese Industrial Policy and High Technology* (Palo Alto, Calif.: Stanford University Press, 1989).

13. The preliminary research for the Kodak case comes from a research paper prepared by Daniel J. Piccinini and JoAnne Kato Colbert, both graduate students at the Kellogg Graduate School of Management of Northwestern University. The preliminary research for the Fuji case comes from a research paper prepared by Cheryl Turnbull, a graduate student at Kellogg.

14. Clare Ansberry, "Kodak Revamping Its 35mm Color Film to Cash In on Market Cachet of Gold," *Wall Street Journal* (April 14, 1988), p. 27.

15. Thomas Moore, "Old Line Industry Shapes Up: Seven Fortune 500 Companies Show How Restructuring Can Make the U.S. Competitive Again," *Fortune* (April 27, 1987), pp. 22–32.

16. "Eastman Kodak: Focus on a New Image," *U.S. News & World Report* (August 24, 1987), p. 40.

17. The following sources were used for this section: Paul Taylor, Terry Dodsworth, and Elaine Williams, "After the Polaroid Ruling: Kodak Looks for a New Exposure," *Financial Times* (January 22, 1986), p. 16. "Is the Kis Instant Empire Headed for a Fall?" *Business Week* (December 22, 1986), pp. 36–37.

18. "Photography," *Standard & Poor's Corporation Industry Survey* (April 1986), pp. L40–L42.

19. Oram, "Eastman Kodak Buys."

20. The following sources were used for this section: Leslie Wayne, "Kodak Agrees to Buy Sterling for $5.1 Billion," *New York Times* (January 23, 1988), pp. 17, 20. Barnaby J. Feder, "Kodak's Offer for Sterling Fits Diversification Strategy," *New York Times* (January 25, 1988), pp. 25–26.

21. William H. Davidson, "The Location of Foreign Direct Investment: Country Characteristics and Experience Effects," *Journal of International Business Studies*, 11:2 (Fall 1980): 9–22.

22. The following sources were used for this section: S. B. Linder, *Essays on Trade and Transformation* (New York: John Wiley & Sons, 1962). Raymond Vernon, Sovereignty At Bay (New York: Basic Books, Inc., 1971), pp. 62–63.

23. Robert C. Christopher, *Second to None: American Companies in Japan* (New York: Ballantine Books, 1986), pp. 5–8, 15, 17, 19, 24–25, 47–51, 75–76, 119, 121–23, and 133–47.

24. Amal Nag, "Chrysler Test Consumer Reaction to Mexican-Made Cars Sold in U.S., *Wall Street Journal* (July 23, 1984), Section 2, p. 1.

25. The following sources were used for this section: Johny K. Johansson and Israel D. Nebenzhal, "Multinational Production: Effect on Brand Value," *Journal of International Business Studies*, 17:3 (Fall 1986): 191–226. Johny K. Johansson and Hans B. Thorelli, "International Product Positioning," *Journal of International Business Studies* 16:3 (Fall 1985): 57–76. A. Nagashima, "A Comparison of Japanese and U.S. Attitudes toward Foreign Products," *Journal of Marketing* 34:1 (January 1970): 68–74.

26. The following sources were used for this section: Johny K. Johansson, Susan P. Douglas, and Ikujiro Nonaka, "Assessing the Impact of Country of Origin on Product Evaluations: A New Methodological Perspective," *Journal of Marketing Research* 22:2 (November 1985): 388–96. Warren J. Bilkey and E. Ness, "Country-of-Origin Effects on Product Evaluations," *Journal of International Business Studies* 13:1 (Spring/Summer 1982): 89–99. G. M. Erickson, J. K. Johansson, and P. Chao, "Image Variables in Multi-Attribute Product Evaluations: Country-of-Origin Effects," *Journal of Consumer Research* 11:2 (September 1984): 694–99.

Chapter 6

1. Heron quoted in Christopher Parkes, "Consumer Trends: 'In the End We Are Big Brand People'," *Financial Times* (January 16, 1989), p. 8.

2. Angus quoted, ibid.

3. Phillips quoted in Christopher Parkes, "Product Development: Propelling Concepts into a Market," *Financial Times* (January 19, 1989), p. 11.

4. Christopher Parkes, "Strengthened by a Sense of Destiny," *Financial Times* (January 16, 1989), p. 10.

5. Parkes, "Consumer Trends."

6. "The Myth of the Euro-Consumer," *Economist* (November 4, 1989), p. 80.

7. Christopher Parkes, "Keeping the Test Tube Brimming with Ideas," *Financial Times* (January 17, 1989), p. 13.

8. Stout quoted in Philip Rawstorne, "Taste Barriers Will Stay after Trade Barriers Fall," *Financial Times* (January 29, 1990), p. 3.

9. The preliminary research for the Unilever case comes from a research paper prepared by Cathy Gilbert, Mauricio Jasso, and Bernardo Araya, all graduate students at the Kellogg Graduate School of Management of Northwestern University.

10. "Concept and Practice of Management in Unilever," internal document of Unilever, 1983.

11. Christopher Parkes, "Unilever Lets in a Shaft of Sunlight," *Financial Times* (May 15, 1986), p. 12.

12. "Why Unilever Wants to Buy American," *Business Week* (October 21, 1985), p. 116.

13. "Unilever Fights Back in the U.S.," *Fortune* (May 26, 1986), p.71.

14. Ibid.

15. "Unilever Aims to Bolster Lines in the U.S.," *Wall Street Journal* (June 9, 1987), p. 6.

16. Philips quoted in Parkes, "Product Development."

17. Ibid.

18. Heron quoted, ibid.

19. Ibid.

20. Ibid.

21. "Why Unilever Wants."

22. Christopher Parkes, "Unilever Seeks Splash of Scent," *Financial Times* (January 11, 1989), p. 23.

23. Parkes, "Product Development."

24. Christopher Parkes, "Powerhouses of Disparate Opportunity," *Financial Times* (January 18, 1989), p. 9.

25. Johny K. Johansson and Ikujiro Nonaka, "Market Research the Japanese Way," *Harvard Business Review* 65:3 (May–June 1987): 16–22.

26. The following sources were used for this section: Advertisers Ride After the Marlboro Man," *Economist* (June 20, 1987), pp. 71–72. Tony Thompson, "When the Client Wants Jam Today," *Financial Times* (July 2, 1987), p. 11. William Hall, "WPP and J. Walter Thompson: British Bulldogs on Madison Avenue," *Financial Times* (June 29, 1987), p. 23.

27. James M. Hulbert, William K. Brandt, and Raimar Richers, "Marketing Planning in the Multinational Subsidiary: Practices and Problems," *Journal of Marketing* 44:3 (Summer 1980): 7–15.

Chapter 7

1. Shrontz quoted in Michael Donne, "Boeing Spreads Its Wings to Match Demand," *Financial Times* (May 10, 1989), p. 8.
2. Smith quoted in Guy de Jonquières, "Bob Smith: Bringing the Drive of Profit to Europe's Airbus," *Financial Times* (March 25, 1989), p. 6.
3. Tom Peters, "Tomorrow's Companies: New Products, New Markets, New Competition, New Thinking," *Economist* (March 4, 1989), p. 19.
4. Michael Donne, "Aerospace: Optimism at New Heights," *Financial Times* (June 7, 1989), p. I of Survey. The figure of 9,935 new jets comes from Paul Betts, "Boeing Lifts Forecast for Jetliner Market," *Financial Times* (March 7, 1990), p. 6.
5. "Planning: Crystal Balls-Up," *Economist* (February 4, 1989), p. 67.
6. Roderick Oram, "The U.S.: Jet Builders Concerned Over Quality," *Financial Times* (June 7, 1989), p. XIV of Survey.
7. Ibid.
8. Roderick Oram, "The Pressure Builds Up at Boeing," *Financial Times* (January 21, 1989), p. 7. Quote is from a senior Boeing strategist.
9. The preliminary analysis for Boeing comes from a research paper prepared by Caren Flewellen, Tanja Herrera, Andrew Mallinger, and Gerald Ng, graduate students at the Kellogg Graduate School of Management of Northwestern University. The preliminary analysis for Airbus comes from research papers prepared by Diane L. Moore, Martin L. Nilsson, George B. Rogers, Mia Igyarto, Luis Mateus, Michael O'Roark, and Kevin Walsh, graduate students at Kellogg.
10. Katherine Hafner, "Bright Smiles, Sweaty Palms," *Business Week* (February 1, 1988), p. 23.
11. Edwin Kiester, Jr., "Suddenly, It's Airbus," *Business Month* (January 1988), p. 19.
12. Hafner, "Bright Smiles." See also, Badiul A. Majumdor, "Upstart or Flying Start? The Rise of Airbus Industrie," *World Economy* 10:4 (December 1987): 499–515.
13. Kiester, "Suddenly."
14. Jeffrey M. Lenorovitz, "Airbus Industrié Challenges U.S. to File Claims in Trade Disputes," *Aviation Week & Space Technology* (January 25, 1988), p. 152.
15. Kiester, "Suddenly," p. 21.
16. Flosdorf quoted, ibid., p. 6.

17. Frank J. Comes, "Airbus Hurts U.S. Planemakers Where It Hurts—at Home," *Business Week* (October 20, 1986), p. 9.
18. Frank J. Comes, "Widebody Wars: Airbus Decides to Go for the Kill," *Business Week* (July 6, 1987), p. 81. See also, David A. Brown, "Manufacturers Discuss Cooperation Despite Aircraft Subsidy Dispute," *Aviation Week & Space Technology* (January 29, 1987), p. 31.
19. The following sources were used for this section: Kenichi Ohmae, "The Global Logic of Strategic Alliances," *Harvard Business Review* 67:2 (March–April 1989): 143–54. Bruce Kogut, "Joint Ventures: Theoretical and Empirical Perspectives," *Strategic Management Journal* 9:4 (July–August 1988): 319–32. S. O. O. Gullander, "An Exploratory Study of Interfirm Cooperation of Swedish Firms," Ph.D. dissertation, Columbia University, 1975. Cited by Kathryn Rudie Harrigan, "Joint Ventures and Competitive Strategy," *Strategic Management Journal* 9:2 (March–April 1988): 142. Paul W. Beamish and John C. Banks, "Equity Joint Ventures and the Theory of the Multinational Enterprise," *Journal of International Business* 18:2 (Summer 1987): 1–16.
20. Kiester, "Suddenly," p. 20.
21. David A. Brown, "Manufacturers Discuss Cooperation Despite Aircraft Subsidy Dispute," *Aviation Week & Space Technology* (June 29, 1987), p. 30. See also Kiester, "Suddenly," p. 20.
22. William Dullforce, "US–EC Air War Breaks Out in GATT," *Financial Times* (May 11, 1989), p. 7.
23. Edwin Kiester, Jr., "We Know How Much It Cost to Build a Plane," *Business Month* (January 1988), p. 20.
24. Paul Betts, "Airbus Conflicts Fly in the Face of Efficiency," *Financial Times* (March 2, 1990), p. 2.
25. Igal Ayal and Jehiel Zif, "Market Expansion Strategies in Multinational Marketing," *Journal of Marketing* 43:2 (Spring 1979): 84–94.

Chapter 8

1. Fidelman quoted in James Buchan and Peter Marsh, "The Winning Mix in Drug Research," *Financial Times* (January 27, 1989), p. 16.
2. Vagelos quoted, ibid.
3. Isaly quoted, ibid.
4. Ibid.
5. Huck quoted, ibid.
6. Ibid.
7. Vagelos quoted, ibid.

8. Ibid.

9. Drucker quoted in George Gilder, "IBM-TV," *Forbes* (February 20, 1989), pp. 72–76.

10. Drucker quoted in Gary Hamel and C. K. Prahalad, "Strategic Intent," *Harvard Business Review* 67:3 (May–June 1989): 71.

11. Steve Lohr, "Merck's Big Venture in Japan," *New York Times* (October 13, 1983), p. 29.

12. Douglas Bernheim and James Shoven, "Taxation and the Cost of Capital: An International Comparison" (Pamphlet published by the American Council on Capital Formation, Washington, D.C., September 1986). The results are based on the tax rates in existence before the 1986 tax reform in the United States. Cited by Michael Prowse, "The Key to Competitiveness," *Financial Times* (October 28, 1986), p. 21.

13. Louis Uchitelle, "Theory of Decline Fails to Hold Up," *New York Times* (December 18, 1989), p. 26.

14. "Merck Wants to Be Alone—But with Lots of Friends," *Business Week* (October 23, 1989), p. 62.

15. The preliminary research for Merck was carried out by Ruth A. Schreiner and Ray A. Carso, both graduate students at the Kellogg Graduate School of Management of Northwestern University.

16. Buchan and Marsh, "The Winning Mix."

17. The preliminary research for Pharmacia was carried out by Joseph H. Gregor and David B. Rollins, both graduate students at the Kellogg Graduate School of Management of Northwestern University.

18. These are discussed as ways to affect the choice of market expansion strategy by Igal Ayal and Jehiel Zif, "Market Expansion Strategies in Multinational Marketing," *Journal of Marketing* 43:2 (Spring 1979): 84–94.

19. The preliminary research for Baxter International was carried out by Paul Alverez, Dennis Burke, C. Drew Caldwell, and Rick Lundgren, all graduate students at the Kellogg Graduate School of Management of Northwestern University.

20. Baxter International Inc., 10-K Filings with the Securities and Exchange Commission, 1988.

21. "Dialysis Today and Tomorrow: A Market Overview," *Clinica* (May 1985): 20.

22. "Proceedings of the Twenty-First Congress of the European Dialysis and Transplant Association," ed., Alex M. Davidson (Florence, Italy: European Renal Association, May 1984), p. 13.

23. The preliminary research for SmithKline Beecham was carried out by David Packham, Mark Thibault, Thomas Soohoo, and Arlene

Wu, all students at the Kellogg Graduate School of Management of Northwestern University.

24. Bauman quoted in "The First Acid Test of the Drug Megamergers," *Business Week* (February 19, 1990), p. 62.
25. Ibid, p. 63.
26. Joann S. Lublin, "SmithKline Beecham's Synergy Sputters," *Wall Street Journal* (March 14, 1990), p. A4.
27. Ibid.
28. Woodhouse quoted, ibid.
29. Mario quoted, ibid.
30. Lublin, "Synergy Sputters."
31. Isaly quoted, ibid.
32. Woodhouse quoted, ibid.
33. Bauman quoted, "The First Acid Test."
34. U.S. Department of Commerce, "U.S. Industrial Outlook 1988" (Washington, D.C.: Government Printing Office, 1988), p. 18–23.
35. "Drug Profits Seem to Be on Steroids," *Business Week* (January 1, 1989), p. 97.
36. "Japan's Next Battleground: The Medicine Chest," *Business Week* (March 12, 1990), p. 69.

Chapter 9

1. Tom Peters, "Tomorrow's Companies: New Products, New Markets, New Competition, New Thinking," *Economist* (March 4, 1989), p. 19.
2. Kenichi Ohmae, "Planting for a Global Harvest," *Harvard Business Review* 67:3 (July–August 1989): 140.
3. Peter F. Drucker, "The Transnational Economy," *Wall Street Journal* (August 25, 1987), p. 30.
4. Alfred Rappaport, *Creating Shareholder Value* (New York: Free Press, 1986). The preliminary analysis for integrating the creation of shareholder value into the test for sustainable competitive advantage was done by William Ovca, a graduate student at the Kellogg Graduate School of Management of Northwestern University.
5. The preliminary research for the study of Black & Decker was carried out by Evangelos Gongolidis, Mauricio Graber, and Andres Ibanez, all graduate students at the Kellogg Graduate School of Management of Northwestern University.
6. "Make or Buy—A Key Strategic Issue," *Long Range Planning* (October 1986): 54–62.

7. "How Black & Decker Got Back in the Black," *Business Week* (July 13, 1987), pp. 86–90.
8. "The New Power at Black & Decker," *Fortune* (January 2, 1989), pp. 65–68. See also "Licensing," *Advertising Age* (June 1, 1987), p. S8.
9. "The New Power."
10. Ibid.
11. "Winning Turn Around Strategy at Black & Decker," *Journal of Business Strategy* (March–April 1988): 30–33.
12. "Small Appliances: Beating Up the Big Boys," *Marketing and Media Decisions* (Winter 1986): 29–33.
13. "Going Global: Choices and Challenges," *Journal of Consumer Marketing* (Winter 1986): 67–70.
14. The preliminary research for the sale of pet food by the Quaker Oats Company in the EEC was carried out by Megan Calvert, Doug Martin, Joe Schlitz, and Soni Simpson-Stanley, all graduate students at the Kellogg Graduate School of Management of Northwestern University.
15. "Quaker Tastes Crunch in Overseas Market," *Advertising Age* (January 28, 1985), pp. 4, 78.
16. Jorge Ribeiro, "Internationalization of the Japanese Palate," *Japan Update* (Winter 1987): 12–14.
17. "Banzais for French Fries," *Forbes* (July 27, 1987), p. 12.
18. Damon Darlin, "Blind Luck, Cartoon Help a U.S. Firm Sell Frozen Potato Products to Japanese," *Wall Street Journal* (May 27, 1987), p. 26.
19. Carla Rapoport, "Exporting to Japan: The Fabricated and Real Barriers to Be Overcome," *Financial Times* (January 22, 1987), p. 16.
20. Carla Rapoport, "Time to Spurn the Sporran," *Financial Times* (January 29, 1987), p. 15.
21. Christopher Lorenz, "How Glaxo Moved into the Fast Lane," *Financial Times* (July 17, 1987), p. 14.
22. "A Japanese Market Ready for a Dose of Foreigners," *Economist* (July 18, 1987), pp. 63–64.
23. Charles Batchelor, "Exporting: 'Hugh' Potential for Overseas Sales," *Financial Times* (March 10, 1987), p. 30.
24. Damon Darlin, "Trade Strategies," *Wall Street Journal* (May 15, 1987), pp. 1, 6.
25. Vernon R. Alden, "Who Says You Can't Crack Japanese Markets," *Harvard Business Review* 65:1 (January–February 1987): 52–56.
26. Michael E. Porter, "From Competitive Advantage to Corporate Strategy," *Harvard Business Review* 65:3 (May–June 1987): 43–59.

Chapter 10

1. Scharp quoted in Christopher Lorenz, "Desperately Seeking the Truly International Manager," *Financial Times* (June 30, 1989), p. 11.
2. Scharp quoted in Lorenz, "The Birth of a 'Transnational': Striving to Exploit an Elusive Balance," *Financial Times* (June 19, 1989), p. 16.
3. Blasius quoted, ibid.
4. Whitman quoted in George Melloan, " 'White Goods' Makers Seek to Counter the Baby Bust," *Wall Street Journal* (May 9, 1989), p. A21.
5. Ibid.
6. Christopher Lorenz, "Trying to Play Coach to Odd Offspring," *Financial Times* (June 28, 1989), p. 11.
7. Christopher Lorenz, "A Struggle Against Creeping Formality," *Financial Times* (June 26, 1989), p. 12.
8. Lorenz, "The Birth."
9. The source for this section was Christopher Lorenz, "An Impossible Organisation, But the Only One That Works," *Financial Times* (June 21, 1989), p. 22.
10. Christopher Lorenz, "Striving to Exploit an Elusive Balance," *Financial Times* (June 19, 1989), p. 16.
11. Takanen quoted in Lorenz, "An Impossible Organisation."
12. Johansson quoted in Lorenz, "An Impossible Organisation."
13. Lorenz, "The Italian Connection: A Stark Contrast in Corporate Manners," *Financial Times* (June 23, 1989), p. 19.
14. Ibid.
15. The following sources were used in this section: Christopher Parkes, "UK Domestic Appliance Industry: Dilemmas of the Final Cycle," *Financial Times* (May 22, 1987), p. 26. Kevin Doe, "Electrolux: Burdens of a Global Viewpoint," *Financial Times* (April 14, 1987), p. 25. "Oven ready," *Economist* (April 18, 1987), pp. 66, 69. Christopher Parkes, "Ariston: How Vittorio Merloni Is Aiming to Make Up Lost Ground," *Financial Times* (August 7, 1987), p. 10.
16. Jean-Emile Denis and Daniel Depelteau, "Market Knowledge, Diversification and Export Expansion," *Journal of International Business Studies* 16:3 (Fall 1985): 77–89. Jan Johanson and Jan-Erik Vahlne, "The Internalization Process of the Firm—A Model of Knowledge Development and Increasing Foreign Market Commitments," *Journal of International Business Studies* 8 (Spring–Summer 1977): 23–32.

17. Ringler quoted in Lorenz, "Desperately Seeking."
18. Scharp quoted, ibid.
19. Johansson quoted, ibid.
20. Peter F. Drucker, "From World Trade to World Investment," *Wall Street Journal* (May 26, 1987), p. 26. See also, "The Transnational Economy," *Wall Street Journal* (August 25, 1987), p. 30.
21. Michael E. Porter, "From Competitive Advantage to Corporate Strategy," *Harvard Business Review* 65:3 (May–June 1987): 43–59. See also Yoram Wind & Thomas S. Robertson, "Marketing Strategy: New Directions for Theory and Research," *Journal of Marketing* 47 (Spring 1983): 12–25.
22. Peter G. P. Walters, "International Marketing Policy: A Discussion of the Standardization Construct and Its Relevance for Corporate Policy," *Journal of International Business Studies* 17:2 (Summer 1986): 55–69. See also John A. Quelch and Edward J. Hoff, "Customizing Global Marketing," *Harvard Business Review* 64:3 (May–June 1986): 59–68.
23. Feona McEwan, "Beecham's Born-Again Brands," *Financial Times* (September 11, 1986), p. 15.
24. P. Doyle, J. Saunders, and V. Wong, "Japanese Marketing Strategies in the UK: A Comparative Study," *Journal of International Business Studies* 17:1 (Spring 1986): 27–46.
25. Lorenz, "Desperately Seeking."

Conclusions

1. Richard Barnet and Ronald Muller, *Global Reach: The Power of Multinational Corporations* (New York: Simon and Schuster, 1974), p. 363.
2. P. O. Gabriel, "MNCs in the Third World: Is Conflict Unavoidable? *Harvard Business Review* 56 (March–April 1978): 83–93.
3. Michael E. Porter, "The Competitive Advantage of Nations," *Harvard Business Review* 68:2 (March–April 1990): 85.

Appendix

1. Feigenbaum quoted in "Smart Advice from Dumb Machines," *Economist* (February 11, 1989), pp. 61–62. Feigenbaum's book is *The Rise of the Expert Company* (New York: Times Books, 1989).
2. Mosteller quoted in Gina Kolata, "Theorist Applies Computer Power to Uncertainty in Statistics," *New York Times* (November 8, 1988), p. B1.

3. Friedman quoted, ibid.

4. David A. Belsley, Edwin Kuh, and Roy E. Welsch, *Regression Diagnostics: Identifying Influential Data and Sources of Collinearity* (New York: John Wiley & Sons, 1980).

5. The source for this section was Bradley Efron, *The Jackknife, the Bootstrap and Other Resampling Plans* (Philadelphia, Pa.: Society for Industrial and Applied Mathematics, 1982).

6. The following sources were used in this section: J. W. Tukey, "Bias and Confidence in Not-Quite Large Samples," *Annals of Mathematical Statistics* 29 (June 1958): 614. D. R. Brillinger, "The Asymptotic Behavior of Tukey's General Method of Setting Approximate Confidence Limits (the Jack-Knife) When Applied to Maximum Likelihood Estimators," *Review of the International Statistical Institute* 32 (1964): 202–06. M. R. Crask and W. D. Perreault, "Validation of Discriminant Analysis in Marketing Research," *Journal of Marketing Research* 14 (1977): 60–68.

7. Bruce Cooil, Russell S. Winer, and David L. Rados, "Cross-Validation for Prediction," *Journal of Marketing Research* 24:3 (August 1987): 271–79.

8. Ian Fenwick and Lyn Amine, "Export Performance and Export Policy: Evidence from the U.K. Clothing Industry," *Journal of the Operational Research Society* 30 (August 1979): 747–54.

9. Igal Ayal, "Marketing Factors in Small Country Manufactured Exports: Are Market Share and Market Growth Rate Really Important?" *Journal of International Business Studies* 13:2 (Fall 1982): 73–85.

10. Cooil, et al., "Cross-Validation."

11. Albert R. Wildt, Zarrel V. Lambert, and Richard M. Durand, "Applying the Jackknife Statistic in Testing and Interpreting Canonical Weights, Loadings, and Cross-Loadings," *Journal of Marketing Research* 19:1 (February 1982): 99–107.

12. Belsley, et al., *Regression Diagnostics.*

13. Alan G. Sawyer and J. Paul Peter, "The Significance of Statistical Significance Tests in Marketing Research," *Journal of Marketing Research* 20:2 (May 1983): 122–33.

14. Paul E. Green, J. Douglas Carroll, and Wayne S. DeSarbo," *Journal of Marketing Research* 15:3 (August 1978): 356–60.

INDEX

About Douglas Lamont...

Douglas Lamont is one of the leading authorities on international business. He is a senior lecturer in international business at the Kellogg Graduate School of Management at Northwestern University. He received a B. S. degree from the Wharton School of Finance and Commerce at the University of Pennsylvania, an MBA from Tulane University, and a Ph.D. in business administration from the University of Alabama. He did postgraduate work in commerical codes of Latin America at the Law School of Tulane University.

Dr. Lamont has written the following books:

- *Managing Foreign Investments in Southern Italy* (Praeger, 1973)
- *Foreign State Enterprises: A Threat to American Business* (Basic Books, 1979)
- *Forcing Our Hand: America's Trade Wars in the 1980s* (Lexington Books, 1986)

In addition, Dr. Lamont has written articles for leading journals, including the *Harvard Business Review*, the *Journal of Marketing*, and the *New York Times*. For many years, he wrote a weekly column on international business for the Chicago *Sun-Times*, and appeared weekly as a business expert on radio stations WIND and WBEZ-FM, the national public radio affiliate in Chicago. He has been a guest on *Wall Street Week*, *The Phil Donahue Show*, *CNN-News*, the *Nightly Business Report*, and other television shows.

Dr. Lamont has provided consultation to such companies as Quaker Oats, FMC, and Maremont, as well as Congressional committees and law firms such as Kilpatrick & Cody. His areas of special interest are foreign trade problems, tariffs and nontariff barriers, export marketing networks, international business negotiations, and international reorganization.